D1222617

DATE DUE

JAN 2017

CHARLESTON COUNTY LIBRARY

3 2 0 3 3 6 8 6 7 3 1 8

WITHDRAWN

CHARLESTON COUNTY LIBRARY

the Aleppo
Cookbook

CHARLESTON COUNTY LIBRARY

the Aleppo
Cookbook

Celebrating the Legendary Cuisine of Syria

Marlene Matar

Interlink Books

To my husband Raja
To our two daughters Rania and Rayya
To the angel of the family, my aunt Suad Ballita

First published in 2017 by

INTERLINK BOOKS
An imprint of Interlink Publishing Group, Inc.
46 Crosby Street, Northampton, Massachusetts 01060
www.interlinkbooks.com

Text copyright © Marlene Matar, 2017
Photography copyright © Marlene Mattar, 2017
Photos pages 189, 192 © Rania Mattar, 2017
Photos pages 6 © Presse750; 9 © Dinosmichail; 54-55, 105, 262-263, 270 © Jackmalipan;
28-29 © Dbajurin; 104 © Longtaildog; 36-37, 246-247 © Dbajurin; 126, 202-203 © Kadirlookatme;
199 © Melica; 750 278- 279 © Presse; 76-77, 119 © Vyskoczilova; 147 © Annachizhova;
331 © Missjelena, Dreamstime.com, 2017
Design copyright © Interlink Publishing, 2017

All rights reserved. No part of this book may be reproduced in any form or by any electronic or
mechanical means, including information storage and retrieval systems, without permission in
writing from the publisher, except by a reviewer who may quote brief passages in a review.

Library of Congress Cataloging-in-Publication Data
Matar, Marlene.
  The Aleppo cookbook : celebrating the legendary cuisine of Syria / by Marlene Matar.
    pages cm
  ISBN 978-1-56656-986-6
  1. Cooking, Syrian. 2. Cooking--Syria--Aleppo. I. Title.
  TX725.S9M38 2014
  641.595691--dc23
                          2014032555

General editor: Michel S. Moushabeck
Editor: Leyla Moushabeck
Food editor: Ruth Lane Moushabeck
Copyeditor: John Fiscella
Proofreaders: Sara Rauch, Jennifer Staltare
Cover design: Julian Ramirez
Book layout and design: Leyla Moushabeck

Printed and bound in China

10 9 8 7 6 5 4 3 2 1

To request our complete 48-page, full-color catalog, please call us toll free at 1-800-238-LINK,
visit our website at www.interlinkbooks.com, or send us an e-mail: info@interlinkbooks.com

TABLE OF CONTENTS

A NOTE FROM THE AUTHOR

This book is not just a collection of recipes. Instead, it is a loving tribute to a little-known cuisine rich in flavors and traditions, one which for so long has been the best-kept secret in Middle Eastern cuisine.

The cuisine of the city of Aleppo belongs to a people who were blessed with a fertile land surrounded by olive, nut, and fruit orchards. Aleppo's location at the intersection of the Silk Road—the ancient trade route between Asia and Europe—made it the marketplace for the exchange of all produce.

Aleppians' great pleasure has been good and rich food marked by traditions and stamped by the people of varied nationalities who passed through the city, enriching it with their contributions. The resulting patchwork of cuisines gave Aleppo culinary prominence.

The book is a tribute as well to my mother's Syrian ancestry, a gratitude deepened by my Aleppian cooking students who were so proud of their food and so gracious in inviting me to taste many of their exquisite dishes. The tastes and smells of these dishes captivated me, and since then I have been stubborn and tenacious in my effort to document Aleppian cuisine.

I had the good fortune of being helped by the Syrian Academy of Gastronomy with a prolonged stay in the second capital of Syria—Aleppo. Over that time I fell in love with the city and its people who are so passionate about their food.

This collection of recipes comes from kitchens of prominent families, cherished restaurants, and great chefs. These recipes are treasured by their owners. I was lucky to gain the confidence of the ladies and chefs who keep them close to their hearts, and they were so generous to share them with me.

This book divulges the mysteries behind the mixture of spices of which Aleppians are so rightfully proud: the sweet red pepper paste that is a bonus to any tomato dish; the dark lemony sauce that is so easy to prepare from dried tamarind; the thick, dark-burgundy pomegranate molasses syrup that is a simmered perfection.

Various basic recipes instruct the reader in how to prepare tomato paste, breadcrumbs, kibbeh paste, kebab, and yogurt; how to cook the perfect chickpeas and simmer pomegranate juice to prepare pomegranate molasses; and how to cook homemade kashta. Others tell how to preserve vine leaves and how to dry mint, okra, and tomatoes, among others.

There are many cold dishes and hot appetizers (mezze), of which some—like Parsley Omelets, a street food particular to Aleppo—are not to be found anywhere else in the region.

Many of the soups are prepared with lentils; some are served as a main dish. There are stews prepared with kibbeh, meat, and a vegetable or fruit, or sumac. These are a cross between a soup and a stew, such as Kibbeh in Pomegranate Molasses or Kibbeh with Quince—my favorite with its sweet-and-sour mélange—or Kibbeh with Eggplants in Sumac Stock.

Some dishes are cooked with fresh pomegranate juice (a great antioxidant), creating an irresistible interplay of sweet and sour. Some are prepared with bulgar as a side dish to replace rice or as a royal dish with eggplants, chickpeas, and nuts. This boiled and cracked wheat is also featured in the Armenian-influenced salad, *Itch*.

Kibbeh plays an important role in Aleppian life, with a variety nonexistent in other Middle Eastern countries, such as Kibbeh Rolls or Grilled Kibbeh with Mint. Aleppian kibbeh are prepared mostly as round balls, which makes them easier to prepare than the elongated classical ones. The book offers another quick option for kibbeh that does not require hollowing the dough, prepared with a mixture of bulgar, pounded meat, and kebab, called Butcher's Kibbeh.

The star of the dessert dishes is Milk Pudding, with its strong Chinese influence showing how the world set out many years ago on the road to becoming "just a small village." The influence of Persian and Chinese cuisines is obvious in the wide assortment of sweets and desserts.

Aleppian cuisine's diversity and richness, coupled with the passion of the city's people to excel, has created a fantastic culinary heritage, crowned by the International Academy for Gastronomy with a Grand Prix of Gastronomic Culture, the only city besides Paris to receive such a distinction.

INTRODUCTION

"You would deny yourself the glory, the wit, and the learning that you were born with, if you had not visited Aleppo." —Bishara al-Khoury, 1935*

"If I was given a choice where to live, I would have said that Aleppo is where I want to spend my life." —Hind Haroon (also attributed to Mohammed al-Thufayri)**

When you are in Aleppo, you can't avoid feeling that this is where life began. It's a city steeped in tradition, history, and culture. Aleppo, *Halab* in Arabic, is an ancient city, one of the oldest continuously inhabited cities in the world. Its rivals for this title are Damascus, Sanaa in Yemen, Jericho in Palestine, and Byblos in Lebanon. But recent excavations could move the city to the top of the list.

Aleppo's rich, ancient history is evident in its nine city gates, in the architecture of its old town, its Great Mosque and other places of worship—Islamic, Christian, and Jewish—its overtowering citadel, its inns and public baths, and its long, meandering *souq*. In 1989 UNESCO declared the Ancient City of Aleppo a World Heritage Site.

~

The Citadel of Aleppo, for instance, is as old as history itself. According to legend, Abraham stopped in Aleppo to milk his cows on Citadel Hill, hence the city's name *Halab* (Arabic for "to milk"). There is lively disagreement as to which civilization laid the first stone of the citadel. But there is some consensus that the citadel was in use at least as far back as the third millennium BC. It was heavily fortified by the Greeks, probably around the third century BC. While every conqueror since then has stamped the citadel with his imprint, the most important renovations were undertaken early in the thirteenth century by the Ayyubid emir Ghazi (Saladin's son), giving the citadel the general form that it has today. It was heavily damaged by the two Mongol invasions, but rebuilt with some additions by the Mamluk governor of Aleppo after the second Mongol invasion. The citadel became one of the most popular historic sites of Aleppo. It was extensively damaged again in the Syrian conflict that began in March 2011.

The Great Mosque of Aleppo, also known as the Omayyad Mosque, was originally built in the eighth century and renovated starting in the eleventh century, with renovations completed in the fourteenth century. It is not far from the Aleppo citadel. The mosque was destroyed by fire in 1159 and devastated by the Mongols in 1260. It was devastated again in April 2013 during the fighting for control of Aleppo.

The *khans* or *caravanserais*, Persian terms for roadside inns, served as resting places for trader caravans, especially along the Silk Road. Over the years, these inns were transformed into impressive compounds that specialized in producing or selling certain goods—for example, the Khan al-Nahassin (*Khan* of Coppersmiths) or the Khan al-Saboon (*Khan* of Soap). They served also as residences for European consuls. The Belgian Consulate, the oldest continuously inhabited house in Aleppo, is situated in Khan al-Nahassin and contains a wealth of antiques and Syrian archeological artifacts.

~

Aleppo grew from its many roots to become a populous city of nearly three million, in excess of five million when one considers greater Aleppo. Located about seventy-five miles inland from the Mediterranean, twenty-four miles south of Turkey, and thirteen hundred feet above sea level, the city has played a major role in the history of the area.

Through the ages it was a major crossroad. The overland Silk Road from China, whose history goes back nearly three thousand years, ended in Aleppo. Over that road, silk, spices, perfumes, and various merchandise moved from China and central Asia to Aleppo, which became the center of distribution to both the surrounding area and to Europe after it started emerging from its dark ages. Aleppo was such an important commercial center that in the mid-thirteenth century the city of Venice signed a trade agreement with it.

In the years that followed, many European merchants established branches in Aleppo, and a number of countries set up consulates. In fact, the first-ever French consulate worldwide was set up in Aleppo

in 1562. In the late seventeenth century, it was estimated that there were seventy-five consulates and commercial attachés in the city at the time. Unfortunately, Aleppo lost that vital role with the opening of the Suez Canal in the mid-nineteenth century.

~

The city's identity reflects its intense history of complex diversity. As far back as 3000 BC, Aleppo was the capital of the Akkadians (a semitic empire in Mesopotamia in the twenty-fourth to the twenty-second centuries BC) and the Amorites (a semitic empire and collection of nomadic tribes west of the Euphrates that existed from the twenty-fourth century BC to the eighteenth century BC), eventually becoming part of the Assyrian Empire. In 333 BC it was conquered by Alexander the Great, became a Roman province three hundred years later, and at one point was the third largest city of the Roman Empire, after Rome and Antioch.

In 637 AD, Aleppo was taken over by the Arabs, and it enjoyed a considerable rise in its fortunes when it became an independent emirate in 944 AD under the emir Sayf el Dawla al-Hamadani, whose coterie included the dean of Arab poets al-Mutanabbi and the eminent philosopher al-Farabi.

Between the eleventh and the onset of the fifteenth century, Aleppo endured a dark period of upheaval. It was besieged twice—in 1098 and 1124—by the Crusaders, who failed to capture it. In 1138 it suffered a devastating earthquake, recorded as the third deadliest and most destructive in history. Aleppo was ransacked and its population massacred by the Mongols under Hulago in 1260, and again under Tamerlane in 1401.

The Ottomans took over Aleppo in 1517, and its fortunes soared, becoming third in importance in the Ottoman Empire after Constantinople and Cairo, indeed more important than Cairo according to some historians.

~

Due to its location and its importance as a trading hub, Aleppo influenced—and was changed by—the different cultures that interacted with it, and its cuisine reflects these varied cultures. Turkish influence is prevalent, not surprisingly, due to the city's proximity to Turkey and to the fact that the hegemony of the Ottoman Empire lasted some four centuries. But long before the Ottoman Empire, and ever since the early days of Islam, Aleppo was a major center for Turkish and Balkan pilgrims on their way to Mecca and Medina to fulfill their religious obligations, just as it was a pilgrimage stop for Christian pilgrims from Europe and Armenia on their way to Jerusalem.

Various Christian denominations have existed in Aleppo since ancient times, among them a large community of Maronites. In fact, the first Maronite patriarch, Saint Youhanna Maron, is said to have been buried in Aleppo's suburb Brad. In the years following the Byzantine reconquest of Antioch in 969, the Maronites, who were settled in the Orontes Valley close to Antioch, were subjected to so much persecution at the hands of the Byzantines that they took refuge in Mount Lebanon and in Muslim-ruled Aleppo, where they felt safer, a tribute to the city's enduring interreligious tolerance.

Aleppo has also always had a significant community of Jews, and many old synagogues have been well-preserved. The Jewish population in Aleppo, however, declined in numbers, as emigrants fled both the famine that struck the region early in the twentieth century and Ottoman rule, and with the establishment of Israel in 1948. Many Aleppian dishes found their way to the US through Aleppian Jewish immigrants who moved to New York in the 1950s.

Armenian influence is also generously evident. The Armenian presence goes back to the first century BC, when the Armenian Empire conquered Syria for a short period. This presence grew significantly in the eleventh century, when a wave of Armenian refugees descended upon Syria after the Seljuks drove the Byzantines out of Armenia. The Cathedral of the Forty Martyrs, built in the fifteenth century, and the magnificent Armenian Catholic cathedral, built in 1840, are standing testimonies to their historic presence. Among the contributions of Armenians to the city is Baron's Hotel, which is the first deluxe hotel built in Aleppo (1909) and whose guests included T. E. Lawrence, who decamped without paying his bill (still framed in the room he occupied), and Agatha Christie, who started writing her popular detective novel, *Murder on the Orient Express*, while staying there. The calamity that befell the Armenians early in the twentieth century resulted in an influx of refugees from Turkey into the various countries of the

Levant, and Aleppo was a first stop. At one point, Armenians formed about twenty-five percent of the population, representing about fifty percent of the city's Christian community.

Aleppo is also host to a sizable community of Kurds who have been part of the area's landscape for centuries, in addition to a number of people from the Caucasus region.

~

Aleppo's reputation as a culinary magnet is not new. Abul Ala al-Maarri, the famous philosopher of the eleventh century, remarked in his book *The Epistle of Forgiveness* (*Risalat al-Ghufran*) that the chefs of Eden must be Aleppians. In modern times, Aleppo became known as "the Pearl of the Arab Kitchen."

Poetry has always been the preferred artistic outlet of the Arabs, and Aleppo has many great poets to its credit. But Aleppo has something else that, to the best of my knowledge, no other city has—the great number of poems dedicated to specific dishes. Aleppians have always had a love affair with their food! They love their food and are proud of it. Before I went to Aleppo, I was given a thick book (seven hundred pages) as a gift. The book is an anthology of poems and songs on any Aleppian dish one can imagine!

The uniqueness of Aleppian cuisine is not surprising, considering the fertility of the land around it and the distinct mix of influences—Arab, Turkish, Armenian, Greek, European, Persian, and more—that converged to make this food so distinctive. In fact, some Aleppian dishes have names that reveal their place of origin, for instance Pistachio *Mortadella* and Leg of Lamb in Vinegar with Bulgar, or *Fakhdeh Dobo* (originating from the Italian word *addobbo*, meaning decoration). Foods of Italian origin probably come from the influence of merchants from the Italian city-states who have had an established presence in the city since the fifteenth century. There is a Chinese Milk Pudding (*Haytaliyeh*) that is still eaten with Chinese cups and spoons. Many Aleppian dishes—including the city's plat de résistance, Meatballs in Sour Cherry Sauce (*Kabab Karaz*)—are sweet-and-sour, reflecting the Chinese practice of adding sugar or fruits to their savory dishes. Foods of Turkish, Armenian, Greek, or Persian origins are too numerous to list.

Perhaps symbolizing the imagination of Aleppian cuisine is the city's unrivalled *souk*. Until nearly fifteen hundred shops were damaged or destroyed in the Syrian conflict in 2012, Aleppo's historic Souk al-Madina was the largest covered market in the Middle East—and in the world. Long, narrow, noisy, seemingly never-ending—about thirteen kilometers (eight miles) in length—the *souk* for centuries has sold everything from essential supplies and provisions to specialty items that can't be found elsewhere; from a cornucopia of foodstuffs, herbs, spices, kitchen equipment, ceramics, and housewares to leather goods, clothing, soaps and perfumes (*attar*), jewelry, accessories, silks, bridal wear, pure cotton and other textiles, rugs, and carpets to crafts such as shoemaking, tailoring, and blacksmithing.

For Aleppians, the *souk* has been the pulse of the city, a place where your senses are overwhelmed by the glitter of gold and silver, the aromas of spices and dried herbs, the fragrances of perfumes, the tastes of nuts and dried fruits, and the buzz of shoppers and shopkeepers. During long shopping trips, you could always appease your hunger with a famous Parsley Omelet (*Ujjet Baqdoones*), topping it with a refreshing glass of *Ayran*, a chilled drink of diluted yogurt. The *souk* has been a place holding lifelong memories of childhood, family and loved ones, and food traditions.

~

It is natural to seek comfort in the fact that, over the millennia, Aleppo has been rebuilt time and again after periods of great turbulence and loss. But when Aleppo reconstructs this time, when its buildings and alleyways are restored, when the sights, sounds, and aromas of its *souk* are recovered, can the spirit, understanding, and know-how that created this heritage of traditional marketplace and cuisine be recovered and preserved as well? Hopefully, this collection of Aleppian recipes can serve as one small contribution to that venture.

---

* Bishara al-Khoury (1885–1968) Lebanese poet, known also as Al-Akhtal al-Saghir (or Bishara Abdullah Khoury, to differentiate him from the president of the Lebanese Republic of the same name).

** Hind Haroon (1927–1995) Syrian poet from Lattaqia. This particular line on Aleppo is also attributed to Mohammed al-Thufayri, an Iraqi poet from Basrah.

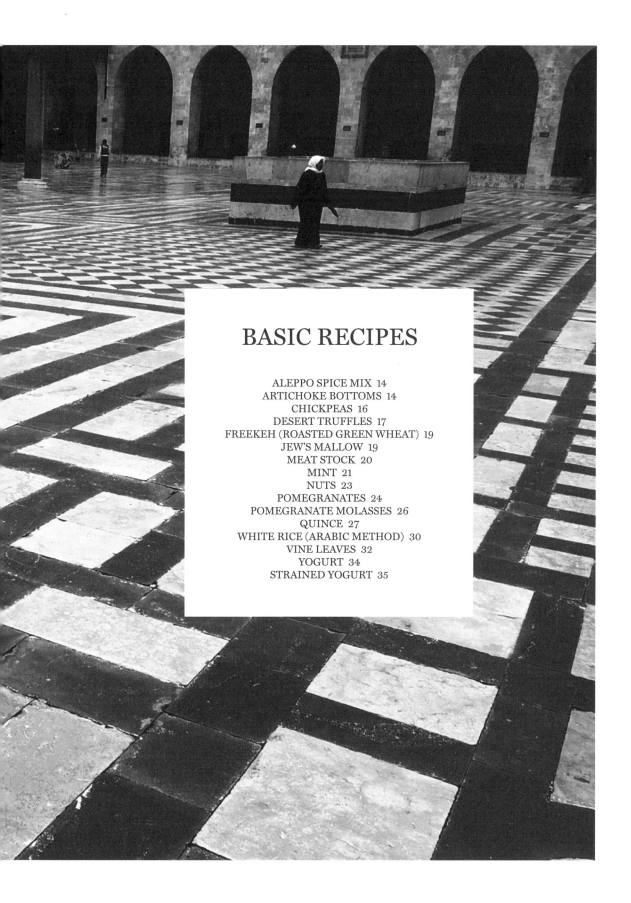

BASIC RECIPES

ALEPPO SPICE MIX
Daqqa

Daqqa (sometimes labeled Aleppo Seven-Spice Powder) is a famous Aleppian blend of spices. It is used widely in Aleppian cuisine and in this book. The main ingredients are allspice, black pepper, cinnamon, nutmeg, and cloves but sometimes other things like red chili, mahlepi (*mahlab*), and/or cardamom are added according to taste. Every household in Aleppo takes pride in its own special blend. The old souqs, in particular Souq al-Attarine, make made-to-order blends, chosen by the customer, to be ground and delivered on the spot.

For the best flavor and aroma, use freshly ground whole spices wherever possible. Roast whole spices in the oven or in a dry nonstick pan over medium heat, shaking the pan. (It takes around 8 minutes in the oven and a few seconds on the stovetop.) Grind to a powder using a spice or coffee grinder, or a mortar and pestle before mixing as below.

MAKES ⅓ CUP/1½ OZ/40 G

2 tablespoons ground allspice

1 tablespoon cinnamon

½ tablespoon ground black pepper

½ tablespoon grated nutmeg

½ tablespoon cardamom pods

¾ teaspoon ground cloves

¾ teaspoon ground mahlepi or ground ginger

ARTICHOKE BOTTOMS
Ardishawkeh

PREPARATION TIME: ABOUT 1 MINUTE PER ARTICHOKE

1. Prepare a bowl of lemon acidulated water: Squeeze the juice of half a lemon into a bowl of water. Reserve the remaining half lemon for rubbing cut edges of artichokes, if necessary (artichokes brown very quickly).

2. Snap the leaves off the artichoke until you reach the thin core of leaves that are attached to the base. Cut the sharp tops off these leaves with kitchen scissors.

3. Cut off part of the stem or cut off the whole stem as required by the recipe (the stem is edible).

4. Peel the skin off the stem and the hard parts of the underside of the heart, rubbing the cut parts with the lemon half as you go.

5. Pull off the leaves exposing the choke (the hairy strands attached to the heart).

6. Scoop out the choke with a spoon.

7. Plunge the prepared bottom into the acidulated water.

CHICKPEAS
Hummus

Test the chickpeas several times during cooking, since the cooking time can vary depending on the quality and size of the dried chickpeas. One cup/7 oz/200 g dried chickpeas makes about 2½ cups/500 g cooked and drained chickpeas.

To cook chickpeas to use whole

1. Place 2 cups dried chickpeas in a bowl and add water to cover by 3 in/8 cm. Add 1 teaspoon baking soda and soak overnight (or see the quick soaking method below).

2. Drain and rinse under running water.

3. Place chickpeas in a pot with water to cover by 1 in/3 cm, and bring to a boil over high heat, skimming off the foam that forms on the surface.

4. Cover pot, lower the heat, and simmer 1–1½ hours, or until chickpeas are soft. Drain and use as needed.

To cook chickpeas for hummus

1. Soak and drain the chickpeas as above.

2. Place chickpeas in a pot with water to cover by 1 in/3 cm. Add 1 teaspoon baking soda and bring to a boil over high heat, skimming off any foam that forms on the top.

3. Pour in ½ cup/120 ml cold water and return to a boil, skimming off the foam. Repeat procedure one more time.

4. Cover pot, lower heat, and simmer 1½ hours, or until chickpeas are very soft (test by pressing a chickpea between two fingers).

5. Drain and reserve the cooking liquid to be used in the recipe. Crush chickpeas while still hot.

To peel cooked chickpeas

1. Peel by hand, or place them in one layer between two paper towels and gently pass a rolling pin over them.

2. Remove top towel; remove and discard peel.

Quick soaking method

1. Place chickpeas in a large pot, add enough water to cover by 4 in/10 cm, and bring to a boil. Reduce the heat and simmer for 2 minutes.

2. Remove from the heat, cover, and set aside for 1 hour before cooking as above.

DESERT TRUFFLES
Kamayeh

To prepare for cooking

1. Soak desert truffles in water for 30 minutes.

2. Strain and gently massage each truffle under running water with the fingers or a soft brush. Wash again and drain. (Some prefer this method to thinly peeled truffles at the expense of taste, some nutrients, and crunchiness.)

3. To chop truffles: Cut into 1 in/2½ cm pieces along the fissures if any, to remove any sand that is embedded. Wash again and drain. (Alternatively, you can keep them whole.)

4. Drop truffles into boiling water for a few seconds and remove with a slotted spoon to a strainer (this step is to make sure that no sand remains). Now, whether whole or chopped, they are ready to be cooked or frozen.

To freeze

5. Dry well with paper towels and freeze in well-sealed plastic bags. They keep well for 6 months.

To cook from fresh or frozen

6. Add the prepared truffles to boiling stock or stew and cook for 4 to 7 minutes. *Or* to add to cooked dishes such as Leg of Lamb with Freekeh (p. 138): Boil in salted water for 4 to 7 minutes, strain, fry briefly in oil, and mix with the freekeh or place on top before serving. *Or* to cook for a salad: Boil in salted water for 4 to 7 minutes, depending on size.

7. Truffles should never be cooked more than a few minutes. (Desert truffles need only a few minutes to cook; they should retain a slight bite.)

FREEKEH (ROASTED GREEN WHEAT)
Freek

To clean, cook, and freeze

1. Remove any stones and impurities from freekeh. Do not wash freekeh, since it will lose its smoky flavor.

2. Cook the grains in boiling water or meat or vegetable stock with a ratio of 1 unit of freekeh to 2 units of liquid (or more depending on age and size of the grains).

3. Cook 20 minutes to 1 hour, depending on the size and age of the grain. Whole grains need more liquid and more cooking time. (You can stir more hot liquid into the cooking grains at any time.)

4. Freeze in sealed containers.

5. Defrost the day before in the refrigerator and reheat over low heat, adding a little boiling water or stock, or alternatively, reheat in a microwave. Mix the cooked freekeh with a little water, cover, and microwave on high for a few minutes.

NOTES

To use freekeh instead of rice as a stuffing for vegetables: Combine ½ cup/3½ oz/100 g medium-grain freekeh with ¾ cup/200 ml water, 1 teaspoon Aleppo spice mix, ½ teaspoon cinnamon, and 1 teaspoon salt. Bring to a boil, lower the heat, and simmer until all the water has been absorbed.

JEW'S MALLOW
Mloukhiyeh

To clean, chop, and freeze fresh leaves

1. Remove the leaves from the stems, and remove any hairs that are on the base of the leaves. Wash, drain, and dry in a salad spinner; then spread on towels for a few hours to dry, turning them a few times.

2. Hold a bunch of leaves firmly on a chopping board and slice them very thinly using a razor-sharp knife in single strokes.

3. Place in plastic bags and refrigerate for 2 days until needed, or freeze.

4. Drop frozen mloukhiyeh directly into boiling stock without defrosting.

5. To dry leaves for Mloukhiyeh with Dried Leaves (p. 261), *see* how to dry mint, p. 21.

MEAT STOCK

Traditionally, many Aleppian stews and soups are cooked in this hearty meat stock made from stewing cuts of meat. The meat is reserved and added to the final dish, giving it another dimension, though if preferred, you can substitute any good quality meat or vegetable stock in these recipes, leaving out the stewed meat. Lamb shanks are best, as they lend a richer flavor, but you can use any stewing cuts of meat.

1 lb/450 g lamb shanks on the bone
    or other stewing cuts and
    2–3 lamb bones
or
1 lb/450 g beef chuck or other
    stewing cuts and 2–3 beef bones
2 tablespoons vegetable oil
    (if making beef stock)

Aromatics

2–3 cinnamon sticks
1 bay leaf
1 medium onion (8 oz/225 g),
    quartered
1 small carrot, chopped (optional)

For lamb stock

1. Place the meat and bones in a large cooking pot with cold water to cover by about 2 in/5 cm.

2. Bring to a boil over high heat, skimming the foam that forms on the surface.

3. Add the aromatics. Cover the pot and simmer very gently (the surface of the liquid should barely tremble) for 1½ hours, or until the meat is very tender and falling from the bone.

4. Remove the meat and set aside, then cut into bite-size pieces.

5. Strain the liquid well and boil, uncovered, to reduce to the amount required by the recipe.

6. If desired, refrigerate stock for a few hours; then remove and discard the fat that collects at the top.

For beef stock

1. Cut the beef into cubes.

2. Heat 2 tablespoons of oil in a skillet over high heat. Fry the meat cubes in batches, stirring after a few seconds.

3. Raise the heat and add the bones, and hot water to cover by 2 in/5 cm. Bring to a boil, skimming off any foam that forms on the surface.

4. Follow steps 3 to 6 above.

To store for later use

Return the meat to the stock to prevent discoloration. Refrigerate or freeze until needed. Defrost and remove the meat before using.

MINT
Na'na'

Mint is called *na'na' al-ward*, rose mint, because it is at its peak in May when the markets are full of damask roses (*ward al-joury*), used to prepare the famous crimson red Rose Petal Jam (p. 285). During this time, you can see bunches of mint hanging from balconies all over Aleppo. The mint dries quickly because of the hot, dry weather. For maximum flavor, gather mint leaves before the plant flowers. Harvest in the early morning or early evening.

To dry using the hanging method (**best for retaining flavor**)

1. Wash mint with the leaves on the stalk. Dry in a salad spinner to remove all water.

2. Gather in small bundles and tie with cotton thread. Place in a paper bag (this helps the mint retain its flavor and color) and hang it upside-down in a dark, warm, shady, and well-ventilated place.

3. About 2 weeks later, when completely dry, pull the leaves off the stalks and rub them between the palms of the hands to crumble them; then pass through a fine strainer. Alternatively, the dried leaves may be kept whole and crumbled as needed, which helps to retain flavor for a longer time.

To dry using the oven

1. Preheat oven to 212°F/100°C.

2. Wash leaves on stalks and dry in a salad spinner. Pull the leaves off the stems and place them in one layer on a baking sheet.

3. Place the leaves in the oven and immediately turn off the oven. Remove after 3–4 minutes.

To dry using the microwave

1. Wash leaves on stalks and dry in a salad spinner.

2. Pull the leaves off the stems and place them on paper towels.

3. Microwave on high for 30 seconds. Repeat the procedure a few more times, stirring the mint each time until completely dry.

To store

1. Always keep dried herbs in glass jars rather than plastic.

2. Check jars frequently to make sure that there are no signs of moisture. Herbs keep for a year but will mold quickly if not completely dry to start with.

NUTS
Qloubat

Useful tips for selecting and cooking nuts

1. Buy good quality nuts.

2. Nuts spoil easily with time. Refrigerate or freeze until needed.

3. Fried nuts like almonds and pine nuts should have a uniform, light-golden color. Almonds take a longer time to fry than pine nuts; pistachios should be fried briefly, just to heat through without coloring; walnuts are best when toasted in the oven or dry-fried in a nonstick skillet.

To peel almonds

1. Place in a bowl, cover with boiling water, and let sit for 1 hour, changing hot water a few times (this keeps the almonds white), or until the skin can be removed easily. Dry with paper towels before frying.

To fry nuts

1. Place a small skillet or pot over medium heat and add oil or ghee.

2. Place a strainer over a bowl (use metal strainer, plastic strainers melt with high heat) near source of heat. You will need a wooden spoon.

3. When the oil is moderately hot, drop the nuts into the pan, without crowding.

4. Stir the nuts constantly until lightly golden in color. Pour the nuts and oil immediately into the strainer. The nuts will darken as they sit. The oil may be used again to fry other nuts.

5. If you are inexperienced with the process, it is better to fry different types of nuts separately. Otherwise fry mixed nuts in this order: Fry almonds until they start to color, stirring continuously. Add pine nuts and fry until the nuts are light golden. Still stirring continuously, add pistachios and fry one second more. Pour nuts and oil into the strainer.

6. Nuts may be fried the day before serving (store in the refrigerator). To reheat, fry in a little oil over low heat until just hot, watching carefully so they don't burn.

POMEGRANATES
Rimman

To remove pomegranate seeds from the fruit

1. Using a sharp knife, cut the pomegranate in half crosswise.

2. Hold the pomegranate half in one hand over a bowl, cut side down. Hold a wooden spoon with the other hand and tap hard on the skin. The seeds will fall into the bowl.

Or

1. Using a sharp knife, cut the pomegranates into quarters.

2. Place the quarters in a bowl of cold water.

3. Shake and crush them slightly in the water.

4. The seeds will separate and the pith will float to the top.

To juice pomegranate seeds (3 methods)

Remove pomegranate seeds and place them in electric fruit juicer. *Or*, pulse seeds in a food processor then strain. *Or*, crush seeds by hand in a strainer set over a bowl.

To freeze pomegranate juice

Place in glass jars leaving about 1 in/3 cm empty space at the top to allow the juice to expand. (Fresh pomegranate juice will keep for about 8 months in the freezer.)

Pomegranate juice substitute

There is no good substitute for pomegranate juice—it has an astringent quality and distinctive flavor, which cannot be duplicated. There is an acceptable substitute for use in cooking. Place in a 1-cup measure: ⅓ cup/75 ml lemon juice, 1 tablespoon sugar, and a dash of salt. Fill with water. Use in place of pomegranate juice in equal measure.

POMEGRANATE MOLASSES
Dibs al-Rimman

YIELDS 2½ CUPS/600 ML
PREPARATION TIME: 20–30 MINUTES
COOKING TIME: 3–4 HOURS

Pomegranate molasses is thick, dark syrup prepared by lengthy simmering of pomegranate juice (*see* p. 24). It can be found in markets all over Syria, but cooking with ready-made syrup is a little tricky, since it can be unreliable. There are variations in the taste, color, and density of pomegranate syrup depending on the variety used to prepare it, the length of time it has simmered, and whether it contains additional ingredients like sugar, citric acid, lemon juice, or food coloring. When cooking with pomegranate syrup, it is important to taste and adjust the flavor by adding more of the syrup, more lemon juice, and/or more sugar, as needed. The reliability of the source is important when choosing ready-made syrup. Making your own allows you to control your preferred flavor.

Pomegranate molasses is usually prepared from sour pomegranates, but some like to use the sweet-and-sour *laffani* variety of pomegranates. It may also be prepared from a mixture of varieties. If using sour pomegranates, sugar may be added at the onset of boiling. Alternatively, thick grape molasses can be added at the end of cooking instead of sugar.

22 lb/10 kg pomegranates

1. Separate the seeds from the pomegranates (*see* p. 24). Be sure to remove all the pith, which tends to give the final result a bitter taste.

2. Pulse the seeds in a food processor or juicer and strain the juice. (In the past, the seeds were placed in a strainer and crushed by hand.)

3. Pour the juice into a wide nonreactive pot (stainless steel works well). Place the pot over medium heat and bring to a boil. Skim the top, lower the heat, and simmer, stirring from time to time, until the juice thickens to the consistency of heavy cream and turns dark red in color.

4. Cool and pour into sterilized bottles; allow to cool fully before sealing.

QUINCE
Safarjal

FOR 11 LB/5 KG QUINCE
PREPARATION TIME: 15–20 MINUTES

To prepare for cooking

Quince is not easy to cut or peel but a cleaver does a good job. Place the quince on a strong cutting board (I usually put the board on the floor) and, holding the quince in one hand stem-side up, cut it in half, lengthwise. Cut the half to two pieces along the core. Remove the hard core.

No need to peel the quince for cooking. Cut each quarter into 1–1½ in/3–4 cm pieces or as desired. Quince cooks in a few minutes and disintegrates when overcooked. Quince grown in the wild takes a longer time to cook than commercially grown quince.

Mashed, cooked quince is great for thickening quince dishes.

To freeze

Follow the steps above to cut. Blanch in boiling water a few seconds. Transfer to cold water then drain. Cool and freeze in plastic bags. You do not need to defrost in order to cook; it can be added to stock from frozen.

WHITE RICE (ARABIC METHOD)
Roz Abiad

SERVES 8–10
PREPARATION TIME: 5 MINUTES
SOAKING TIME: 30 MINUTES
COOKING TIME: 15 MINUTES
RESTING TIME: 20 MINUTES

Rice was cultivated in China more than 3,000 years ago, while the rice plant may have originated in Southern India, then spread north and to China. It reached North America toward the end of the seventeenth century.

The Arabs encouraged the use of rice in Egypt and Morocco and introduced it to Europe through Spain. It is a symbol of good fortune and is showered on the bride and groom after a marriage ceremony.

White rice, plain, flavored with nuts or cinnamon, or Rice Pilaf with Vermicelli (p. 110) is served with many dishes and stews.

3 cups/1 lb 5 oz/600 g short
    grain rice
3 tablespoons/1½ oz/45 g butter
3 tablespoons vegetable oil
3 cups/700 ml boiling water
1 tablespoon salt, or to taste
A sprinkle of cinnamon or fried nuts
    (*see* p. 23) to garnish (optional)

To wash rice

1. Place rice in a bowl and fill with water.

2. Pass fingers through rice gently so as not to break rice grains. Tilt the bowl and pour off water.

3. Pour clean water again and repeat procedure 3–5 times, or until water is clear.

4. Place clean water over rice and soak for 30 minutes.

5. Place in a strainer and set aside 10 minutes to 2 hours.

To cook the washed rice

1. Place butter and oil in a pot over medium to low heat.

2. Add rice and stir gently using a wooden spoon for about 30 seconds until the rice is heated through.

3. Stir in the water and salt and bring to a boil.

4. Cover the pot tightly, lower heat to very low, and cook for 15 minutes.

5. Remove from heat and let rest, covered, for 10 minutes.

6. Fluff rice with a fork, cover, and let rest 10 minutes more.

7. Fluff again and spoon onto a serving platter; decorate with cinnamon or fried nuts, if using.

NOTES

- Mixing two kinds of rice gives best results. To use short- and long-grain rice: Follow the recipe above, replacing 1 cup/2½ oz/100 g of the short-grain rice with 1 cup/2½ oz/100 g unwashed long-grain rice. Cook together following the steps above, using 4 cups/1 liter water.
- To cook rice without soaking: Use ¼ cup/60 ml extra water for each cup of rice.
- To reheat rice not in cake form: This is best done in a microwave oven. Mix with 2–3 tablespoons cold water and cook on high for 2 to 3 minutes.

VARIATIONS

- To form a rice ring with nut garnish: Fry nuts (*see* p. 23) and place in the bottom of a ring-shaped mold or bundt pan. Cook rice as per the recipe above and spoon on top of the nuts, pressing on rice gently. Flip onto a serving platter and serve immediately. To serve after a few hours: Reheat, covered, in a medium oven for about 30 minutes; or turn into a serving platter, remove mold, and reheat in the microwave.
- To cook rice in the oven: Cooking rice in the oven often yields better results. Preheat the oven to 350°F/180°C. Follow the steps to wash the rice, and follow cooking steps 1–3. Making sure that the water you added to the rice is boiling, cover rice with a piece of wax paper in the pot, cover the pot, and bake for 20 minutes in the preheated oven. Remove from heat, switch off the oven, and let the rice sit covered for 10 minutes. Fluff with a fork, cover, and return to the still-hot oven until serving. (Rice will stay hot for a good 1½ hours.)

VINE LEAVES
Waraq 'Inab

FOR 5 LB/2 KG LEAVES
PREPARATION TIME: 15–20 MINUTES
RESTING TIME FOR METHOD 2: 2–3 DAYS

In Aleppo, grapevine leaves are most commonly filled with stuffing of rice, meat, and spices, and rolled into cigar shapes (*see* p. 210). Grapevine leaves are available fresh from the vine during late spring and early summer. That is when the leaves are at their best—green and tender. They are also available in supermarkets preserved in salted water or in vacuum jars.

To prepare fresh leaves for cooking

Cut off the stems and blanch leaves in boiling salted water for 30 seconds. Then, using a slotted spoon, transfer to cold water and drain.

To freeze

Method 1: Do not wash leaves. Use scissors to cut off the stems. Stack leaves in bunches and gather them in plastic bags, pressing on them to remove as much air as possible, and then freeze. They keep for about 8 months in the freezer and need to be blanched in boiling water before use.

Method 2: I use the method below, which keeps the leaves for a longer time, makes them easier to handle, and more convenient to use.

1. Do not wash leaves. Cut off stems, gather into bundles of 3½ oz/100 g, and tie with cotton threads (*see* Photo). Place the bundles close together in a large heatsafe bowl.

2. Place a pot over high heat with enough water to cover the bundles. For each 8 cups/2 liters of water, add 6 tablespoons/2½ oz/75 g coarse salt, 3 tablespoons sugar, and 2 teaspoons citric acid (or ¼ cup/60 ml white vinegar).

3. Bring to a rolling boil. Pour the boiling water over the bundles and cover with an upturned plate with a heavy weight on top. Leave at room temperature for 2 to 3 days, making sure that the leaves in the inner part of the bundles have changed color (the thicker the bundle the more time is needed).

4. Drain the bundles and press each with both hands to extract all the liquid; then freeze in plastic bags.

5. To reconstitute: Place in cold or lukewarm water and leave until defrosted. No need to blanch before using.

YOGURT
Laban

MAKES 4 CUPS/1 LITER
PREPARATION TIME: 5 MINUTES
RESTING TIME: 4–8 HOURS

Yogurt is widely used in Aleppian cuisine as a sauce base, and yogurt mixed with dried mint is a popular accompaniment to kibbeh dishes. In past days and before refrigerators were available, a thick sauce called *douberkeh* was made by mixing salt and goat's milk and boiling until it thickened. The sauce was kept in special containers for up to a year for use in dishes that required yogurt. This is still prepared in many villages.

The plain yogurt sold in the West is sweeter than the yogurt available in the Arab world. Sheep's milk is the best to use in the preparation of yogurt; it stabilizes during cooking and does not need a thickening agent. But goat's milk, cow's milk, and low-fat varieties can also be used.

4 cups/1 liter milk

3 tablespoons plain yogurt with active cultures

1. Place the milk in a stainless steel pot over medium heat and bring to a boil, stirring a few times.

2. Remove from the heat and set aside until it reaches a little above body temperature: between 107 and 113°F/42 and 45°C. (In our grandmothers' times, the method to test the temperature was to dip a finger in the yogurt; it is ready when no discomfort is felt after counting to 10.)

3. Mix a few tablespoons of the warm milk with the plain yogurt; return mixture to the warm milk, and mix well.

4. Place the mixture in a nonreactive container (like a glass jar) and cover. To keep the heat in for a longer time, wrap the container in a thick (preferably woolen) cloth.

5. Place the container in a warm, draft-free place, undisturbed for about 4 hours, or 6 if the weather is cold.

6. Store yogurt in a covered container in the refrigerator.

STRAINED YOGURT
Labneh

MAKES UP TO 1 CUP/240 ML (DEPENDING ON HOW LONG YOU STRAIN)
PREPARATION TIME: 5 MINUTES; 5–6 HOURS TO DRAIN

Labneh, sometimes called Arab yogurt cheese, is plain yogurt that has been drained of some of its whey to create a thick, soft mixture, the texture of thick sour cream or thin cream cheese. Most *labneh* available in supermarkets is prepared from cow's milk yogurt, while some is prepared from lamb's milk yogurt. Some *labneh* is drained further, shaped in small balls, and preserved in olive oil in glass jars. To make your own *labneh*, you will need cheesecloth or a fine mesh strainer lined with strong paper towels.

2 cups/1 lb/450 g plain yogurt

1 teaspoon salt, or to taste

To serve (optional)

Olive oil
Arabic flatbread
Sliced scallions
Sliced tomatoes
Black olives
Sliced radish
Mint leaves

1. Mix the yogurt and salt.

2. Place the mixture in the center of a square of cheesecloth and tie in a bundle. Hang the cheesecloth on the faucet over the sink, and leave to drain for a few hours or overnight (the time depends on the climate, and the consistency you need). Alternatively, the mixture can be spooned into a strainer lined with paper towels and placed over a bowl in the refrigerator.

3. Once it has reached the desired consistency, taste and season with more salt, if desired.

4. To serve, spoon into a shallow bowl and drizzle with olive oil. Serve with toasted flatbread and sliced scallions, tomatoes, black olives, radishes, and fresh mint leaves.

5. Store in a sealed container in the refrigerator for up to 10 days. (To extend its life, mix in a little more salt and olive oil.)

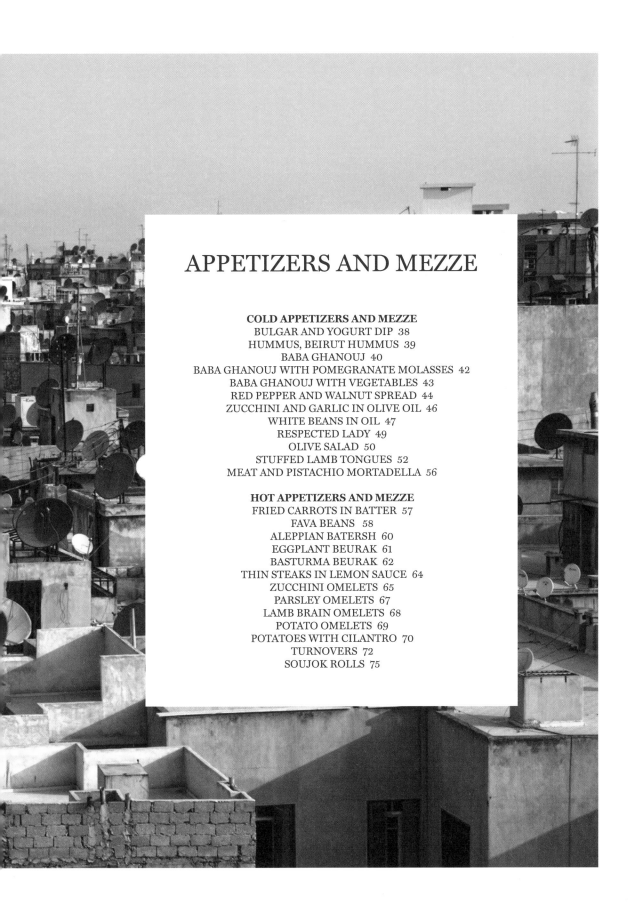

APPETIZERS AND MEZZE

BULGAR AND YOGURT DIP
Kishkeh Khadra

SERVES 4–6 AS PART OF A MEZZE OR 2 AS A LIGHT MEAL
PREPARATION TIME: 10 MINUTES
RESTING TIME: 5 HOURS OR OVERNIGHT

Kishek is a fine powder made by fermenting wheat with yogurt, or sometimes yogurt and milk. It is popular in Syria and Lebanon. *Khadra* means green. The name of the recipe, *Kishkeh Khadra*, refers to the unfermented version of the dish. The dish is nourishing and very simple to prepare with easily available ingredients: yogurt, bulgar, parsley, mint, and walnuts. Serve it with Arabic flatbread, black olives, scallions, and tomatoes. It is also delicious with toast or crackers. Try it in the morning for breakfast, in the afternoon as a bite between meals, or in the evening as part of a light dinner. This dish can be prepared up to two days before serving and stored in the refrigerator: mix in a few tablespoons of yogurt if it thickens.

½ cup/3½ oz/95 g fine bulgar

2 cups/1 lb/450 g plain yogurt, preferably sheep's yogurt (or an equal mixture of yogurt and Strained Yogurt, p. 35)

1 teaspoon salt, or to taste

½ cup/2 oz/60 g walnuts, soaked in water for at least 30 minutes

1–2 garlic cloves (4–8 g), crushed

¼ cup/½ oz/15 g chopped parsley

2 teaspoons dried mint, or ¼ cup/ ½ oz/15 g chopped fresh mint

½ small onion (2 oz/60 g), finely chopped

3 tablespoons olive oil, and more to drizzle on top

Dried or fresh mint, ground red pepper, and olive oil, to garnish

1. Wash the bulgar, squeeze dry, and mix with the yogurt and salt. Refrigerate 4 hours or overnight. (The bulgar will absorb the moisture and soften.)

2. Place a strainer over a bowl and line it with muslin or absorbent paper towel. Spoon the bulgar/yogurt mixture into the strainer and refrigerate for 1 hour. Discard the whey that collects in the bowl. (The mixture should be the consistency of slightly whipped cream.)

3. Coarsely chop the walnuts, keeping a couple whole for the garnish, and combine with the bulgar-yogurt mixture along with the rest of the ingredients. Taste and adjust seasoning.

4. Place on a serving platter, drizzle with olive oil, garnish as desired, and serve cold with Arabic flatbread and olive oil.

HUMMUS
Hummus bi-Tahina

MAKES 5 CUPS/2 LB/1 KG
PREPARATION TIME: 10 MINUTES
RESTING TIME: OVERNIGHT
COOKING TIME: 1½ HOURS

Hummus is an essential part of a mezze in most Arab countries. In this age of globalization it has traveled beyond the Middle East and is now a much-loved dish in many countries of the world. It is really easy to prepare; simply mixing cooked, crushed chickpeas with tahini, lemon juice, and garlic. Without a doubt, the best hummus is homemade!

The most time-consuming part is cooking the chickpeas and then crushing them to a silky smooth texture. To achieve this one needs to have two things: good quality chickpeas that have been cooked until very soft, and a good food processor (for a finer texture, you can add a few tablespoons of yogurt to the hot chickpeas and use a blender). The rest is simply adding tahini, crushed garlic, and lemon juice. Canned chickpeas are not recommended, as they do not fulfill the first rule.

You can prepare a large batch of hummus, leaving out the garlic, and store it in containers in the freezer to be defrosted when needed. Add the crushed garlic just before serving. You can adjust the quantities to your liking.

2 cups/14 oz/400 g good quality
    dried chickpeas
2 teaspoons baking soda
¾ cup/180 ml lemon juice
¾ cup/180 ml tahini
5 garlic cloves (¾ oz/20 g), crushed
1½ teaspoons ground cumin
    (optional)
1 teaspoon salt, or to taste
2–4 tablespoons/30–60 ml olive oil
A sprinkle of Aleppo pepper or
    paprika (optional)

1. Soak and cook chickpeas according to the instructions on p. 16. Drain and reserve the cooking liquid.

2. Using a food processor or immersion blender, blend the hot chickpeas to a creamy texture.

3. Add the lemon juice, tahini, crushed garlic, and cumin, if using. Process until well mixed.

4. Add enough cooking liquid to form a soft paste. Taste and adjust the seasoning, adding salt, if necessary.

5. Spoon onto a serving platter. Make a well in the center using the back of a spoon. Drizzle with olive oil and sprinkle with Aleppo pepper or paprika, if using.

6. Serve cold with Arabic flatbread or toasted bread, scallions, and radish.

VARIATIONS: BEIRUT HUMMUS (*HUMMUS BEIRUTY*)

• Mix 1¼ cups/8 oz/225 g hummus with 3 oz/90 g finely chopped pickles; 1 large, firm tomato (6½ oz/185 g), seeded and finely chopped; 1 cup/2 oz/60 g finely chopped parsley; and 1½ teaspoons ground cumin. Drizzle with about 2 tablespoons olive oil before serving.

BABA GHANOUJ
Baba Ghannooj bi-Tahina

SERVES 6 AS PART OF A MEZZE
PREPARATION TIME: 10 MINUTES
COOKING TIME: 20 MINUTES

Tahini, garlic, and lemon juice are zesty companions to roasted eggplant in this easy-to-prepare dip. To reduce the calories, substitute half the amount of tahini with yogurt or Strained Yogurt (p. 35), if desired. This dish can be prepared up to two days before serving.

1 lb 5 oz/600 g eggplant

2 garlic cloves (¼ oz/8 g)

¾ teaspoon salt, or to taste

3–4 tablespoons/45–60 ml
    lemon juice

⅓ cup/75 ml tahini

2 tablespoons plain yogurt,
    mixed with a fork

To garnish (optional)

Seeds of half a pomegranate,
    or 1 small tomato, chopped
Chopped parsley leaves
Olive oil

1. Using the tip of a small knife or the tines of a fork, prick each eggplant in a few places to allow steam to escape (the eggplant will burst if skin is not pierced). Remove the leaves of the green cap, leaving the stem attached.

2. Insert a skewer into the eggplant allowing a handle to protrude at one end to hold on to. (Make sure you use a towel or oven mitt as the metal may get very hot!) Place the eggplant directly over an open flame, turning it every few minutes to char the skin all over (this infuses the eggplant with a smoky flavor). Alternatively, broil or grill for at least 20 minutes, turning once, until the skin is charred and the pulp is soft.

3. While still hot, peel the eggplant under cold running water, and cut crosswise into rough chunks.

4. Crush the garlic with salt and place in the food processor or large mortar, along with the eggplant pulp, lemon juice, tahini, and yogurt. Pulse or pound the ingredients, keeping the texture coarse. Taste and adjust the seasoning.

5. Spoon the mixture into a serving bowl or platter, drizzle with oil, and decorate with pomegranate seeds or tomato, parsley, and olive oil (if using). Serve cold with Arabic flatbread.

VARIATIONS

Verjuice (sour grape juice) or sour pomegranate juice can be used instead of the lemon juice.

BABA GHANOUJ WITH POMEGRANATE MOLASSES
Baba Ghannooj bi-Dibs al-Rimman

SERVES 6–8 AS PART OF A MEZZE
PREPARATION TIME: 20 MINUTES
RESTING TIME: 30 MINUTES
COOKING TIME: 10 MINUTES

Fried and crushed eggplant slices are mixed with pomegranate molasses and garlic to yield this succulent dip. This is best served with Arabic flatbread.

2–3 eggplants (about 2 lb/1 kg)

1½ teaspoon salt, or to taste

Vegetable oil, for frying

4 garlic cloves (½ oz/15 g), crushed

3 tablespoons pomegranate
    molasses

¼ teaspoon ground black pepper

Olive oil, to serve

1. Cut the green stems off the eggplants; peel and slice lengthwise into slices ½ in/1½ cm thick.

2. Sprinkle slices with salt on both sides and leave to sweat for 30 minutes in a strainer or on paper towels.

3. Wipe the eggplants with paper towels and fry in hot oil until golden. Using a slotted spoon, transfer cooked slices to a strainer.

4. Place each slice between paper towels and press with the palms of the hands to remove excess oil.

5. Place the eggplant slices in a food processor with the crushed garlic, pomegranate molasses, and black pepper and pulse a couple of times. (Alternatively, finely chop the eggplant slices, crush with a fork, and mix with the rest of the ingredients.) Taste and adjust the seasoning.

6. Spoon onto a platter, drizzle with olive oil, and serve with Arabic flatbread.

BABA GHANOUJ WITH VEGETABLES
Baba Ghannooj bi-Khodar

SERVES 6 AS PART OF A MEZZE
PREPARATION TIME: 15 MINUTES
COOKING TIME: 20 MINUTES

Ghannooj in Arabic means "coquettish," referring to how the sturdy eggplant becomes so tender and compliant after being cooked and bared of its skin.

In this recipe the eggplant is not weighed down by other players but stands by itself, accompanied by only a few finely chopped vegetables. The eggplant can be steamed or boiled for this dish, but grilling directly over an open flame gives it a sublime smoky taste. It is the dish of choice for the health and calorie conscious. Choose eggplants that are shiny and firm with small seeds.

2–3 eggplants (about 2 lb/1 kg)

¼ cup/1½ oz/40 g finely chopped sweet green pepper

¼ cup/1½ oz/40 g finely chopped sweet red pepper

¼ cup/1¾ oz/50 g seeded and finely chopped tomatoes

¼ cup/½ oz/15 g finely chopped parsley leaves

For the dressing

¼ cup/60 ml olive oil

2–3 tablespoons lemon juice

2 garlic cloves (¼ oz/8 g), crushed

¼ teaspoon ground white pepper

1 teaspoon salt, or to taste

To garnish (optional)

Olive oil

Pomegranate seeds

1. Using the tip of a small knife or the tines of a fork, prick the eggplant in few places to allow steam to escape (it will burst if skin is not pierced). Remove the leaves of the green cap, keeping the stem attached.

2. Insert a skewer into the eggplant allowing a handle to protrude at one end to hold on to. (Make sure you use a towel or oven mitt as the metal may get very hot!) Place the eggplant directly over an open flame, turning it every few minutes to char the skin all over (this infuses the flesh with a smoky flavor). Alternatively, broil or grill for at least 20 minutes, turning once, until the skin is charred and the flesh is soft.

3. While still hot, peel the eggplant under cold running water.

4. Chop the eggplant flesh and place in a bowl with the peppers, tomatoes, and parsley.

5. Combine the dressing ingredients, mix well, and stir into the eggplant mixture. Taste and adjust seasoning.

6. Spoon onto a serving plate, garnish with olive oil and pomegranate seeds (if using), and serve at room temperature with Arabic flatbread.

RED PEPPER AND WALNUT SPREAD
Muhammara

SERVES 4–5 AS PART OF A MEZZE
PREPARATION TIME: 15 MINUTES

With a brilliant red color and intense flavors that fuse together to tantalize the palate, Red Pepper and Walnut Spread is the star of the Aleppian mezze and a seductive companion to many dishes. It is popular throughout the Levant—in South Lebanon it is served as an accompaniment to Pan-Baked Kibbeh (p. 177), and in western Turkey it is known as *acuka*—but it is Aleppo that claims it as its own.

The principal ingredients are red pepper paste, chopped walnuts, pomegranate molasses, cumin, breadcrumbs, and olive oil. It may also include chopped onion, garlic, lemon juice, and tahini, which soften the flavors of the main ingredients. It looks so easy to prepare, but in fact it can be an intricate process to adjust the balance of flavors, which depend heavily on the quality of the ingredients and the taste buds of the chef. One can only imagine the spectrum of variations; in Aleppo there are as many versions of this recipe as there are cooks.

If red pepper paste is not available, fresh or dried sweet red peppers may be used instead (*see* Notes). Care must be taken when using pomegranate molasses. I use the genuine Aleppian product, which has a pure, lemony, sweet taste that is not impaired by the addition of sugar, citric acid, or dyes. You may need to add lemon juice to sweeter pomegranate molasses varieties.

This versatile spread can be served with bread or vegetables as an appetizer or mezze dish (adjust the texture by adding more water or oil), or as an accompaniment to meat or kibbeh dishes, or with Meat and Pistachio Mortadella (p. 56). I sometimes serve it smeared on Arabic flatbread, then grilled, or as a canapé in baked filo or Arabic flatbread cups: fill the baked cups with Red Pepper and Walnut Spread just before serving (*see* Photo).

1 cup/3 oz/80 g breadcrumbs
    (*see* Notes)

⅓ cup/75 ml red pepper paste

2 tablespoons pomegranate molasses

1 tablespoon ground cumin

1 tablespoon Aleppo pepper or
    paprika

1 tablespoon sugar

½ cup/120 ml best quality extra
    virgin olive oil

Up to 2 tablespoons lemon juice,
    if needed

1 teaspoon salt, or to taste

Scant 1 cup/3½ oz/100 g walnuts

Extra olive oil, for drizzling

Pine nuts, whole walnuts, and/or
    mint leaves, to garnish (optional)

1. Using a fork, mix all the ingredients up to and including lemon juice (if using) in a medium-size bowl.

2. Gradually add enough water to make a smooth, moist paste (about ⅓ cup/75 ml). Taste and add the salt.

3. Coarsely chop half of the walnuts. Finely chop the remaining half. Add the walnuts to the bowl and mix well.

4. Spoon the paste onto a serving platter and smooth the top, making a design with a small spoon, if desired. Drizzle with olive oil, decorate with nuts and/or mint, if using, and serve at room temperature. Red Pepper and Walnut Spread keeps well for 10 days in the refrigerator. You may need to mix in a little more water the next day to soften.

NOTES

- Store-bought breadcrumbs are finely ground and weigh about 5 oz/135 g per cup. Dried breadcrumbs prepared at home usually weigh about 3 oz/80 g per cup. The amount of water used in the recipe depends on the kind of breadcrumbs.

ZUCCHINI AND GARLIC IN OLIVE OIL
Mtawamet al-Koosa

SERVES 6–8 AS PART OF A MEZZE
PREPARATION TIME: 10 MINUTES
RESTING TIME: 30 MINUTES
COOKING TIME: 10 MINUTES

This is a healthy vegetarian dish of zucchini cores, onion, and garlic, all sautéed in olive oil. It is usually prepared after cooking Stuffed Zucchini (p. 216), to use up the scooped out cores, but it can be prepared with coarsely grated whole zucchini, and sometimes even eggplant (*see* Variations). Serve with Arabic bread.

1 lb/450 g coarsely grated zucchini (or the cores of about 4 lb/2 kg zucchini, chopped)

1 teaspoon salt, or to taste

Scant ½ cup/100 ml olive oil

1 small onion (4 oz/115 g), finely chopped

4 garlic cloves (½ oz/15 g), crushed

¼ teaspoon ground black pepper

2 teaspoons dried mint

½ teaspoon Aleppo pepper or paprika

1. Mix the grated or chopped zucchini with the salt and set aside for 30 minutes. Squeeze gently to remove excess moisture.

2. In a pot, heat the olive oil over medium to low heat. Fry the onion until tender, stirring.

3. Add the zucchini and continue stirring until tender (a few minutes). Add the crushed garlic and black pepper and fry for a few minutes more, stirring frequently.

4. Remove the pot from the heat and mix in the dried mint. Taste and add salt, if needed; then allow to cool.

5. Spoon the mixture onto a serving platter, sprinkle with Aleppo pepper or paprika, and serve cold.

VARIATIONS

For Eggplant and Garlic in Olive Oil, replace the zucchini with eggplant cores or grated eggplant. Add about 1 cup/5½ oz/ 160 g cooked chickpeas towards the end of cooking. You can also fry 3–4 eggs with the eggplant.

WHITE BEANS IN OIL
Fasoliah Baida bi-Zeit

SERVES 6 AS PART OF A MEZZE
PREPARATION TIME: 5 MINUTES
COOKING TIME: 15 MINUTES

White beans are known for their high fiber content and richness in protein, vitamins, and minerals. Here, they are combined with onion, garlic, and tomatoes to make a healthy, nourishing appetizer. In Greece, this dish is prepared using very large white beans called *plaki*. In Turkey, it is made with red beans.

1 very small onion (3 oz/85 g), finely chopped

1 carrot, finely chopped

¼ cup/60 ml olive oil

5 garlic cloves (¾ oz/20 g), crushed

2 tablespoons tomato paste

2 tablespoons red pepper paste

1 teaspoon sugar

¼ teaspoon ground white pepper

1 teaspoon salt, or to taste

15 oz/450 g can cannellini, great northern, or navy beans (or soaked and cooked dried beans; *see* Notes)

Lemon wedges, to serve (optional)

1. In a large pot, fry the onion and carrot in olive oil over medium heat until tender. Add the garlic and fry for a few more seconds.

2. Pour 2 cups/480 ml water into the pot, then add the rest of the ingredients, except the beans and lemon wedges, and bring to a boil.

3. Lower the heat, cover the pot, and simmer for about 15 minutes, or until the carrots are cooked and the liquid has reduced.

4. Drain and wash the canned beans and add them to the mixture in the pot.

5. Bring to a boil and simmer for 1 minute, stirring once or twice.

6. Spoon into a serving dish and serve cold with lemon wedges on the side if desired, and Arabic flatbread to scoop the white beans.

NOTES

To cook dried white beans: Soak 1 cup/8 oz/225 g dried beans in twice their volume of water for 8 hours or overnight. Strain the beans and rinse them thoroughly. Place the beans in a pot and cover with water by 1 in/3 cm. Bring to a boil, lower the heat, and simmer for 45 minutes, or until tender. Drain and continue with the recipe as above.

RESPECTED LADY
Sit Geleila

SERVES 6–8 AS PART OF A MEZZE
PREPARATION TIME: 10 MINUTES

This is a simple dish of pickled turnips, onions, and cumin. It is normally served as part of a mezze, and sometimes as a side dish. Pickled turnips are widely used in Aleppo as well as in many parts of the Arab world. In the US, they can be found in most Middle Eastern grocery stores. Beets are added to the jar to produce their characteristic bright pink color. You can prepare this dish ahead (add the scallions or onion just before serving).

14 oz/400 g drained pickled turnips

2 scallions, sliced, or ½ small onion
    (2 oz/60 g), finely chopped

1 teaspoon ground cumin

3 tablespoons/15 ml olive oil

1. Slice turnips into thin matchsticks and place in a bowl.

2. Mix in the rest of the ingredients.

3. Serve cold or at room temperature.

VARIATIONS

- Chopped tomatoes can be added to the pickled turnips.
- Pomegranate molasses can be added along with the oil.
- You can make this salad with pickled cucumbers instead of turnips.

OLIVE SALAD
Salatet Zeitoon

SERVES 6 AS PART OF A MEZZE
PREPARATION TIME: 15 MINUTES

Syria ranks fourth in the world in the production of olives and is the original home of the olive tree, which has been cultivated there for thousands of years. Olives are grown mainly in the Harem region and the Kurd Mountains, near Afrin. They are harvested in early autumn and processed for storage in glass jars.

An important staple, they are found on every table in the Arab world, usually as part of breakfast or mezze. If you like green olives then you must try them in a salad the way they are prepared in Aleppo—hot, sweet, and sour. Pomegranate seeds are sometimes added to this salad.

6 oz/170 g pitted green olives
(avoid bitter olives)

1 tablespoon red pepper paste

3 tablespoons olive oil

2 teaspoons pomegranate molasses

2 teaspoons tomato paste

2 scallions (white and tender green
parts), thinly sliced

1 small tomato (3½ oz/100 g), seeds
removed, diced

¼ cup/1 oz/30 g coarsely chopped
walnuts

1 teaspoon sugar

¼ teaspoon ground black pepper,
or to taste

Salt, if needed

1 tablespoon chopped parsley, to
garnish

1. In a bowl, combine and mix all the ingredients, except for the parsley. Taste and adjust seasoning.

2. Spoon onto a serving platter, decorate with chopped parsley, and serve with Arabic flatbread.

STUFFED LAMB TONGUES

Lsanat Dobo

SERVES 8 AS PART OF A MEZZE
PREPARATION TIME: 20 MINUTES
RESTING TIME: 30 MINUTES
COOKING TIME: 1–2 HOURS

Aleppians use every edible part of the lamb, producing excellent recipes. Tongue meat is favored for its strong muscular texture and assertive flavor. In this unusual cold appetizer, lamb tongues are stuffed with pistachios and garlic and cooked in an aromatic stock.

Traditionally, this recipe is prepared with tongues that still have part of the upper muscles (*lagh-lough*) attached; the fat from the upper muscles is a welcome addition. However, if whole tongues are difficult to find, the recipe can be prepared without the upper muscles.

This is an old recipe that has lately been overlooked in favor of the easier method, serving the tongues sliced without stuffing. Though not traditional, you may also choose to substitute beef tongues for this recipe, which are more readily available in the West (*see* Variations).

1 lb/450 g lamb tongues
    (about 6), including upper
    muscles, if possible
Ice-cold water, for soaking

For the stuffing

5 garlic cloves (¾ oz/20 g), coarsely
    chopped
¼ cup/1 oz/33 g shelled unsalted
    pistachios
½ teaspoon Aleppo spice mix or
    seven-spice powder
¼ teaspoon ground black pepper
¾ teaspoon salt, or to taste

For the stock

½ cup/120 ml red wine vinegar
5 cloves
3 cardamom pods
½ in/1 cm piece of dried or fresh
    ginger (optional)
2 bay leaves
½ teaspoon black peppercorns
1 cinnamon stick
½ small onion (2 oz/60 g), peeled
1 small dried lime (*lomi*), pierced
    with the tip of a knife (optional)
½ teaspoon salt, or to taste

1. Soak the tongues in ice-cold water for 30 minutes and drain.

2. Place the tongues in a pot with water to cover and bring to a boil over medium heat. Simmer for a few seconds, or until foam forms on the top. Drain and wash the tongues.

To stuff the tongues

3. Using the tip of a small knife, make an incision in the middle of the thickest end of the tongue. Rotate the knife, making incisions in a star shape, to hollow out a cavity. Insert the handle of a wooden spoon into the cavity, and carefully rotate to widen it as much as possible; the small part at the end is difficult to reach with a knife. (An easier method is to make a 1½ inch/2 cm slit along the length of the tongue, though this makes for a less attractive dish.)

4. Mix stuffing ingredients. Stuff each tongue, pushing it in with your finger to fill the cavity. Sew or tie the opening with cotton thread.

To cook and serve

5. Place tongues in a pot with 4 cups/1 liter water and add the stock ingredients. Bring to a boil, skimming any foam that forms on the top. Lower the heat, cover the pot, and simmer slowly for 1½ hours, or until tender.

6. Remove tongues, reserving the stock for later use (*see* Notes). While still warm, remove the skin from each tongue. Cool and cut each tongue into lengthwise slices. Serve cold.

NOTES

- The tongue stock can be used to cook bulgar or rice as an accompaniment, if desired; strain the stock before using, mixing in some beef stock if it is too sour.
- To freeze this dish: After removing the outer skin, wrap each tongue in plastic wrap and freeze. Defrost in the refrigerator 24 hours before serving. Serve as above.

VARIATIONS

SLICED LAMB TONGUES (UNSTUFFED)

Follow the steps above, omitting the stuffing (keeping the tongues whole). Cool and thinly slice the tongues. Serve with a dressing of lemon juice, olive oil, and a hint of crushed garlic.

STUFFED BEEF TONGUE

Replace the lamb with 1 beef tongue (around 3 lb/1½ kg). Increase the water to 6 cups/1.5 liters, increase the vinegar to 1 cup/240 ml, and double the quantity of all the aromatics ingredients except the dried lime (if using). Double the stuffing ingredients and add 2 teaspoons of water to the mixture. Follow the instructions as above, simmering for 2 hours, or until tender. You can make delicious gravy from the leftover cooking stock, if desired.

MEAT AND PISTACHIO MORTADELLA
Mortadella

MAKES 2 ROLLS, EACH 6 IN X 2½ IN/15 X 6 CM
PREPARATION TIME: 20–30 MINUTES
COOKING TIME: 40 MINUTES
RESTING TIME: 2 HOURS

Aleppo's response to the Italians! This recipe most likely predates the Italian version, but it is called by the Italian name. It is easy to prepare and very handy to have if guests drop in without notice, as often happens in Aleppo. It makes a good appetizer; it is beautiful as part of a mezze, ideal for a buffet, and tasty in a sandwich. Typically, lamb is used but it can also be prepared with beef or chicken (*see* Variations). You can use any leftover cooking stock to prepare Bulgar Pilaf with Chickpeas (p. 112) or Bulgar Pilaf with Vermicelli (p. 110).

1 lb/450 g finely ground lean lamb or beef (pulse in a food processor or pound to obtain a fine texture)
¼ cup/¾ oz/20 g breadcrumbs
4 garlic cloves (½ oz/15 g), crushed
1 tablespoon Aleppo spice mix or seven-spice powder
1 teaspoon cinnamon
¼–½ teaspoon ground black pepper
1 egg yolk
Pinch red food-coloring powder (optional)
1½ teaspoons salt, or to taste
½ cup/3 oz/80 g unsalted shelled pistachios, lightly toasted
½–1 red chili, seeds removed and finely chopped (optional)
¼ cup/60 ml vegetable oil

For the stock

4 cups/1 liter cold water
1 cup/240 ml white or cider vinegar
½ small onion (2 oz/60 g), quartered
1 small carrot, chopped
1 bay leaf
1 cinnamon stick
1½ teaspoons salt, or to taste

To make the rolls

1. Mix all the ingredients except the oil. Knead briefly then divide into 2 portions.

2. With moistened hands, form one portion into a ball, pressing on it to avoid the formation of air holes. Push the pistachios back in if they surface.

3. Working on a floured surface, form one portion into a roll about 6 in/15 cm long, and level the surface with dampened hands. Repeat the procedure with the second portion of meat. Refrigerate, covered for at least 2 hours.

To cook and serve

4. Fry the rolls in the oil, turning them to color all over.

5. Place the stock ingredients in a pot. Bring to a boil over high heat; then turn down the heat and simmer for 1 minute. Place the meat rolls in the stock and simmer, uncovered, for 30 minutes, turning them once.

6. Remove rolls and reserve the stock for another use. Allow to cool. (You can place a weighted plate on top of the rolls while they cool to remove any holes, but this is not essential if the rolls are properly shaped.) Once cool, refrigerate until cold.

7. Thinly slice the rolls and serve cold.

VARIATIONS

- For Chicken Mortadella, use 1 lb/450 g chicken breast and thigh meat instead of the meat; pound them to a paste, remove sinews, and continue as above.
- 5 oz/150 g skinless boneless chicken breast can be cut lengthwise into 2 inch strips, seasoned, and placed in the center of the meat rectangle before rolling.

FRIED CARROTS IN BATTER
Jazar bi-Rawbeh

SERVES 8–10 AS PART OF A MEZZE
PREPARATION TIME: 15 MINUTES
COOKING TIME: 10 MINUTES

It is a wonder how humble ingredients like carrots and flour can produce such a tasty and appetizing dish. This recipe can be easily halved for smaller parties.

1 lb/450 g carrots (black carrots,
    if you can find them), washed,
    dried, and peeled
¾ cup/180 ml canola or peanut oil

For the batter

1 cup/4½ oz/125 g all-purpose flour
½ teaspoon ground white pepper
¼ teaspoon Aleppo spice mix or
    seven-spice powder
1½ teaspoons salt, or to taste

1. Thinly slice the carrots lengthwise.

2. Make the batter: Sift the flour, spices, and salt into a bowl. Make a well in the center. Gradually pour 1 cup/240 ml water into the well, stirring with a wire whisk until no lumps remain (this can also be done in a food processor).

3. Heat the oil until moderately hot (320°F/160°C). Dip one carrot slice in the batter and fry to test the coating. If the coating is too thin, sift 1–2 teaspoons more flour into the mixture and try again. If too thick, mix in 1–2 teaspoons water.

4. Start dipping and frying a few slices at a time; do not crowd the pan, as this lowers the temperature, causing the carrots to absorb too much oil. Each batch takes a few minutes; remove the carrots as soon as they are cooked through, and transfer to a strainer. You can prepare the recipe several hours in advance up to this step. (To reheat: Immediately before serving, deep-fry the carrots again in very hot oil [350°F/180°C] for a few seconds until crisp and golden.)

FAVA BEANS
Fool Medammas

SERVES 4 AS A BREAKFAST OR 8 AS PART OF A MEZZE
PREPARATION TIME: 20–25 MINUTES
RESTING TIME: OVERNIGHT
COOKING TIME: 3 HOURS (SEE VARIATIONS FOR QUICKER METHOD)

Medammas means concealed, and *fool* is the Arabic word for fava beans (also known as broad beans). Fava beans are the oldest cultivated beans, loaded with nutrients and used widely in the Middle East (there are 2 varieties: a smaller variety is used in Lebanon, while a larger variety is preferred in Aleppo).

This dish is a popular breakfast all over the Arab world, and it is also sometimes served as part of a mezze. In Aleppo it is also a street food, popularized by the famous Hajj Abou-Abdo, who has been preparing this dish for the last fifty years in his small shop in Sahet al-Hatab (Lumber Square). People stand in line to buy the beans, cooked in a large brass urn and served in small earthenware bowls.

The beans can be served simply with a little lemon juice, crushed garlic, ground cumin, and a drizzle of olive oil, but this recipe is the way they are served in restaurants or hotels or for guests. To save time, you can use canned fava beans (*see* Variation).

3 cups/14 oz/400 g large dried fava
    beans, soaked overnight
1½ teaspoons baking soda
2 teaspoons salt, or to taste

For the tahini sauce

⅓ cup/75 ml tahini
Scant ½ cup/100 ml lemon juice
½ teaspoon salt, or to taste

For the lemon-garlic sauce

½ cup/120 ml lemon juice
4 garlic cloves (½ oz/15 g), crushed
½ teaspoon salt, or to taste

To serve

Arabic flatbread
2 small firm tomatoes (7 oz/200 g),
    seeds removed, finely diced
3 scallions (1 oz/30 g), finely
    chopped
2 tablespoons ground cumin
¼ cup/½ oz/15 g chopped parsley
1 tablespoon Aleppo pepper or
    paprika
½ cup/120 ml olive oil

1. Drain and rinse the soaked beans. In a pot, cover them with water by 2 in/5 cm. Bring to a boil over high heat. Lower the heat, cover the pot, and simmer for 1 hour.

2. Drain and rinse the cooked beans, and place them in a pot for a second cooking. Pour in hot water to cover by 2 in/5 cm and add the baking soda. Bring to a boil, lower the heat, and simmer slowly for 2 hours, or until very tender, adding more hot water as needed. (Once done, the cooking liquid should barely cover the beans.) Remove from heat and mix in the salt.

3. Mix the tahini sauce ingredients with 6 tablespoons/90 ml water and spoon into a serving bowl.

4. Mix the lemon-garlic sauce ingredients with scant ½ cup/ 100 ml water and pour into a small serving bowl.

5. To serve: Place the beans and their cooking liquid in a serving bowl. Serve hot, with the rest of the serving ingredients on the side so that each person can arrange his or her dish as desired.

VARIATIONS: A QUICKER METHOD

Replace the dried beans with 2 cans (28 oz/800 g) cooked fava beans, omitting the baking soda. Rinse and drain the beans and place them in a medium pot with water to cover. Simmer for 8–10 minutes until the beans are heated through and the water has been mostly absorbed. Add the salt, if needed. Follow the recipe from step 3.

ALEPPIAN BATERSH
Batersh Halab

SERVES 4 AS A MAIN DISH OR 6 AS PART OF A MEZZE
PREPARATION TIME: 5 MINUTES
RESTING TIME: 1 HOUR
COOKING TIME: 20 MINUTES

I will never forget the lunch I had at the home of Chef Khaldoun Tchalabi, where his friends and family gathered to taste his excellent dishes. Everyone clapped and hailed as each dish emerged from the kitchen. I can still taste his succulent *Batersh*—perfectly grilled eggplants mixed with yogurt, tahini, and garlic, and topped with a layer of fried ground meat in a thick tomato sauce. All this pleasure was garnished with lots of golden fried pine nuts.

    Batersh originated in Turkey, where it is called *Ali Nazik*. It was prepared in Hama before it found its way to Aleppo. In Turkey, cheese is added to the eggplant to thicken it; in Aleppo, strained yogurt and a few tablespoons of tahini are mixed with the eggplant flesh. It can be served as an appetizer, a main dish, or as an accompaniment to meat or chicken dishes. In Turkey, it is served with rice.

1–2 large eggplants, (2 lb/1 kg)

1 cup/8 oz/225 g *Labneh* (Strained
    Yogurt, *see* p. 35) or thick Greek
    yogurt

¼–⅓ cup/60–75 ml tahini

4 garlic cloves (½ oz/15 g), crushed

1 teaspoon salt, or to taste

For the top layer

Scant ½ cup/100 ml olive oil

1 small onion (4 oz/115 g), finely
    chopped

14 oz/400 g lean ground lamb or
    beef

3 garlic cloves (⅓ oz/12 g), crushed

½ teaspoon ground black pepper

1 teaspoon salt, or to taste

¼ cup/60 ml tomato paste

½ teaspoon sugar

1 tablespoon pomegranate molasses

2 tablespoons pine nuts

A few parsley leaves, to garnish

1. Prick the eggplant in a few places and broil for 20 minutes, turning once, until the skin is charred and the pulp is soft. Holding the eggplant by the stem, peel under cold running water. Place the pulp in a strainer set over a bowl for about an hour to drain off some of the liquid.

2. Cut the eggplant crosswise and place in the bowl of a food processor with the yogurt, tahini, garlic, and salt. Pulse a few times until a coarse paste has formed. Spoon onto a serving platter, flatten slightly, and set aside. (Recipe may be prepared to this step a day in advance, refrigerated, and brought to room temperature before proceeding.)

For the top layer and to serve

3. Heat half the oil in a pot and fry the onion over low heat until tender. Raise the heat to high and add the meat, crushed garlic, black pepper, and salt. Sauté, stirring, until the meat loses its pink color.

4. Pour 1 cup/240 ml water into the pot and add the tomato paste and sugar. Cover and cook on low heat for 10–15 minutes. Stir in the pomegranate molasses. Taste and adjust seasoning.

5. Fry the pine nuts in the rest of the oil over low heat until golden.

6. Spoon the meat and sauce on top of the crushed eggplant layer, then sprinkle the pine nuts on top with the frying oil. Garnish with parsley and serve immediately.

EGGPLANT BEURAK
Banjane Beurak

SERVES 8 AS PART OF A MEZZE
PREPARATION TIME: 20 MINUTES
RESTING TIME: 60 MINUTES IN TOTAL
COOKING TIME: 15 MINUTES

Börek (sometimes spelled *beurak, burek, boereg, piroq*) is a Turkish word for a type of savory stuffed pastry. In this recipe, the dough is replaced with eggplant and the stuffing is cheese and dried ground red pepper, making a hot appetizer that melts in the mouth.

This recipe traditionally uses *jibneh khadra*, meaning "green cheese." This is a fresh, young white cheese that also forms the basis of other cheeses. It is salty and similar to halloumi in flavor and texture, though slightly more tender. Other kinds of mild white cheeses can also be used in this recipe.

1 lb/450 g small eggplants (about 8)

1 teaspoon salt, or to taste

1 cup/240 ml vegetable oil

For the stuffing

1¾ oz/50 g white cheese such as
  halloumi, mozzarella, or feta;
  grated or crumbled

2 teaspoons finely chopped parsley

1 teaspoon Aleppo pepper or paprika

¼ teaspoon allspice

¼ teaspoon ground white pepper

½ teaspoon salt (less if the cheese
  is salty)

To coat

¼ cup/1 oz/30 g all-purpose flour

1 egg mixed with 1 tablespoon water,
  ½ teaspoon salt, and ¼ teaspoon
  cinnamon

1 cup/3 oz/80 g breadcrumbs mixed
  with ½ teaspoon Aleppo pepper
  or paprika

1. Peel the eggplants, cutting off the green leaves and part of the stem, leaving about ½ in/1 cm. Unless they are very thin, cut each eggplant in half lengthwise. Cut a lengthwise slit on the side of each eggplant or half.

2. Place the eggplants in a strainer or over paper towels and sprinkle with salt. Set aside for 30 minutes. Wipe eggplants using paper towels.

3. Shallow fry the eggplants in about ¼ cup/60 ml of the oil until light golden in color, turning once. Cool.

4. Combine all the stuffing ingredients.

5. Open the slit of the eggplants and work it a little to widen the opening. Push as much stuffing inside as possible.

6. Carefully dip each eggplant in flour, then in the egg mixture, and then in the breadcrumbs. Refrigerate for 30 minutes. (The recipe can be prepared one day ahead up to this step.)

7. Deep-fry the cooled eggplants in hot vegetable oil until golden, turning them a few times for even coloring (their color will darken after removing them from the oil). Strain the oil between batches, if necessary.

8. Serve immediately; they will only stay crisp for about an hour.

BASTURMA BEURAK

Beurak al-Basturma

MAKES 22
PREPARATION TIME: 15–20 MINUTES
COOKING TIME: 20 MINUTES

In this dish, filo pastry is stuffed with cheese and basturma (*see* p. 338) and baked in the oven. It is a handy appetizer, since it can be premade and frozen, and baked as needed.

5 filo leaves cut into 22 strips
   (12 x 2½ in/30 x 6 cm each)
5 tablespoons/2½ oz/70 g butter,
   melted

For the stuffing

5 oz/150 g reduced-salt white cheese
1¾ oz/50 g basturma, thinly sliced
1 teaspoon dried mint
½ teaspoon Aleppo pepper or
   paprika
Dash ground white pepper or
   cayenne

1. Preheat the oven to 400°F/200°C.

2. In a food processor, mix stuffing ingredients to fine crumbs.

3. Brush the first strip of filo with melted butter. (Cover the remaining strips with plastic wrap or a damp cloth as you work.)

4. Place about 1 teaspoon stuffing on one side of a strip of filo, and fold on the diagonal to form a triangle. Continue folding in this way until you reach the end of the strip. Repeat until you have used all the filo strips and stuffing.

5. Brush triangles with melted butter and bake for 20 minutes, or until golden. Serve hot as an appetizer, or with salad.

THIN STEAKS IN LEMON SAUCE
Sharhat Mtaffayeh

SERVES 4–5 AS PART OF A MEZZE
PREPARATION TIME: 15–20 MINUTES
COOKING TIME: 10–15 MINUTES

This dish is known as *barzowlat* or *sharhat*, meaning slices. The word *mtaffayeh* means, "it has been extinguished," referring to the process of dousing the heat of the meat in a sauce. These thin, sautéed lamb steaks are served in a lemon-oil sauce as part of a hot mezze.

The dish can be served as lunch or dinner if accompanied with boiled or fried potatoes. Any piece of tender lamb, mutton, veal, or beef will do; the secret is to flatten it as much as possible before cooking, and dress it with a perfectly seasoned sauce.

2 skirt steaks or thin slices of lamb
    steak, about 7 oz/200 g each
¼ teaspoon ground black pepper
½ teaspoon salt, or to taste
¼ cup/60 ml vegetable oil

For the sauce

1 garlic clove (4g), crushed
½ teaspoon ground cumin
¼ cup/60 ml lemon juice
1 teaspoon cornstarch (optional)
1 teaspoon pomegranate molasses
¼ cup/60 ml olive oil
¾ teaspoon salt, or to taste

1. Cut each steak into 4 equal pieces.

2. Using a mallet, pound until thin and sprinkle both sides with black pepper and salt.

3. In a skillet set over high heat, fry the steaks in the oil in two batches for 30 seconds each side (you can alternatively grill them over charcoal).

4. Remove steaks, leaving the oil in the skillet, and partially cover to keep warm.

To prepare sauce and finish dish

5. Return the skillet to medium heat and fry the crushed garlic and cumin for a few seconds. Pour in the lemon juice.

6. Mix the cornstarch, if using, with ¼ cup/60 ml water and pour into the skillet, stirring. The sauce will thicken as it comes to a boil. Stir in the pomegranate molasses, olive oil, and salt. Taste and adjust seasoning.

7. Bring the sauce to a boil once more; then remove the pan from the heat.

8. Arrange the meat on a serving platter and strain the sauce on top. Serve immediately.

ZUCCHINI OMELETS
Ujjet Koosa

MAKES 8–10 PATTIES
PREPARATION TIME: 15 MINUTES
COOKING TIME: 15 MINUTES

These fried omelet patties are usually prepared from leftover zucchini cores after making Stuffed Zucchini (p. 216), but they are so good that many prepare them from coarsely grated whole zucchini. They are usually served as a part of a hot mezze or as a side dish. They can be prepared one day in advance and reheated or eaten at room temperature with Arabic flatbread. *See* Variations for Oven-Baked Zucchini Omelet.

1 lb/450 g coarsely grated zucchini
    (or the cores of about 4 lb/2 kg
    zucchini)

1 tablespoon salt, or to taste

2 large eggs

⅓ cup/1 oz/30 g finely chopped
    scallions or white onion

⅓ cup/¾ oz/20 g finely chopped
    parsley

¼ cup/½ oz/15 g finely chopped
    mint, or 2 teaspoons dried mint

3 tablespoons/¾ oz/20 g all-
    purpose flour

¼ teaspoon cinnamon

½ teaspoon allspice

½ teaspoon ground black pepper

¼ cup/60 ml vegetable oil

1. Place 5 cups/1.2 liters water and the salt in a medium-size pot over high heat and bring to a boil. Add the zucchini and bring to a boil again. Lower the heat and simmer for 3 minutes. Drain and place zucchini in cold water. Drain again and squeeze dry.

2. In a large bowl, mix the zucchini with the rest of the ingredients except the oil.

3. Place the vegetable oil in a skillet over medium heat; when hot, pour in about 2 tablespoons of zucchini mixture to form a patty, adding as many patties as the pan can hold. (You can use egg fry rings to obtain a neat, even appearance.) Fry until the underside is golden then turn to fry the other side. Transfer to absorbent paper towel to drain.

4. Serve hot or at room temperature.

VARIATIONS: OVEN-BAKED ZUCCHINI OMELET

Follow steps 1 and 2 above. Preheat the oven to 350°F/180°C. Grease a 9 in/23 cm cake pan with ¼ cup/60 ml vegetable oil. Spoon the egg mixture into the pan, level the top, and bake for 30–40 minutes, or until cooked through. Cut into slices and serve hot or at room temperature.

PARSLEY OMELETS
Ujjet Baqdoones

MAKES 26 BITE-SIZE OMELETS OR 1 LARGE OMELET
PREPARATION TIME: 15 MINUTES
RESTING TIME: 1 HOUR
COOKING: 20 MINUTES

Eggs, parsley, mint, garlic, and onion are the few simple ingredients that are combined in these delicious bite-size omelets. They are prepared in every household in Aleppo, particularly Christian households, who make them for Fridays during Lent and on Holy Saturday just before Easter. If you pass the souq you will smell the perfume of these omelets filling the place.

They are traditionally prepared in a special skillet called *ouweinat,* meaning eyeglasses, denoting the round indentations that give these omelets their beautiful shape. If you are able to find one (they have been spotted in Spain and Canada, or try looking for a Danish pancake pan), make sure it is a copper or nonstick pan, half-fill each indentation with oil, and follow the stovetop instructions below.

The omelets are delicious served on a bed of shredded lettuce with Arabic flatbread and a salad of choice. You can serve yogurt on the side, either plain or mixed with shredded lettuce, or combined with garlic and dried mint (*see* Garlic Yogurt, p. 98).

1 cup/2 oz/60 g finely chopped
    parsley
¼ cup/½ oz/15 g finely
    chopped mint
¼ cup/2 oz/60 g finely
    chopped onion
3 garlic cloves (⅓ oz/12 g), crushed
1 teaspoon dried mint
1 teaspoon allspice
1 teaspoon Aleppo pepper or paprika
1 teaspoon salt, or to taste
6 medium eggs (about 2 oz/
    60 g each)
About ⅓ cup/75 ml vegetable oil

NOTES

The ratio of chopped parsley to eggs is important; less parsley and the omelets will not hold their shape.

1. In a bowl, combine the parsley, fresh mint, onion, garlic, dried mint, allspice, Aleppo pepper, and salt. Add the eggs one by one, beating with a fork or whisk after each addition. Set the mixture aside for one hour to rest.

For bite-size omelets (on the stovetop)

2. Heat ¼ cup/60 ml of the oil in a large skillet over medium to high heat. Gently drop about 2 tablespoons of the mixture into the pan for each omelet, being careful not to crowd the pan, and fry until golden, watching carefully so they don't burn. Turn them over and fry the other side. Transfer the cooked omelets to absorbent paper towels. Repeat, in batches, until all the mixture has been used, replenishing the oil as needed.

For one large omelet (in the oven)

2. Preheat the oven to 400°F/200°C.

3. Grease a 9 in/23 cm baking pan with ⅓ cup/75 ml vegetable oil and place it in the oven for a few minutes, or until the oil is warm. Spoon the egg mixture into the pan, level the top, and bake for 30 minutes, or until the eggs have just set.

4. Place under a hot broiler to color top, watching carefully so it doesn't burn.

5. Allow to cool, and cut into slices.

LAMB BRAIN OMELETS
Ujjet Zwaz

MAKES 23 BITE-SIZE OMELETS
PREPARATION TIME: 15 MINUTES
RESTING TIME: 1 HOUR
COOKING TIME: 25 MINUTES

Lamb's brains are considered a delicacy in the Arab world. They are sometimes boiled and served as a salad, or sliced and fried *à l'Anglaise*. They are at their best when prepared in omelets.

5 lamb brains (1 lb/450 g)

Ice-cold water, for soaking

3 tablespoons white wine vinegar

5 white peppercorns

2 bay leaves

½ small onion (2 oz/60 g),
    quartered

1 small cinnamon stick

1 tablespoon salt, or to taste

6 large eggs

½ teaspoon allspice

¾ teaspoon ground white pepper

2 tablespoons/1 oz/30 g butter, or
    more if needed

2 tablespoons vegetable oil, or more
    if needed

1. Place the brains in a bowl and cover with ice-cold water and 2 tablespoons of the vinegar. Set aside for 30 minutes.

2. Remove and discard the red veins from the brains: holding a vein between two fingers, pull gently to dislodge.

3. Place brains in a pot with water to cover. Add the rest of the white vinegar, peppercorns, bay leaves, onion, cinnamon stick, and 2 teaspoons of the salt.

4. Bring to a boil over high heat. Lower heat to medium and simmer the brains for about 8 minutes.

5. Using a slotted spoon, transfer the brains to a strainer. Cool and refrigerate 30 minutes.

6. Crack the eggs into a bowl and beat briefly. Mix in the allspice, white pepper, and the rest of the salt.

7. Chop the brains to 1 in/2.5 cm cubes and mix them into the eggs.

8. In a large skillet, heat the oil and butter over medium heat. Pour in about 2 tablespoons of the egg mixture to form a patty, adding as many patties as the pan can hold without crowding. (You can use egg fry rings to obtain a neat, even appearance.) Fry until the underside is golden then turn to fry the other side. Remove to absorbent paper towel to drain. Repeat, in batches, until all the mixture has been used, replenishing the butter and oil as needed.

9. Serve hot, or cold as sandwich fillers.

POTATO OMELETS
Ujjet Batata

MAKES 27 BITE-SIZE OMELETS OR 1 LARGE OMELET
PREPARATION TIME: 15 MINUTES
COOKING TIME: 35–40 MINUTES

These easy-to-prepare omelets are flavored with potatoes, onions, and various spices. For instructions to fry them in an *ouweinat*, a traditional Aleppian skillet, *see* Parsley Omelets, p. 67. Serve these omelets hot with a fresh green salad.

4 small-medium potatoes
    (1 lb 10 oz/750 g)
1 tablespoon salt
1 teaspoon white vinegar
6 large eggs
1 very small onion (3 oz/85 g),
    grated
1½ tablespoons ground coriander
½ teaspoon Aleppo pepper or
    paprika
1 teaspoon ground cumin
½ teaspoon Aleppo spice mix or
    seven-spice powder
¼ teaspoon ground black pepper
4 garlic cloves (½ oz/15 g), crushed
1½ teaspoons salt, or to taste
About ½ cup/120 ml vegetable oil

1. Place the potatoes in a large pot, with enough water to cover them by 2 in/5 cm. Add the salt and white vinegar.

2. Bring to a boil over high heat, reduce the heat to low, and cook the potatoes, partially covered, for about 20 minutes, or until tender. Drain. Peel and mash with a fork while still hot.

3. Briefly whisk the eggs; mix them with the potatoes and the rest of the ingredients except the oil.

For bite-size omelets (on the stovetop)

4. Heat ¼ cup/60 ml of the oil in a large skillet over medium heat. Gently drop about 2 tablespoons of the mixture into the pan for each omelet, being careful not to crowd the pan, and fry until golden, watching carefully so they don't burn. Turn them over and fry the other side. Using a slotted spoon, transfer the cooked omelets to absorbent paper towels.

5. Repeat, in batches, until all the mixture has been used, replenishing the oil as needed.

For one large omelet (in the oven)

4. Preheat the oven to 400°F/200°C.

5. Grease a 9 in/23 cm baking pan with ⅓ cup/75 ml vegetable oil and place it in the oven for a few minutes, or until the oil is warm. Spoon the egg mixture into the pan, level the top, and bake for 30 minutes, or until the eggs have just set.

6. Place under a hot broiler to color top, watching carefully so it doesn't burn.

7. Allow to cool, and cut into slices.

POTATOES WITH CILANTRO
Batata bi-Kouzbara

SERVES 6 AS PART OF A MEZZE
PREPARATION TIME: 15 MINUTES
COOKING TIME: 20–25 MINUTES

This is the Aleppian version of a dish popular throughout the Middle East. The use of the deep red pepper paste gives it an extraordinary color and taste. It uses fresh cilantro, a modern addition to this old recipe, which traditionally uses ground coriander (*see* Notes).

1 lb/450 g potatoes

Peanut or vegetable oil,
    for deep-frying

3 garlic cloves (⅓ oz/12 g), crushed

1 teaspoon ground cumin

2 teaspoons red pepper paste

½ teaspoon salt, or to taste

¼ cup/60 ml olive oil

¼ cup/½ oz/15 g finely chopped
    cilantro (*see* Notes)

1. Peel the potatoes and cut into ¾ in/2 cm cubes.

2. Place cubes in boiling salted water and simmer for 3 minutes. Drain well, removing as much moisture as possible.

3. Deep-fry the potato cubes in hot peanut or vegetable oil until golden. Using a slotted spoon, transfer to paper towels.

4. Mix the crushed garlic, ground cumin, red pepper paste, and salt. Fry ingredients in olive oil over medium heat for a few seconds, stirring.

5. Mix in the chopped cilantro and fry for a few seconds more, stirring. Add the fried potato cubes and fry for a few seconds until the potatoes are hot. Taste and adjust seasoning.

6. Serve hot or warm.

NOTES

To use ground coriander instead of cilantro: Add 1 tablespoon of ground coriander with the spices in step 4.

TURNOVERS
Sambousek

MAKES 36 PIECES (18 MEAT-FILLED AND 18 CHEESE-FILLED)
PREPARATION TIME: 30–35 MINUTES
RESTING TIME: 30 MINUTES
COOKING TIME: 20–25 MINUTES

Sambousek are savory flaky pastries stuffed with spiced ground meat or cheese. They were made as early as the tenth century, and were mentioned in the medieval Arabic cookbook of al-Baghdadi. They are usually prepared in half-moon shapes, sometimes in triangular form, with the edges crimped. They are a popular snack food throughout the Arab world. In Iran, these filled pies are known as *sanbosag*; and versions exist as far east as India with the samosa.

Aleppo prides itself on its *sambousek*. Aleppian meat *sambousek* have a particularly distinctive flavor due to the addition of pomegranate molasses, Aleppo pepper, and walnuts, which enhance the flavor, color, and give the turnovers their much-desired crunch. They can be baked or shallow fried, and you can easily halve this recipe, or adjust it to make more meat pies or more cheese pies to your liking.

For the dough

¼ cup/60 ml melted butter
¼ cup/60 ml olive oil
2 cups/9 oz/250 g all-purpose flour
½ teaspoon salt

For meat stuffing

1 very small onion (3 oz/85 g), finely
    chopped
2 tablespoons olive oil
8 oz/225 g lean ground lamb or beef
¼ cup/1 oz/30 g chopped walnuts or
    ¼ cup/1½ oz/40 g pine nuts
1 teaspoon Aleppo spice mix or
    seven-spice powder
½ teaspoon cinnamon
¼ teaspoon ground black pepper
¾ teaspoon salt, or to taste
1 tablespoon pomegranate molasses

To prepare the dough

1. Melt the butter over low heat and pour into a bowl. Add the olive oil, flour, and salt.

2. Rub mixture with your hands until flour particles are well covered with the oil.

3. Gradually pour in about ¼ cup/60 ml water, mixing just until a soft dough is formed (handle the dough as little as possible).

4. Knead briefly on a floured surface then cover and set aside for 30 minutes to rest in the refrigerator.

5. Roll on a lightly floured surface until paper-thin. Using a pastry cutter or the rim of a glass, cut the dough into rounds about 3 in/8 cm in diameter.

To prepare meat stuffing

6. Fry the onion in olive oil over low heat until tender (about 10 minutes). Add the meat, pine nuts (if using), Aleppo spice mix or seven-spice powder, cinnamon, black pepper, and salt. Raise the heat and fry until meat is cooked. Mix in the pomegranate molasses and walnuts (if using). Cool.

To prepare cheese stuffing

7. Combine the ingredients in a large bowl and mix well.

For cheese stuffing

8 oz/225 g grated Akkawi or feta
    cheese (*see* Notes)

1 teaspoon Aleppo pepper or paprika

2 tablespoons finely chopped parsley
    or 1 teaspoon dried mint

Vegetable oil, for shallow frying or
    melted butter, for brushing

To fill and cook the turnovers

1. Place 1 tablespoon of the stuffing in the center of each round, then fold each round in half, covering the stuffing.

2. Seal the edges together with the tines of a fork, or make a festoon edge by pinching a small piece and folding it along the boundaries.

3. To fry: Heat the vegetable oil in a large pan and shallow fry, in batches, until light golden in color on both sides.

4. To oven-bake: Preheat the oven to 400°F/200°C. Brush the turnovers with melted butter and place on an ungreased baking sheet. Bake for about 20 minutes, or until pale golden. Best served hot or warm.

NOTES

- Akkawi cheese is a semi-soft white cheese native to Palestine and named after the city Akka. It is produced mainly from cow's milk in Syria, Lebanon, and Cyprus, but it can be found internationally in Middle Eastern grocery stores. Grate the Akkawi cheese and soak it in several changes of water to remove salt and drain well before using (alternatively, you can slice the cheese before soaking, drain, and blend in a food processor).
- Feta cheese can also be used: Mix with one egg or mild white cheese if the feta is too salty for your taste.

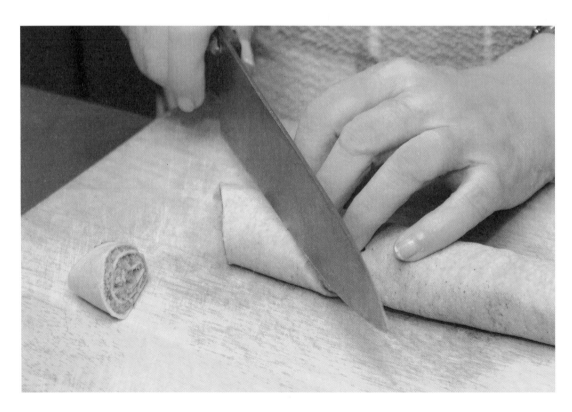

SOUJOK ROLLS
Lafaif al-Soujok

MAKES ABOUT 30 HORS D'OEUVRES
PREPARATION TIME: 25 MINUTES
RESTING TIME: ½–1 HOUR
COOKING TIME: 5–8 MINUTES

One hot day in July, I went to a beautiful restaurant in the heart of Jdeideh called Zmorrod (Arabic for emerald) with my photographer friend, Dikran. Dalal Touma, a charming and vivacious lady, decided to turn this ancient and majestic house into a jewel of a restaurant. We were treated to these delectable bites of soujok, rolled in Arabic flatbread. The kitchen was impeccable and the chefs hospitable and generous with information about soujok and these delicious rolls.

Soujok is a heavily spiced regional specialty, prepared with kebab meat and a variety of spices. (For more about soujok and Aleppian soujok, *see* the Glossary.)

For the soujok

1 lb/450 g lean ground lamb (pulse
    in a food processor to achieve a
    fine texture)
1 tablespoon ground coriander
1 teaspoon ground nutmeg
1 teaspoon red pepper paste
1 teaspoon Aleppo pepper or paprika
1 teaspoon ground cumin
1 teaspoon Aleppo spice mix or
    seven-spice powder
2 teaspoons crushed garlic
½ teaspoon salt, or to taste

For the rolls

2–3 Arabic flatbreads, pockets split
    open and separated
Vegetable oil, for deep-frying

1. In a bowl, combine and mix the soujok ingredients.

2. Cut each flap of bread into a 9 in/22 cm square.

3. Divide soujok mixture evenly between the bread squares and spread over the whole inner surface.

4. To roll the soujok: Fold about ¼ in/½ cm of one side of the square over the stuffing, pressing on it well. Continue to roll the bread tightly. Cover with plastic wrap, twisting the sides, and freeze the roll until it has hardened just enough to hold its shape when sliced (½–1 hour). Repeat with the rest.

5. Cut each roll on the diagonal into ½ in/1½ cm slices, attaching each with a toothpick.

6. Deep-fry in hot oil directly from frozen (including the toothpick) then transfer to a strainer. Serve hot or warm as part of an appetizer or buffet.

NOTES

- Arabic flatbread is very thin, which makes it ideal in this recipe. In Aleppo, it is common to only use the lighter-colored, thinner side of the bread for rolling, since the color darkens when fried. If you can't find Arabic flatbread, you can use pita (which is similar, but typically a little thicker). Split the pocket open and use the thinner part. If using ovular pita breads, cut into rectangles and roll, starting on the long edge.
- This soujok mixture is very popular in the Arab world. It is excellent fried with eggs, or formed into sausages, sliced, and used to top pizza.

SOUPS

BIRD'S HEAD SOUP
Shorbet Ras Asfoor

SERVES 6
PREPARATION TIME: 15 MINUTES
COOKING TIME: 15 MINUTES
RESTING TIME: 20 MINUTES

Bird's Head Soup has nothing to do with birds; the name refers rather to meatballs that are as small as a bird's head. It is a simple light soup with simple ingredients that can be prepared in 15 minutes. It is often served with kibbeh.

1 lb/450 g lean ground lamb or beef

2 teaspoons Aleppo spice mix or
  seven-spice powder

¾ teaspoon cinnamon

¼ teaspoon ground black pepper

1½ teaspoons salt, or to taste

¼ cup/60 ml vegetable oil

7½ cups/1.8 liters lamb or beef stock
  or water

½ teaspoon tomato paste

½ cup/3½ oz/100 g short-grain rice,
  preferably Egyptian

A handful of chopped parsley, to
  serve (optional)

1. In the bowl of a food processor, combine the meat, Aleppo spice mix or seven-spice powder, cinnamon, black pepper, and salt to taste. Process until a fine, dough-like paste is formed.

2. With moistened hands, form the mixture into balls a little larger than a hazelnut (you should have about 65).

3. In two batches, fry the meatballs briefly in the oil, shaking the pan gently. Remove with a slotted spoon.

4. In a large pot, combine the stock or water and tomato paste and bring to a boil over high heat. Add the meatballs and rice. Lower the heat to medium, cover the pot, and simmer for about 10 minutes. Taste and adjust seasoning.

5. Remove the soup from the heat and keep covered for 20 minutes (the rice will swell and release its starch into the soup).

6. To serve: Reheat if needed and ladle into bowls. Sprinkle with chopped parsley, if using, and serve hot.

VARIATIONS

5½ cups/1.3 liters of stock and 2 cups/480 ml of tomato juice can be used in place of the 7½ cups/1.8 liters of stock.

CREAMY LENTIL SOUP
Shorbet Adess Msaffayeh

SERVES 7–8
PREPARATION TIME: 15 MINUTES
COOKING TIME: 40 MINUTES, PLUS 5 MINUTES FOR FRIED BREAD

Going back to Biblical times, lentil soups have been popular all over the Middle East. At one time they were among the favorite dishes of the poor, but today they are widely appreciated as a good source of protein, fiber, iron, potassium, and vitamin B. In Aleppo, lentil soup is passed through a vegetable mill to produce a creamy texture, and served with ground cumin, lemon juice, and golden-fried bread. (If you would rather not fry the bread, keep it whole, toast until brown, and break it into bite-size pieces.)

This dish can be made in advance, stored in the refrigerator, and reheated before serving. Store the fried bread in an airtight container at room temperature.

¼ cup/60 ml olive oil

1 small onion (4 oz/115 g),
   finely chopped

2¼ cups/15 oz/425 g brown lentils,
   picked and washed

1 tablespoon ground cumin

¼ teaspoon ground black pepper

½ teaspoon salt, or to taste

For the fried bread

1 loaf Arabic flatbread, cut into
   ¾ in/2 cm squares

½ cup/120 ml peanut or
   vegetable oil

To serve

2 tablespoons ground cumin,
   or to taste
Lemon slices

1. Heat the oil in a medium-size pot over medium heat and fry the onion until golden, stirring frequently (about 8 minutes).

2. Raise the heat, add the lentils, 8 cups/2 liters water, and the cumin and black pepper, and bring the mixture to a boil, stirring a few times.

3. Lower the heat, add the salt, cover the pot, and simmer for about 30 minutes, stirring a few times until the lentils are cooked.

4. Place the lentil mixture in a vegetable mill over a clean pot. Rotate the handle until the soup is pushed down into the pot and only the skins are left in the mill. Discard skin. (Alternatively, purée with a hand blender or food processor and pass through a strainer.)

5. Bring the soup back to a boil over medium heat, stirring a few times. Taste and adjust the seasoning, adding a few tablespoons of hot water if a thinner soup is desired.

6. Make the fried bread garnish: Heat the oil in a skillet or small pot over high heat. When the oil is hot, fry the bread until golden, stirring. Using a slotted spoon, transfer the bread to a strainer.

7. Garnish the soup with fried bread and serve hot with cumin and lemon slices on the side.

BULGAR AND SPINACH SOUP
Shorbet Burghol bi-Sabanekh

SERVES 6
PREPARATION TIME: 15 MINUTES
COOKING TIME: 20 MINUTES

This is a highly nutritious and tasty soup similar in flavor to Mloukhiyeh (*see* Mloukhiyeh with Chicken, p. 133) but easier to prepare. It is packed with healthy ingredients: spinach, bulgar, cilantro, garlic, and lemon juice, and is low in fat. The soup can be prepared with Swiss chard leaves instead of spinach.

1 lb/450 g spinach leaves, roughly chopped
¾ cup/4½ oz/125 g coarse bulgar, washed and drained
7 cups/1.8 liters chicken, beef, or vegetable stock
3 tablespoons ground cumin
3 tablespoons ground coriander (optional)
1 teaspoon allspice
½–1 teaspoon ground black pepper
1 tablespoon salt, or to taste
Scant ½ cup/100 ml olive oil
9 garlic cloves (1½ oz/40 g), crushed
1¼ cups/2½ oz/75 g finely chopped cilantro
Scant ½ cup/100 ml lemon juice
1 lemon, cut into slices, to serve

1. In a large pot combine the spinach, bulgar, stock, cumin, coriander (if using), allspice, black pepper, and salt. Bring to a boil over high heat, cover tightly, lower the heat, and cook for 20 minutes, adding a little hot water if needed. Remove from heat.

2. Heat ⅓ cup/75 ml of the olive oil in a skillet over medium heat and fry the garlic and cilantro for 30 seconds. Mix into the soup and continue cooking, uncovered, for a few minutes more. Taste and add the lemon juice and more salt, if needed.

3. Ladle soup into serving bowls, drizzle with the rest of the olive oil, and serve hot with lemon slices.

RED LENTIL AND LEMON SOUP
Shorbet Adess bi-Hamod

SERVES 5–6
PREPARATION TIME: 15 MINUTES
COOKING TIME: 1 HOUR

This is a healthy and satisfying soup of split red lentils, carrots, Swiss chard, lemon juice, garlic, and cilantro. It is usually served during the first day of Christian Lent, along with Lentils with Bulgar and Caramelized Onion (p. 244). Sometimes the lemon juice is replaced with verjuice (sour grape juice), and called *Shorbet Adess bi-Husrom*, Sour Grape Soup. It is often served with Arabic flatbread on the side.

There are mentions of this recipe as early as the Old Testament, where we learn that Esau, the son of Isaac and twin brother of Jacob, much favored this soup, especially after coming home from hunting. It was so good that Jacob persuaded Esau to exchange his right to the inheritance of the land of Canaan for a kettleful.

½ cup/120 ml olive oil

8 garlic cloves (1 oz/30 g), crushed

1 tablespoon ground coriander

1 teaspoon ground cumin

¼–½ teaspoon ground black pepper

1½ cups/10 oz/300 g split red lentils, picked and washed

2½ cups/12 oz/350 g peeled and sliced carrots

3 cups/9 oz/250 g chopped Swiss chard (stems and leaves)

9 garlic cloves (1½ oz/40 g), peeled and sliced lengthwise if large

1 cup/2 oz/60g finely chopped cilantro leaves and tender stems

⅓ cup/75 ml lemon juice

1 tablespoon salt, or to taste

1. In a large pot, heat the olive oil over medium heat and fry the crushed garlic, coriander, cumin, and black pepper for about 2 minutes, stirring frequently. Do not allow the garlic to color.

2. Pour 8 cups/2 liters water into the pot and add the lentils. Bring the mixture to a boil and stir. Lower the heat to simmer, cover, and cook for about 30 minutes, or until the lentils have disintegrated in the water.

3. Remove from the heat, process the mixture in a blender until smooth, and return to the pot.

4. Add the carrots and simmer for 10 minutes.

5. Add the Swiss chard and simmer for a further 15–20 minutes, or until the carrots are tender.

6. Add the sliced garlic, chopped cilantro, lemon juice, and salt. Simmer for 1 minute. Taste and adjust the seasoning.

7. Serve hot.

RED LENTIL AND RICE SOUP
Makhloota

SERVES 6
PREPARATION TIME: 10 MINUTES
COOKING TIME: 45 MINUTES

A delicious, thick soup prepared with split red lentils, ground meat, rice, and cumin. The soup can also be made without the meat.

1½ cups/10 oz/300 g split red
    lentils, picked over and washed
8 cups/2 liters homemade or
    reduced-salt chicken or
    vegetable stock
⅓ cup/2½ oz/70 g short-grain rice,
    washed and drained
6 tablespoons/90 ml olive oil
1 small onion (4 oz/115 g),
    finely chopped
½ lb/250 g ground lamb or beef
1½ tablespoons ground cumin
1 teaspoon allspice
¼ teaspoon ground black pepper
1¾ teaspoons salt, or to taste

For the fried bread (optional)

1 loaf Arabic flatbread
½ cup/120 ml peanut or vegetable
    oil

To garnish (optional)

Aleppo pepper or paprika
A handful of chopped parsley
Lemon slices

1. Place the lentils and stock in a medium pot over high heat and bring to a boil. Lower the heat, cover the pot, and simmer for 30 minutes.

2. Remove the lentils from the heat and purée them in a blender or food processor.

3. In a small-medium pot, combine the rice with 1 cup/240 ml water and bring to a boil. Cover the pot, lower the heat, and cook for 15 minutes, then set aside.

4. In a soup pot, heat the oil and fry the onions on low heat, stirring frequently, until they start to color.

5. Raise the heat, add the meat, cumin, allspice, black pepper, and salt, and fry for a few minutes, or until the meat loses its pink color.

6. Pour the lentils on top of the onion-meat mixture. Add the cooked rice, stir well, and bring to a simmer.

7. Lower the heat, cover the pot, and cook the soup for 15 minutes, stirring a few times at the beginning and end of cooking.

8. Make the fried bread: Cut the bread into ¾ in/2 cm squares. Heat the oil in a skillet or small pot over high heat. When the oil is hot, fry the bread until golden, stirring. Using a slotted spoon, transfer the bread to a strainer. (Alternatively, you can keep it whole, toast until brown, and then break it into bite-size pieces.)

9. Pour the soup into serving bowls, garnished to your liking, and serve with fried or toasted bread and lemon slices on the side.

LENTIL, OLIVE OIL, AND DUMPLING SOUP
Richtayeh

SERVES 4
PREPARATION TIME: 10 MINUTES
COOKING TIME: 40–45 MINUTES

This simple lentil and bread dumpling soup is usually served at the beginning of Christian Lent. Some flavor the soup with cilantro, cumin, or pomegranate molasses, but I like the version below. The recipe goes back to ancient times, when it was prepared with homemade bread dough. Nowadays, fresh pasta is often used as a quick and easy alternative.

¾ cup/5 oz/150 g whole white or
    brown lentils
1 cup/5 oz/150 g finely chopped
    onion
½ cup/120 ml olive oil
¼ recipe Arabic Flatbread dough
    (p. 272) or 2 oz/60 g lasagna
    noodles or pappardelle
1 teaspoon allspice
¼ teaspoon ground black pepper
2 teaspoons salt, or to taste

1. In a large pot, heat the lentils and 3 cups/700 ml water over medium heat and bring to a boil. Cover, lower the heat, and simmer for about 30 minutes, or until the lentils are tender.

2. Fry the onion in olive oil, stirring until golden. Add to the pot with the lentils.

3. If using Arabic Flatbread dough: Roll thinly, cut into squares or rectangles, and sprinkle with flour. Add to the soup with 2 cups/480 ml water. If using pasta: Boil in 2 cups/480 ml salted water until al dente. Drain the pasta, reserving 2 cups of the cooking liquid. Cut into squares or rectangles and add to the lentils with the reserved cooking liquid.

4. Add the allspice, black pepper, and salt.

5. Continue simmering the soup for 10 minutes, adding hot water if needed.

6. Serve hot.

GARLICKY PURSLANE SOUP WITH CHICKPEAS AND WHEAT
Shorbet Baqleh

SERVES 8–10
SOAKING TIME: OVERNIGHT
PREPARATION TIME: 20 MINUTES (WITH COOKED OR CANNED CHICKPEAS)
COOKING TIME: 45 MINUTES

This is a healthy and satisfying vegetarian soup much appreciated on cold days. It is quick to prepare when you use canned chickpeas and precooked wheat berries. I usually cook a large batch of these two ingredients and freeze them so I can make this soup in a snap.

Purslane is cultivated for food in many parts of the Middle East, Europe, and Central America. It grows wild in many parts of the US. If purslane is not available, you can substitute Swiss chard or spinach.

1 cup/7 oz/200 g hulled wheat berries, soaked overnight

2 cinnamon sticks

2¼ cups/15 oz/425 g split red lentils

4 small ripe tomatoes (14 oz/400 g), finely chopped

¼ cup/60 g tomato paste

3 tablespoons red pepper paste

1 teaspoon allspice

¼ teaspoon ground black pepper

2 tablespoons salt, or to taste

14 oz/400 g can chickpeas, drained, or 1 cup/7 oz/200 g dried chickpeas, soaked, cooked, and drained (*see* p. 16)

¼ cup/60 ml lemon juice, or to taste

40 garlic gloves (6 oz/160 g), crushed (yes, a lot of garlic!)

2 tablespoons dried mint

2–3 bunches purslane (to make 10 oz/300 g leaves), washed

1. Drain the wheat berries and place them in a pot over high heat with 4 cups/1 liter water. Add the cinnamon sticks. Bring to a boil, lower the heat, and simmer, covered, for about 35 minutes, or until the kernels open. Uncover and cook for 10 minutes more, until the liquid has reduced and the broth has thickened.

2. In a large pot, combine 8 cups/2 liters of water with the lentils, tomatoes, tomato paste, red pepper paste, allspice, black pepper, and salt and bring to a boil. Cover, lower the heat, and simmer for 20 minutes, or until the lentils are cooked and have almost disintegrated into the liquid.

3. Stir in the chickpeas, wheat berries, lemon juice, crushed garlic, dried mint, and purslane leaves. Simmer for a few minutes, or until the leaves are just cooked. Taste and adjust the seasoning.

4. Serve hot.

SALADS AND VEGETABLE SIDE DISHES

ITCH FOR EVERYDAY
Kibbet al-Hammam Lakil Yome

SERVES 10
PREPARATION TIME: 35 MINUTES
RESTING TIME: 2 HOURS
COOKING TIME: 35 MINUTES

The Lebanese have the famous parsley-laden bulgar salad, *tabbouleh*, sharpened with lemon juice. In southeastern Turkey they choose instead to mix their bulgar into tomatoes and red pepper for a dish called *kisir*. The Armenians make their bulgar salad with fresh mint and lemon juice, calling it *itch*, meaning to drink; in Aleppo, it is prepared with pomegranate molasses, cumin, and spices. It is thought that *itch* is of Kurdish origin.

The name *Kibbet al-Hammam*, meaning "bath kibbeh," comes from the tradition of bringing this salad to the hammam (or public bath), to be eaten while gathering and gossiping about the latest news in town. Hammams were of great importance in Roman and Byzantine times, and remained so for the Arabs and Turks.

This salad makes a great appetizer served in lettuce leaves, or lettuce leaves can be served on the side for scooping, but *itch* is just as tasty eaten on its own.

2 cups/12 oz/350 g coarse bulgar, preferably white

¾ cup/180 ml olive oil

2½ cups/14 oz/400 g finely chopped onions

4 teaspoons salt, or to taste

1½ cups/9 oz/260 g finely chopped sweet green pepper

2 teaspoons ground cumin

1 tablespoon Aleppo spice mix or seven-spice powder

¼ cup/60 ml tomato paste

¼ cup/60 ml red pepper paste

7 cups/2¾ lb/1.3 kg finely chopped tomatoes

¼ cup/60 ml pomegranate molasses

1 tablespoon sugar

½–1 teaspoon ground black pepper, or to taste (use less if using hot red pepper paste)

1½ cups/3 oz/80 g finely chopped parsley

¾ cup/1¾ oz/50 g finely chopped mint or 2 heaped tablespoons dried mint

Lettuce leaves, to garnish (optional)

1. Wash the bulgar and soak it in water for 10 minutes. Squeeze dry and set aside.

2. In a medium-size pot, heat the olive oil over very low heat. Add the onions and half of the salt. Cook gently, stirring a few times, until the onions are very tender but not colored (this may take 20–30 minutes).

3. Add the green pepper, cumin, and Aleppo spice mix or seven-spice powder and fry briefly, stirring.

4. Add the tomato and red pepper pastes and fry for a few seconds.

5. Add the chopped tomatoes, pomegranate molasses, sugar, and black pepper (the salad should be slightly spicy), and cook until the mixture comes to a boil.

6. Add the bulgar and more salt, as needed, and give the mixture a good stir. Cover the pot, remove from the heat, and set aside for about 2 hours, stirring a few times until the bulgar absorbs the liquid and the mixture has cooled. Taste and adjust seasoning.

7. Mix in the parsley and mint.

8. Spoon the salad onto a serving platter and serve cold with lettuce leaves, if using.

ITCH FOR INVITATIONS
Kibbet al-Hammam lil A'azayem

SERVES 6
PREPARATION TIME: 20 MINUTES
FIRST RESTING: 30 MINUTES PLUS 2 HOURS
COOKING TIME: 25 MINUTES

Similar to Itch for Everyday (previous page), Itch for Invitations is a delicious bulgar salad, but with fewer ingredients and a slightly different flavor and texture, thanks, in part, to the addition of walnuts. It is beautifully presented in the form of a cake, and can be prepared one day in advance.

1 cup/6½ oz/185 g fine bulgar

1 small-medium onion (5oz/150 g), finely chopped

¼ cup/60 ml olive oil

1 tablespoon ground cumin

1 lb/450 g tomatoes, finely chopped, plus more to garnish

¼ cup/60 ml pomegranate molasses

3 tablespoons red pepper paste

2 teaspoons dried mint

2 teaspoons salt, or to taste

½ cup/1½ oz/40 g finely chopped scallions (white and tender green parts)

¾ cup/2½ oz/75 g walnuts, coarsely chopped (optional)

¼ cup/½ oz/15 g finely chopped parsley, plus more to garnish

Cherry tomatoes, to garnish (optional)

Lettuce leaves, to garnish (optional)

1. Briefly wash the bulgar and squeeze dry. Place in a bowl.

2. In a medium-size pot, fry the onion in olive oil over very low heat until tender but not colored (this may take 20–30 minutes). Add the cumin and fry for a few more seconds.

3. Raise the heat to medium, add the tomatoes, and stir for 30 seconds, or until the tomatoes release their juice.

4. Add the bulgar to the pot and stir briefly.

5. Stir in the pomegranate molasses, red pepper paste, mint, and salt, and cook for a few more seconds.

6. Remove the pot from the heat, cover, and set aside for 30 minutes, or until the bulgar absorbs the liquid. (Recipe can be prepared one day ahead to this step and refrigerated until needed.)

7. Mix in the chopped scallions, walnuts, if using, and parsley. Taste and adjust seasoning.

8. Spoon the *itch* into a circular cake pan, pressing to compact, and refrigerate for 2 hours. Turn it out onto a serving platter, decorate with parsley and cherry tomatoes, and serve with lettuce leaves on the side for scooping (though it is just as good eaten simply with a spoon or fork).

ARMENIAN SALAD
Salata Armaniyeh

SERVES 6
PREPARATION TIME: 15 MINUTES

The most colorful of all salads; cucumbers, tomatoes, sweet red and green peppers, and onions are all diced and served with parsley in a lemony dressing. It is great for making ahead, since it does not wilt when mixed a few hours in advance (add the chopped parsley just before serving).

6 small cucumbers (10 oz/300 g), diced

6 small tomatoes (1 lb 5 oz/600 g), diced

1 large sweet red pepper (6 oz/170 g), diced

1 large sweet green pepper (6 oz/170 g), diced

1 small onion (4 oz/115 g), thinly sliced into half-moons, or 3 scallions, finely chopped

¼ cup/½ oz/15 g coarsely chopped parsley

For dressing

¼ cup/60 ml lemon juice

¼ cup/60 ml olive oil

1 garlic clove (4 g), crushed

½ teaspoon ground cumin

1 tablespoon sumac

1½ teaspoons salt, or to taste

To garnish

Romaine lettuce leaves, washed and dried

1. Combine the salad ingredients in a bowl (if making ahead, add the parsley just before serving).

2. Combine and mix the dressing ingredients.

3. To serve: Pour the dressing over the salad and mix. Garnish with whole lettuce leaves.

CARROT SALAD
Salatet Jazar

SERVES 6
PREPARATION TIME: 10 MINUTES
COOKING TIME: 15–20 MINUTES

Carrots come in a variety of colors: white, yellow, red, purple, and black. They all contain a good amount of the very beneficial carotene. Black carrots are a sweet variety. During the season, there is an abundance of black carrots in Aleppo. This salad can be prepared with carrots of any color.

2 lb/1 kg small carrots, peeled and
    cut into lengths, if large
1 teaspoon salt, or to taste
1 teaspoon cumin seeds

For the dressing

¼ cup/60 ml lemon juice
6 tablespoons/90 ml olive oil
2 garlic cloves (¼ oz/8 g), crushed
¼ teaspoon ground black pepper
1 teaspoon sugar
1 teaspoon salt, or to taste

1. Place the carrots in a pot with water and the salt. Bring to a boil over high heat. Lower the heat and simmer until the carrots are almost cooked (they should have a slight bite to them). Drain and place in a bowl.

2. Heat the cumin seeds in a dry nonstick pan until they start to pop. Add them to the carrots in the bowl.

3. Mix the dressing ingredients and add to the carrots while they are still hot. Taste and adjust the seasoning and allow to cool.

4. Serve cold.

CABBAGE SALAD
Salatet Malfoof

SERVES 4
PREPARATION TIME: 15 MINUTES

Cabbage has the triple blessing of being an antioxidant, available all year round, and staying fresh for weeks in the refrigerator. This salad can be tossed with the dressing up to 30 minutes before serving.

5 cups shredded white cabbage
    (1 cabbage/11 oz/325 g)
¼ cup/60 ml red wine vinegar or
    lemon juice
6 tablespoons/90 ml olive oil
1 garlic clove (4 g), crushed
½ teaspoon ground cumin
¼ teaspoon hot paprika
1 teaspoon salt, or to taste
A few cherry tomatoes, to garnish

1. Remove hard outer leaves of the cabbage and discard. Remove the tender leaves and cut off the tough ribs. Stack a few leaves at a time and cut into fine shreds. Place in a bowl.

2. In a small jar, combine the red wine vinegar, olive oil, crushed garlic, cumin, paprika, and salt, cover, and shake to mix the ingredients. Pour the dressing over the cabbage and mix well.

3. Taste, adjust seasoning, transfer to a serving platter, and garnish with cherry tomatoes.

GARDEN TOMATO SALAD
Salata Bustaniyeh

SERVES 6
PREPARATION TIME: 10–15 MINUTES
RESTING TIME: 30 MINUTES

This simple tomato salad is a pleasure to look at and a good accompaniment to many dishes. I like to scoop it up with Arabic flatbread, allowing the bread to absorb the juices.

3½ lb/1½ kg firm red tomatoes
5 scallions (white and tender green parts) or 1 small white onion

For the dressing

⅓ cup/75 ml lemon juice
1½ teaspoons salt, or to taste
1–2 teaspoons ground cumin
¼ cup/60 ml olive oil

1. Place a strainer over a bowl. Chop the tomatoes into small cubes. Transfer to the strainer using your fingers, leaving as many seeds as possible on the chopping board. Discard the seeds and drain the tomatoes for 30 minutes.

2. Thinly slice the scallions or onion, and place in a bowl with the tomatoes.

3. To prepare the dressing, mix the lemon juice with salt and cumin then stir in the olive oil.

4. Dress the salad just before serving.

DESERT TRUFFLE SALAD
Salatet Kamayeh

SERVES 8 AS AN APPETIZER
PREPARATION TIME: 10 MINUTES IF TRUFFLES ARE CLEAN AND READY TO COOK
COOKING TIME: 6–8 MINUTES

This is the crown jewel of all salads, adding richness to any table. It has an advantage over other salads in that it can be prepared a few hours ahead (add the chopped parsley just before serving). The dressing is simple so as not to interfere with the exquisite flavor of the truffles.

Desert truffles are available canned or frozen in Middle Eastern specialty shops. For this salad, it is important that they are of the best quality.

Heaped tablespoon salt
About 6 large, ready-to-cook desert truffles (1 lb/450 g; *see* p. 17)
2 tablespoons olive oil
Dash of allspice
Dash ground white pepper
2 tablespoons chopped parsley
Arugula leaves, to garnish (optional)

1. In a large pot, heat 6 cups/1.5 liters water and the salt over high heat. Bring to a boil and drop in the truffles. Simmer for about 6–8 minutes (depending on the size), and remove to a strainer. Cool.

2. Slice truffles into ¼ in/½ cm thick slices and place in a bowl.

3. Mix in the rest of the ingredients and place on a serving platter. Serve cold or at room temperature.

PURSLANE SALAD
Salatet Baqleh

SERVES 4
PREPARATION TIME: 10 MINUTES

Purslane is a succulent herb that contains a high amount of alpha-linolenic acid, one of the highly appreciated omega-3 acids that are abundant in oily fish. It can be grown easily on balconies or patios in small pots. In parts of the US, it even grows wild as a weed. Spinach and arugula are possible substitutes for purslane in this salad.

In Turkey, purslane salad (*semizotu aalatasi*) is prepared with sweet red and green peppers, and sometimes pomegranate molasses is added to the dressing.

6 cups/5½ oz/160 g purslane leaves, cleaned and dried

8 small cherry tomatoes (3½ oz/100g), halved, or 1 small tomato, chopped

½ teaspoon Aleppo pepper or paprika

For the dressing

1 tablespoon lemon juice

3 tablespoons olive oil

2 teaspoons ground coriander

2 teaspoons ground cumin

½ teaspoon salt, or to taste

1. In a large bowl, mix the dressing ingredients. Add the purslane leaves and toss.

2. Place on a serving platter with the tomatoes and sprinkle with Aleppo pepper or paprika.

3. Serve immediately.

GARLIC YOGURT
Laban Mtawwam

MAKES ABOUT 2¼ CUPS/1 LB 2 OZ/550 G
PREPARATION TIME: 5 MINUTES

This is a very tasty, refreshing condiment, perfect for hot summer days. It is made to accompany stuffed dishes, such as Stuffed Swiss Chard (p. 211), Stuffed Ajjour (p. 204), and Stuffed Vine Leaves with Rice and Lamb (p. 210), but not those cooked in a pomegranate molasses sauce.

Sheep's milk yogurt is best for this recipe, but goat's milk yogurt, cow's milk yogurt, or fat-free yogurt can be used if preferred.

A variation with cucumber is known throughout the Middle East, Greece, and India. The Armenians call it *jajik*, the Greeks *tzatziki*, and the Indians *raita*. In Turkey it is prepared with lettuce and served as a salad and called *yogurtlu semizotu salatasi*.

2½ cups/1 lb 4 oz/550 g plain yogurt
   (preferably sheep's milk)
2 teaspoons dried mint
   (or use a heaped tablespoon
   chopped fresh mint leaves)
2 garlic cloves (¼ oz/8 g), crushed
1¼ teaspoons salt, or to taste

1. Place the yogurt in a small bowl and whisk until smooth.

2. Stir in the rest of the ingredients. Taste and adjust the seasoning.

3. Serve cold.

VARIATIONS: CUCUMBER AND GARLIC YOGURT

Add 4–5 chopped or grated baby cucumbers (7½ oz/210 g) to the mixture. Shredded lettuce may be used instead of cucumber.

ARTICHOKE AND FAVA BEAN SALAD
Salatet Shawki wa-Fool Akhdar

SERVES 4–5 AS A SIDE OR 8 AS PART OF A MEZZE
PREPARATION TIME: 15–20 MINUTES
COOKING TIME: 10 MINUTES

Also called broad or field beans, fresh fava beans start appearing in grocery stores in spring but are at their peak in July. They come in green pods, and each bean is covered with a thick skin. For this salad, choose pods that contain large beans. It takes some work to peel the pods and then the skin, but the result is worth it. When peeled, the beans have a delicate flavor and a beautiful vivid green color.

When fresh fava beans are not in season, you can buy them frozen. This salad can be prepared several hours ahead; add the chopped parsley just before serving.

3¼ lb/1.5 kg fresh fava bean pods, shucked, or 1½ cups/9 oz/250 g frozen fava beans

Ice-cold water, for soaking

2 teaspoons salt

1 tablespoon all-purpose flour

1 lb/450 g frozen artichoke bottoms (about 8; or *see* p. 14 to prepare from fresh)

5 cherry tomatoes (3½ oz/100 g), quartered, or 1 small tomato, seeds removed, chopped

Chopped parsley, to garnish (optional)

For the dressing

1 garlic clove (4 g), crushed

¼ cup/60 ml lemon juice

⅓ cup/75 ml olive oil

¼ teaspoon ground cumin

1½ teaspoons salt, or to taste

1. Blanch the fava beans in a pot of boiling, salted water for 2 minutes. Drain and immediately transfer to ice-cold water. Drain again.

2. Using your fingers or a small knife, slip the outer skin off each bean.

3. In a small pot, heat about 5 cups/1.2 liters water over high heat. Add the salt and flour. Stir with a wire whisk until the mixture comes to a boil.

4. Add the artichoke bottoms and cook, stirring a few times until tender (about 10 minutes). Drain and immediately plunge the artichoke bottoms into ice-cold water. Drain and quarter them.

5. Mix the artichokes with the beans and tomatoes.

6. Mix the dressing ingredients and gently mix into the salad. Garnish with chopped parsley, if using, and serve cold or at room temperature.

ROASTED RED PEPPER SALAD
Salatet Fleifleh Hamra

SERVES 6
PREPARATION TIME: 25 MINUTES
COOKING TIME: 30–35 MINUTES
RESTING TIME: 20 MINUTES

This vibrant red salad is made with grilled red peppers and plenty of walnuts. It is easy to prepare and ideal to serve as part of a mezze, or as an accompaniment to kibbeh dishes, kebab, and grilled meat. It can also be served as a dip or as a topping for hors d'oeuvres.

The salad can be prepared a few days in advance and keeps well in the refrigerator (decorate just before serving).

3¼ lb/1.5 kg Syrian red peppers or
    any sweet red peppers
2 garlic cloves (¼ oz/8 g), crushed
1 tablespoon pomegranate molasses
1 tablespoon red pepper paste
⅓ cup/75 ml olive oil
½ cup/2 oz/60 g chopped walnuts
¼ teaspoon ground red chili powder
¾ teaspoons salt, or to taste

To garnish

A few whole walnuts
A few mint sprigs

1. Remove the stalks of the red peppers and cut each lengthwise into 4 sections. Remove and discard the seeds and white filaments.

2. Preheat a charcoal grill or the broiler. Grill the peppers, skin-side down, until the skins are charred. If broiling: Line a baking sheet with aluminum foil and arrange the peppers skin-side up. Place the baking sheet 2–4 in/5–10 cm under the broiler for 30 minutes, or until the pepper skins are charred.

3. Place peppers, while still hot, into a bowl and cover with a plate or plastic wrap. Set aside for 10 minutes. Peel the peppers and place in a strainer to drain for another 10 minutes. (The final weight should be about 1 lb/450 g.)

4. Finely chop the peppers or place them in a food processor and pulse once or twice. Transfer to a bowl.

5. Combine the red peppers with the garlic, pomegranate molasses, red pepper paste, olive oil, chopped walnuts, chili powder, and salt. Taste and adjust seasoning.

6. Place on a serving platter and garnish with walnuts and mint sprigs. Serve cold.

VARIATIONS

- For Roasted Red Pepper Dip, purée the peppers to a paste instead of finely chopping.
- You can also grill a fresh hot red chili with the red peppers instead of using ground red chili powder.

POTATO SALAD
Salatet Batata

SERVES 4–5
PREPARATION TIME: 15 MINUTES
COOKING TIME: 30–45 MINUTES

Potato salad is a familiar dish in many countries. It is satisfying, inexpensive, and easy to prepare. Aleppian potato salad is perked up with ground red pepper and cumin. Serve it with grilled meat or kebab or as part of a mezze. It is a healthier, lighter alternative to mayonnaise-based potato salad.

2 lb/1 kg potatoes

2 teaspoons salt

1 teaspoon white vinegar

For the dressing

¼ cup/60 ml lemon juice

½ cup/120 ml olive oil

½ small onion (2 oz/60 g),
    finely chopped

4 scallions (1½ oz/40g),
    finely chopped

¼ cup/½ oz/15 g chopped parsley

1 teaspoon Aleppo pepper or
    paprika, plus more to garnish

1½ teaspoons ground cumin

½ teaspoon allspice

½ teaspoon white pepper

1½ teaspoons salt, or to taste

1. Place the potatoes in a large pot with water to cover by 2 in/5 cm. Stir in the salt and white vinegar.

2. Bring to a boil over high heat. Reduce heat to low, partially cover, and cook the potatoes until tender. Drain.

3. Mix dressing ingredients in a large bowl.

4. While still warm, peel and cut the potatoes into bite-size pieces and toss with the dressing in the bowl (you can use a wooden spoon or just hold the bowl with two hands and flip the mixture). Taste and adjust seasoning, if necessary.

5. Sprinkle with paprika or Aleppo pepper and serve warm or cold.

VARIATIONS

You can add any number of ingredients to this potato salad according to your taste. I like to add finely chopped sweet red pepper, enhancing the flavor, texture, and color of the dish. Some add boiled and quartered eggs.

WHITE BEAN SALAD
Salatet Fasoliah Baida

SERVES 6 AS PART OF A MEZZE
PREPARATION TIME: 10 MINUTES

This salad is prepared in many parts of the Middle East. In Aleppo, cumin and red pepper paste give it a new dimension and a vibrant color. It is usually served with Arabic flatbread as part of a mezze, or as a side dish. I have used canned white beans here, but *see* Variations to use fresh or dried beans. It can be made up to two days in advance and stored in the refrigerator (garnish just before serving).

2 x 15 oz cans white beans
(3 cups/700 g), drained and
rinsed
2 tablespoons red pepper paste
1½ teaspoons ground cumin
2 teaspoons cumin seeds (optional)
2 garlic cloves (¼ oz/8 g), crushed
3 tablespoons lemon juice
½ cup/120 ml olive oil
¼ teaspoon ground black pepper
¾ teaspoon salt, or to taste

To garnish

1 tablespoon chopped parsley
2 tablespoons red pepper paste
mixed with 2 tablespoons
olive oil

1. In a bowl, combine the beans with the rest of the ingredients except the garnish.

2. Mix well, taste, and adjust seasoning.

3. Garnish as desired and serve cold.

VARIATIONS

- To use dried beans: Soak 1¼ cups/250 g dried beans and ½ teaspoon baking soda in plenty of water overnight. The next day, drain and rinse the beans. In a large pot, cover the beans with fresh water (no salt added) and bring to a boil, skimming the white foam that rises to the top. Lower the heat to medium and simmer until tender. (For this salad, I like to cook them until they split and open to allow them to absorb more sauce.) Drain the beans and mix them with the sauce ingredients while they are still hot.
- When they are in season, I like to prepare this salad with fresh beans instead (use any broad white beans like cannellini, great northern, or navy beans). In a large pot, cover the beans with fresh water (no salt) and bring to a boil. Lower the heat to medium and simmer until tender. Proceed with the recipe as above.

SWISS CHARD STEMS IN TAHINI SAUCE
Dloo' Siliq bi-Taratore

SERVES 3 AS A SALAD OR 6 AS PART OF A MEZZE
PREPARATION TIME: 10–15 MINUTES
COOKING TIME: 2–3 MINUTES

This salad of Swiss chard stems in tahini sauce is often prepared alongside dishes that use only the leaves, such as Stuffed Swiss Chard (p. 211) or Vegetarian Stuffed Swiss Chard (p. 228).

Swiss chard is like two vegetables in one, but sadly many cooks discard the stems. Like the leaves, the stems are laden with nutrients such as vitamins A and K. According to the US Department of Agriculture, one cup of Swiss chard supplies 38% of the daily requirements of magnesium and 22% of iron.

The white-stemmed variety is most common in the Middle East, but you can also use the yellow- or red-stemmed varieties in this recipe.

2 lb/1 kg Swiss chard stems

1 tablespoon salt for every 8 cups/ 2 liters of water (to set the green color)

Ice-cold water, for soaking

For the tahini sauce

½ cup/120 ml tahini

¼ cup/60 ml lemon juice

1–2 garlic cloves (4–8 g), crushed

1 teaspoon salt, or to taste

1. Wash the stems and remove any threads that cling to them: Hold a small knife at the top of the stem, cut away a bit, and pull the thread down along the length of the stem. Repeat from the other end of stem.

2. Cut stems into bite-size pieces.

3. Boil a large pot of salted water to the proportion listed here, and drop the stems in the water. When the water comes back to a boil, lower the heat and simmer for a few minutes until tender but not mushy.

4. Drain and immediately plunge the stems into the ice-cold water to cool. Drain again and set aside in the strainer.

5. Combine all the sauce ingredients and mix in ¼ cup/60 ml water (or a few teaspoons more if the sauce is too thick; add more tahini if the sauce is too thin).

6. Dry stems with paper towels to remove any remaining water.

7. Mix stems with sauce and serve cold.

CHICKEN IN TAHINI SAUCE
Dajaj Taratore

SERVES 8 AS PART OF A MEZZE OR BUFFET
PREPARATION TIME: 15–20 MINUTES
COOKING TIME: 15–20 MINUTES

Preparing parts of this dish in advance (like cooking the chicken the day before) makes it a quick and excellent part of a cold mezze. This Aleppian chicken salad-type dish can be served as an appetizer or as a light meal.

14 oz/400 g skinless boneless chicken breasts (the breasts of one chicken)

½ cinnamon stick

2 allspice berries

1 bay leaf

1 garlic clove (4 g; optional)

½ small onion (2 oz/60 g)

1 small carrot, chopped

2 parsley stems

½ teaspoon salt, or to taste

For the tahini sauce

¼ cup/60 ml tahini, or to taste

6 tablespoons/90 ml lemon juice, or to taste

½ teaspoon salt, or to taste

1–2 garlic cloves (4–8 g), crushed

To garnish (optional)

2 tablespoons pine nuts, fried in vegetable oil (*see* p. 23)

1 tablespoon chopped parsley

1. Place the chicken in a pot. Cover with water, add the spices, garlic (if using), onion, carrot, parsley, and salt, and bring to a boil. Lower the heat, cover, and simmer for 10–20 minutes, or until the chicken is tender.

2. Remove from the heat and set aside to cool in the stock.

3. Remove the chicken from the pot. Drain the stock and reserve for another use.

4. Using your fingers, shred the chicken into long thin strips and arrange on a serving platter.

For the tahini sauce

5. Place the tahini in a bowl and gradually add 6 tablespoons/ 90 ml water, mixing with a wire whisk.

6. Add the lemon juice and stir to mix. The sauce will thicken slightly; then it will thicken a little more as it sits. (It can be further thickened with the addition of few teaspoons of tahini, or diluted with a few teaspoons lemon juice or water.)

7. Mix in the salt and crushed garlic. Taste and adjust seasoning.

To garnish

8. Spoon the sauce over the shredded chicken.

9. Garnish as desired and serve cold.

GRAINS

RICE PILAF WITH VERMICELLI
Roz bi-Shi'ariyeh

SERVES 8–10
PREPARATION TIME: 5 MINUTES
SOAKING TIME: 30 MINUTES
COOKING TIME: 15 MINUTES
RESTING TIME: 20 MINUTES

3 cups/1 lb 5 oz/600 g short-grain rice

¼ cup/2 oz/45 g broken vermicelli

3 tablespoons/1½ oz/45 g butter

3 tablespoons vegetable oil

3 cups/700 ml boiling water

1 tablespoon salt, or to taste

Cinnamon, fried nuts (*see* p. 23),
    or fried vermicelli, to garnish
    (optional)

1. Follow the instructions on p. 30 to wash and cook the rice, with the following modification: add the vermicelli pieces after step 6 and fry in the butter and oil until lightly golden, before adding the rice. Continue with steps 7–11.

2. Fluff with a fork, decorate with cinnamon, fried vermicelli nests, or fried nuts, and serve hot.

BULGAR PILAF WITH VERMICELLI
Burghol bi-Shi'ariyeh

SERVES 4–5
PREPARATION TIME: 10 MINUTES
COOKING TIME: 25 MINUTES
RESTING TIME: 10 MINUTES

This simple pilaf is served as an alternative to rice, and is delicious with yogurt and a salad.

2 cups/12 oz/350 g coarse bulgar

½ cup/120 ml olive oil

1 cup/3 oz/85 g vermicelli

½ teaspoon ground black pepper

2 teaspoons salt, or to taste

2 tablespoons/1 oz/30 g butter

1. Wash the bulgar and place in a strainer.

2. In a medium-size pot, add the olive oil and fry the vermicelli over medium to low heat until light golden, stirring continuously. Add the bulgar and black pepper and stir for a few minutes.

3. Pour 3 cups/700 ml water into the pot and bring to a boil. Add the salt, cover the pot, and cook on very low heat for 20 minutes.

4. Remove from the heat and mix in the butter. Replace the lid and set aside for 10 minutes, allowing the grains to swell and absorb all the moisture. Check they are cooked (*see* Notes on p. 112), and serve hot.

BULGAR PILAF WITH CHICKPEAS
Burghol bi-Hummus

SERVES 4–5
PREPARATION TIME: 10 MINUTES
COOKING TIME: 25 MINUTES
RESTING TIME: 10 MINUTES

This healthful side dish can be served with stews or meat dishes as an alternative to rice, but it is also a delicious vegetarian main dish, served with yogurt and salad.

2 cups/13 oz/360 g coarse bulgar

¼ cup/60 ml olive oil

1 small onion (4 oz/115 g), finely chopped

½ teaspoon ground black pepper

½ teaspoon ground cumin

3 cups/700 ml stock or water

2 teaspoons salt, or to taste

2½ cups/400 g/14 oz cooked or canned chickpeas (*see* p. 16)

2 tablespoons pine nuts, fried in vegetable oil (*see* p. 23)

1. Wash the bulgar and set aside in a strainer.

2. In a medium-size pot, heat the oil and fry the onion over medium heat, stirring frequently, until it starts to color. Add the bulgar, black pepper, and cumin, and continue to fry for a few more seconds.

3. Pour the stock or water into the pot and bring to a boil. Add salt, if desired, lower the heat to very low, cover the pot, and cook for 20 minutes.

4. Remove from the heat and mix in half of the chickpeas. Replace the lid and set aside in a warm place for 10 minutes, allowing the grains to swell and absorb all the moisture. Check the texture of the bulgar (*see* Notes).

5. Place the rest of the chickpeas in the base of a 9 in/22 cm round cake pan and top with the bulgar, pressing it in with the back of a spoon.

6. To serve: Place an upturned serving platter on top of the pan and, holding them together, quickly flip them. Carefully remove the pan, leaving the molded pilaf on the platter. Garnish with the fried pine nuts and serve hot.

NOTES

Bulgar may require more cooking time or liquid, depending on the size and freshness of the grains. Before serving, taste the bulgar to check that it is the desired texture. If it is not tender, stir in ¼ cup/60 ml hot water and cook over low heat for another 10 minutes, repeating the procedure until the bulgar is the desired texture.

FREEKEH PILAF
Freek Mfalfal

SERVES 4–6 AS A SIDE DISH
PREPARATION TIME: 10 MINUTES
COOKING TIME: 50 MINUTES–1 HOUR
RESTING TIME: 30 MINUTES

Freekeh is roasted green durum wheat. It is green in color with a chewy texture and an appealing sweet and smoky flavor. This hearty pilaf makes an excellent side dish, especially for desert truffle dishes and Lamb Shanks and Onions in Yogurt Sauce (p. 265).

¼ cup/60 ml olive oil

1 cup/5 oz/150 g chopped onion

2 cups/12 oz/350 g freekeh

1 teaspoon allspice

1 teaspoon cinnamon

½ teaspoon ground black pepper

1 teaspoons salt, or to taste

4 cups/1 liter beef, chicken, or
    vegetable stock

1. Heat the olive oil over medium to low heat and fry the onion until light golden in color. Add the freekeh, allspice, cinnamon, black pepper, and salt. Continue frying for a few seconds.

2. Pour in the stock and bring to a boil. Lower the heat, cover the pot, and gently simmer for about 45 minutes–1 hour, stirring a few times after about 20 minutes.

3. Check the freekeh—if it needs more cooking time, stir in about ¼ cup/60 ml of hot stock and simmer, covered, for around 10 more minutes. Taste and adjust seasoning.

4. Remove from heat and replace the lid, covering it with a thick towel to keep the heat in. Set aside for 30 minutes.

5. Spoon onto a serving platter and serve.

FREEKEH WITH RICE AND LAMB
Tatbiqa

SERVES 7–8
PREPARATION TIME: 30 MINUTES
COOKING TIME: ABOUT 1 HOUR
RESTING TIME: 10 MINUTES

This is an ancient Aleppian recipe consisting of rice, freekeh, and spiced meat served in layers. Traditionally, the prized freekeh was placed at the bottom of a serving platter and completely covered with white rice, perhaps to surprise guests. Here, I have used the modern presentation: serving the grains in the form of a cake, topped with lamb. This dish can easily be made in advance, and can be served with yogurt and a salad. You can use ground beef in place of the lamb, or *see* Variations to use chicken.

2 cups/14 oz/400 g short-grain
    white rice
2 tablespoons/1 oz/30 g butter
2 tablespoons vegetable oil
2½ cups/830 ml boiling water
1 tablespoon salt, or to taste
1 recipe Freekeh Pilaf (p. 113)

For the topping

¼ cup/60 ml olive or vegetable oil
    or ghee
1 lb/450 g lean ground lamb
    (or beef)
2 teaspoons Aleppo spice mix or
    seven-spice powder
½ teaspoon ground black pepper
2 teaspoons salt, or to taste

To serve

¼ cup/1½ oz/40 g pine nuts
¼ cup/1 oz/30g flaked almonds
Vegetable oil, for frying

1. Wash and drain the rice. Using the listed measures, follow steps 6–11 on page 30.

2. Prepare the topping: Heat the oil or ghee in a medium-size pot and fry the meat over high heat until browned but not dry. Add the Aleppo spice mix, black pepper, and salt; fry for a few more seconds. Remove from the heat.

3. Fry the nuts in oil and drain (*see* p. 23).

4. Spoon the rice into a 9 in/22 cm round cake pan, pressing it in gently with the back of a spoon. Spoon the freekeh over the rice. (The recipe can be prepared a few hours ahead to this point, and reheated in a medium-hot oven before serving.)

5. To serve: Place an upturned serving platter on top of the cake pan and, holding them together, quickly flip them. Carefully remove the cake pan, leaving the molded pilaf on the platter. Spoon the meat over the rice and sprinkle the top with fried nuts. Serve hot.

VARIATIONS: FREEKEH WITH RICE AND CHICKEN

Boil a whole chicken with your preferred spices, using the stock to cook the rice and freekeh. Discard the skin and bones, separate the meat into pieces, and use in place of the cooked lamb.

GAZIANTEP BULGAR PILAF
Burghol Antabli

SERVES 6–8
PREPARATION TIME: 15–35 MINUTES
COOKING TIME: 30–50 MINUTES
RESTING TIME: 30 MINUTES

Gaziantep is a city in southeastern Turkey, close to the Syrian border and only sixty miles from Aleppo. It is one of the oldest continuously inhabited cities in the world and one of the most famous culinary regions of Turkey.

This vegetarian pilaf combines bulgar, sweet peppers, and tomatoes. It is typically topped with fried eggplants, but it can also be made with coarsely ground lamb or beef. It is delicious served simply with yogurt and a salad, or alongside meat or poultry dishes.

6 tablespoons/90 ml olive oil

1¼ cups/7½ oz/190 g finely chopped onion

1 cup/6 oz/170 g finely chopped sweet green pepper

1½ cups/9 oz/260 g finely chopped sweet red pepper

2 tablespoons red pepper paste

1 tablespoon tomato paste

2½ cups/1 lb/485 g finely chopped red tomatoes

2 teaspoons allspice

½ teaspoon ground black pepper

½ teaspoon cinnamon

2½ teaspoons salt, or to taste

2 cups/12 oz/350 g coarse white bulgar, rinsed and drained

2 cups/480 ml hot water

For the eggplants (optional)

1¾ lb/800 g eggplants (about 2)

1½ teaspoons salt, or to taste

½ cup/120 ml vegetable oil

1. Heat the oil in a large pot and fry the onion over medium heat until almost tender.

2. Add the green and red peppers and fry for a few seconds. Add red pepper and tomato pastes and fry for a few seconds more. Add the tomatoes, allspice, black pepper, cinnamon, and salt.

3. Stir for about 30 seconds, or until the tomatoes are heated through.

4. Pour the hot water into the pot along with the bulgar, and bring to a boil. Lower the heat, cover, and cook for 30 minutes, stirring once or twice. Taste and adjust the seasoning.

5. Remove from the heat and keep the pot covered for 15 minutes, allowing the bulgar to absorb all the moisture. Remove the cover and check that the bulgar is the correct texture (*see* Notes on p. 112).

6. Prepare the eggplants, if using: cut off the stems and green caps and peel the eggplants. Cut into 1½ in/4 cm cubes. Sprinkle with salt and place in a colander for 30 minutes.

7. Wipe the eggplants with paper towels. Heat the oil over medium heat and fry the eggplants until browned and tender.

8. To mold the bulgar, spoon half the bulgar mixture into a 9 in/22 cm Bundt pan (or pan of your choice). Press gently on the top with the back of a spoon to compress. Add the second half of the bulgar and repeat. (The recipe can be prepared a few hours ahead to this point, and reheated in a medium-hot oven before serving.)

9. To serve: Place an upturned serving platter on top of the pan and, holding them together, quickly flip them. Carefully remove the pan, leaving the molded pilaf on the platter. Arrange the fried eggplants on top.

TRAVELING JEW
Yahoudi Msefar

SERVES 6–7
PREPARATION TIME: 20 MINUTES
RESTING TIME: 45 MINUTES
COOKING TIME: 40–45 MINUTES

This is an old recipe from the repertoire of Aleppian heritage, prepared with bulgar, meat, and vegetables. It is customarily served with yogurt and a salad. The dish can be prepared without meat, if preferred.

2 cups/12 oz/350 g coarse bulgar
1–2 eggplants (1½ lb/700 g)
3½ teaspoons salt, or to taste
⅓ cup/75 ml vegetable oil
¼ cup/60 ml olive oil
1 small onion (4 oz/115 g),
    finely chopped
2 large sweet red peppers
    (12 oz/350 g), finely chopped
2½ cups/1 lb/450 g peeled and
    finely chopped tomatoes
12 oz/350 g ground lamb or beef
2 teaspoons ground allspice
1 tablespoon ground coriander
½ teaspoon cinnamon
½ teaspoon ground black pepper
1 tablespoon tomato paste
3½ cups/830 ml hot water or stock
1 cup/9 oz/250 g cooked chickpeas
    (1 drained 14 oz/400 g can)
¼ cup/1½ oz/40 g pine nuts, fried in
    vegetable oil (*see* p. 23)

1. Wash the bulgar, squeeze it dry, and place it in a bowl.

2. Peel the eggplant, leaving strips of skin at ½ in/1 cm intervals. Cut into 1½ in/4 cm cubes. Place in a colander, sprinkle with some of the salt, and set aside for 30 minutes.

3. Wipe eggplants with paper towels. Heat the vegetable oil and shallow-fry until cooked and golden. Transfer to a colander.

4. Heat the olive oil in a pot over medium heat. Add the onion and red peppers. Add a little of the salt and stir for about 2 minutes. Add the chopped tomatoes.

5. Raise the heat, add the meat, allspice, coriander, cinnamon, and black pepper. Stir using a wooden spoon to separate meat pieces, being careful not to let the meat dry out.

6. Mix in the tomato paste, bulgar, and hot water or stock, and bring to a boil.

7. Reduce heat to medium, cover the pot, and simmer gently for 30 minutes, stirring the mixture twice. Taste and adjust seasoning.

8. Remove the pot from the heat, mix in the chickpeas, cover the pot, and set aside for 15 minutes. Remove the lid and taste to check that the bulgar is cooked. If it is not quite tender, stir in ¼ cup/60 ml boiling water and cook, covered, over medium heat for a further 10 minutes.

9. Add the fried eggplants and half of the pine nuts and mix gently. Spoon into a serving dish, garnish with the remaining pine nuts, and serve hot.

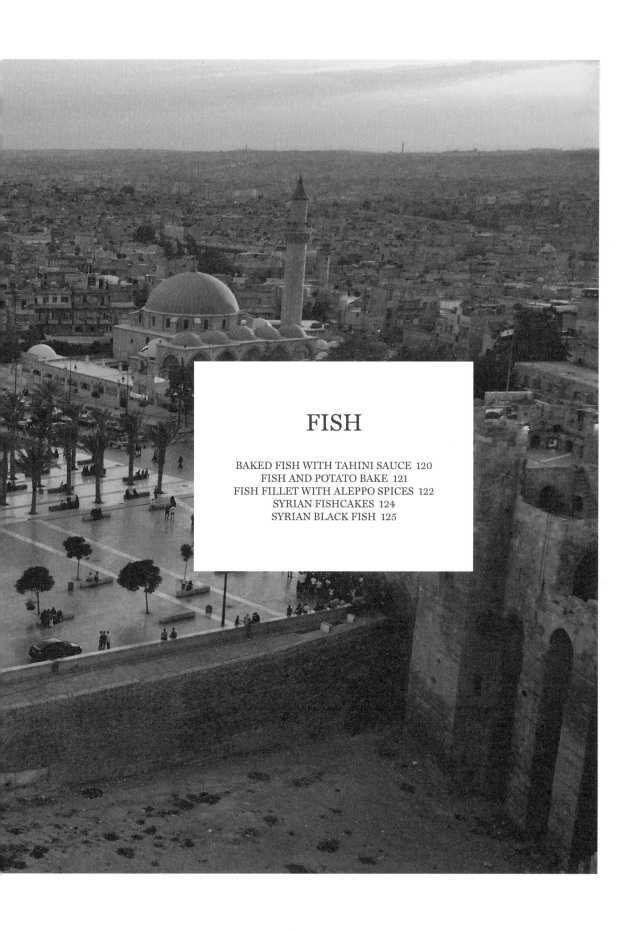

FISH

BAKED FISH WITH TAHINI SAUCE
Samak Taratore

SERVES 6–8 AS PART OF A MEZZE
PREPARATION TIME: 20–25 MINUTES
COOKING TIME: 20 MINUTES
RESTING TIME: 10 MINUTES

This is a delicious chilled dish of baked and flaked fish fillet covered in a creamy tahini sauce. It is easy to prepare and ideal as part of a mezze. The recipe can be easily doubled and served as a buffet dish.

¼ teaspoon allspice

1 teaspoon salt, or to taste

1½ lb/700 g skinless boneless white
fish fillets (such as cod, haddock,
or sea bass)

3 tablespoons olive oil

For the tahini sauce

½ cup/120 ml tahini,
or more to taste

¼ cup/60 ml lemon juice,
or more to taste

2 garlic cloves (¼ oz/8 g), crushed

½ teaspoon salt, or to taste

To garnish

3 tablespoons pine nuts, fried in
vegetable oil (*see* p. 23)

Thinly sliced cucumber or chopped
parsley (optional)

Prepare the fish

1. Preheat the oven to 400°F/200°C.

2. Mix the allspice and salt. Sprinkle the fish with the mixture and rub with 2 tablespoons of the olive oil.

3. Brush a baking pan with the rest of the oil and place in the oven for a few minutes, or until hot.

4. Place fish in the hot pan and bake for 20 minutes, or until cooked.

5. Transfer the fish to a cutting board and set aside for 10 minutes until just warm. Flake with a fork and allow to cool.

Prepare the tahini sauce

6. Place tahini in a bowl and add gradually whisk in ½ cup/ 120 ml water.

7. Add the lemon juice and continue to whisk; the sauce will thicken slightly. It will thicken a little more as it sits. If it is too thick, dilute with a few teaspoons lemon juice or water, or if too thin, thicken with a few teaspoons of tahini.

8. Mix in the crushed garlic. Taste and season with salt.

To serve

9. Mix 2–3 tablespoons/30–45 ml of the tahini sauce with the fish flakes. Add more lemon juice or salt, if desired.

10. Gather the fish flakes firmly in portions and arrange on a platter in the form of a fish. Cover with the rest of the sauce and top with the fried pine nuts.

11. Garnish with thinly sliced cucumber or chopped parsley.

FISH AND POTATO BAKE
Samak Mashwi wa-Batata

SERVES 4–5
PREPARATION TIME: 20 MINUTES
COOKING TIME: 1 HOUR

In this quick and easy recipe, fish is baked with onions and potatoes in a thick tomato sauce. I use whole sea bass, but you may choose any other white fish, or fish fillets (*see* Variations).

3¼ lb/1½ kg whole sea bass, cleaned, scaled, and gutted

2½ teaspoons salt, or to taste

½ lemon, cut into thin slices

6 tablespoons/90 ml olive oil

About 2 small onions (7 oz/200 g), thinly sliced into half-moons

14 oz/400 g can whole tomatoes, chopped

2 tablespoons red pepper paste

1 teaspoon Aleppo pepper or paprika

1–2 tablespoons lemon juice

2 teaspoons sugar

¼ teaspoon ground black pepper, or more to taste

2 medium potatoes (14 oz/400 g), thinly sliced

1. Preheat the oven to 400°F/200°C.

2. Using a sharp knife, cut a few slanted slashes on one side of the fish. Sprinkle the cavity and slashes with ½ teaspoon salt. Insert lemon slices into the slashes.

3. In a skillet, heat 3 tablespoons of the olive oil over medium heat and fry the onions until not quite tender, stirring frequently. Remove from the heat and set aside.

4. In the bowl of a food processor, combine the tomatoes, red pepper paste, Aleppo pepper or paprika, lemon juice, sugar, salt, and pepper. Pulse until coarsely puréed.

5. Mix the sauce with the fried onions. Add the potato slices and ½ cup/120 ml water.

6. Pour the sauce mixture into an ovenproof dish large enough to hold the fish (do not add the fish yet). Cover with aluminum foil and bake for 30 minutes.

7. Remove the dish from the oven, uncover, and arrange the fish on top of the mixture. Drizzle with the rest of the olive oil. Return to the oven and bake for 30 minutes, or until the fish is cooked through. (The potatoes and onions can be baked a few hours in advance, but the fish must be baked just before serving.)

8. Spoon the potatoes and sauce onto a serving platter and arrange the fish on top. Serve hot.

VARIATIONS

The dish is also excellent with filleted fish: Substitute the whole fish with 2 lb/1 kg fish fillets. Boil the potatoes, cool, and cut into ½ in/1 cm slices before adding to the sauce, omitting the water. Bake fish for 10–15 minutes, depending on thickness.

FISH FILLET WITH ALEPPO SPICES
Sharhat al-Samak bi-Tawabel Halab

SERVES 4–5
PREPARATION TIME: 15–20 MINUTES
COOKING TIME: 20–25 MINUTES

Here, filleted fish is baked with a crumbly topping of Aleppian spices, garlic, sweet red peppers, and pine nuts. It is excellent served with potatoes. You can also make a delicious sauce from the juices.

1 lb 10 oz/750 g white fish fillet, such as cod or sea bass
1 teaspoon salt, or to taste
¼ teaspoon ground white pepper
1 tablespoon olive oil

For the crumble

3 tablespoons/½ oz/15 g freshly made breadcrumbs
2 tablespoons ground coriander
3 tablespoons pine nuts, coarsely chopped
1½ tablespoons Aleppo pepper or paprika
2 teaspoons red pepper paste
½ cup/3 oz/90 g finely chopped sweet red pepper
4 garlic cloves (½ oz/15 g), crushed
½ teaspoon salt
3 tablespoons olive oil

To serve (optional)

2 tablespoons pine nuts, fried in 2 tablespoons vegetable oil (*see* p. 23)
A handful of parsley leaves
Cooked baby potatoes

For the sauce (optional)

1 teaspoon cornstarch

1. Preheat the oven to 475F°/240C°.

2. Sprinkle the fish with salt and white pepper then brush with olive oil. Place the fish on an oiled rack in a baking pan.

3. Mix the crumble ingredients and arrange on top of the fish.

4. Bake the fish for 20 minutes, or until cooked, loosely covering the fish with foil halfway through cooking.

5. Remove the pan from the oven and arrange the fish fillet on a serving platter.

6. To make the sauce: Pour the juices that collected in the pan into a small pot and place over medium heat. Mix the cornstarch with 1 teaspoon water and gradually pour into the pot, stirring continuously until it boils and thickens. Taste and adjust the seasoning.

7. Serve the fish hot, arranged on a platter and garnished with fried nuts, parsley, and potatoes drizzled with sauce, if using.

SYRIAN FISHCAKES
Aqras Samak wa Batata

MAKES 7
PREPARATION TIME: 20–25 MINUTES
COOKING TIME: 30 MINUTES

These excellent fish and potato patties can be served as a light meal, accompanied by a salad and cold mezze dishes such as Hummus (p. 39) or Baba Ghanouj (p. 40). They are also good to serve to children who won't eat fish! The mixture can be prepared in bite-size fingers, or as small croquettes to serve as hors d'oeuvres. They can be frozen and fried directly from frozen when needed and are a great way to use up leftover fish.

1 lb/450 g skinless boneless fillets of
    white fish, such as cod or
    sea bass
1 teaspoon salt, or to taste
1 large potato (12 oz/350 g)
1 egg yolk
3 tablespoons chopped parsley
1 teaspoon lemon zest
1½ teaspoons ground coriander
1 teaspoon ground cumin
¼–½ teaspoon ground black pepper
3 eggs, beaten
½ teaspoon cinnamon
2 drops of white vinegar
    (or any other vinegar)
¾ cup/2 oz/60 g breadcrumbs
⅓ cup/1½ oz/40 g all-purpose flour
About ½ cup/120 ml vegetable oil

1. Cook the fish with ½ teaspoon of the salt, according to your preferred method—it can be baked (*see* Baked Fish with Tahini Sauce, p. 120), poached, or pan-fried. Flake into small pieces.

2. Place the potatoes in a pot with cold water and a pinch of salt. Bring to a boil, lower the heat, and cook for 20 minutes, or until tender.

3. Drain the potatoes, peel, and mash while hot. Cool.

4. Using a fork, mash the flaked fish to a pulp. Mix with the mashed potatoes and mix in the egg yolk, parsley, lemon zest, coriander, cumin, pepper, and the rest of the salt.

5. In a bowl, mix the beaten eggs with the cinnamon, vinegar, and salt.

6. Place the breadcrumbs and flour on separate plates.

7. Prepare the fishcakes: Divide the fish mixture into 7 pieces. Using dampened hands, roll each piece into a ball, and flatten into discs about 4 in/10 cm in diameter.

8. Lightly coat each fishcake in flour; then dip in the egg mixture, then in the breadcrumbs, turning until well coated. Place on a plate or tray and refrigerate for 30 minutes, or until needed. (At this time, you can freeze them, separated by wax paper.)

9. To fry and serve: Heat the oil in a skillet until moderately hot. Place a few fishcakes in the skillet and fry until golden and crisp on one side. Gently flip over and fry the other side.

10. Serve hot or warm with a salad or cold appetizers.

SYRIAN BLACK FISH
Samak Aswad

SERVES 2–3
PREPARATION TIME: 10 MINUTES
RESTING TIME: 6–8 HOURS (OR OVERNIGHT)
COOKING TIME: 5–8 MINUTES

Samak aswad, meaning "black fish," is a species of freshwater catfish found in a lake on the river Euphrates. They are widely available in Aleppo, but you can make this recipe with other species of catfish, or with any other white fish, if preferred.

The fish is usually marinated, dipped in flour, and fried. It is a delicious meal, served with potatoes and a salad.

The recipe below is an old one, in which the fried fish was preserved in its marinade for winter consumption. With the advent of the refrigerator, however, this is not necessary anymore.

1 lb/450 g skinless catfish steaks
  with bones (about 4, each
  ¾ in/1½ cm thick)
¼ cup/1 oz/30 g all-purpose flour
1 cup/240 ml vegetable oil

For the marinade

¼ cup/60 ml cider vinegar or
  lemon juice
¼ cup/60 ml olive oil
2 garlic cloves (¼ oz/8 g),
  thinly sliced
1 bay leaf
1 teaspoon lemon zest
1 tablespoon ground coriander
1 teaspoon ground cumin
½ teaspoon ground white pepper
1 teaspoon salt, or to taste

1. In a bowl, mix the marinade ingredients.

2. Place the fish in the marinade and turn to coat well. Cover and refrigerate for 6–8 hours or overnight.

3. Place the flour on a plate. Remove the fish steaks from the marinade and dip in the flour to lightly coat on both sides.

4. In a skillet, heat the oil over medium heat. Fry the fish for about 2 minutes on each side, or until lightly golden.

5. Serve hot.

POULTRY

GRILLED CHICKEN
Dajaj Mashwi

SERVES 8
PREPARATION TIME: 10 MINUTES
MARINATING TIME: 4 HOURS OR OVERNIGHT
COOKING TIME: 45 MINUTES

In this tasty dish, chicken in a simple marinade of garlic, lemon juice, and olive oil is grilled over charcoal for an authentic smoky flavor, and served in a rich sauce made from the marinade. I serve this with baby potatoes, boiled in their skins and topped with butter or olive oil.

2 small chickens, about 2 lb/
    1 kg each, quartered
¾ cup/180 ml good quality low-
    sodium chicken stock

For the marinade

9 garlic cloves (1½ oz/40 g), crushed
½ cup/120 ml lemon juice
½ cup/120 ml olive oil
1 teaspoon ground white pepper
1 tablespoon salt, or to taste

1. Cut each piece of chicken in half. Remove the wings and reserve for another use.

2. Holding your knife perpendicular to the chicken pieces, make several 1 inch/2cm deep cuts through the skin and flesh.

3. Mix the marinade in a nonreactive bowl (like glass), add the chicken, and turn until well coated with the marinade. Cover and refrigerate for 4 hours or overnight.

4. Remove the bowl from the refrigerator one hour before grilling and preheat the barbecue (preferably charcoal).

5. Remove the chicken from the marinade, making sure that no garlic pieces are left on the skin. Strain and reserve the leftover marinating liquid.

6. Grill the chicken pieces until cooked through and set aside, keeping them warm.

7. In a wide pot, combine the reserved marinade with the chicken stock. Bring to a boil over medium heat and boil without stirring until the liquid has reduced to a sauce.

8. Place the chicken pieces on a platter and spoon the sauce on top.

VARIATIONS: TO OVEN-BAKE

Follow the instructions to step 4. Preheat the oven to 250°F (180°C). Place the chicken in a baking pan in one layer with the marinade and stock. Bake, uncovered, for about 45 minutes, brushing the chicken with the sauce a few times during cooking.

CHICKEN AND OLIVES
Dajaj bi-Zeitoon

SERVES 4–5
PREPARATION TIME: 20 MINUTES
COOKING TIME: 1 HOUR

Green olives are abundant in Aleppo and they marry so well with chicken in this delicious, easy-to-prepare stew. The quality of the olives is crucial to the dish; avoid bitter ones, since they will ruin the flavor. If the olives are very salty, soak them in warm water before adding them, and taste before adding salt. This is excellent served with rice.

¼ cup/60 ml olive oil

1 whole chicken (3 lb/1.5 kg), quartered

About 4½ cups/1 liter hot water

1 cup/5 oz/150 g finely chopped onion

2 tablespoons flour

½ teaspoon cinnamon

½ teaspoon allspice

¼ teaspoon ground black pepper

4 garlic cloves (½ oz/15 g), crushed

1¼ cups/6 oz/170 g pitted green olives, halved

2 teaspoons salt, or to taste

¼ cup/60 ml lemon juice

For the stock

2 cinnamon sticks

2 cardamom pods (optional)

5 allspice berries

2 bay leaves

1 garlic clove (4 g; optional)

1 small carrot, chopped

2 parsley stems

1 very small onion (3 oz/85 g), quartered

1. Heat the oil in a large sauté pan, and brown the chicken pieces all over. Remove the chicken, reserving the oil left in the pan.

2. Place the chicken in a large pot with enough hot water to cover, and bring to a boil, skimming off any foam that forms on the surface.

3. Add the stock ingredients, cover the pot, lower the heat, and simmer very gently for 40–50 minutes until the chicken is cooked and tender.

4. Remove the chicken pieces and set aside to cool, before removing the skin and bones.

5. Strain the stock and return it to the pot. Boil, uncovered, until the stock is reduced to 3 cups/700 ml.

6. In the oil reserved from browning the chicken, fry the onion over medium heat, stirring until tender.

7. Stir in the flour, cinnamon, allspice, and black pepper and fry for a few seconds. Add the garlic and fry for a few more seconds, stirring.

8. Gradually pour the hot stock over the onion mixture. Bring to a boil, stirring continuously. Lower the heat, cover the pot, and simmer gently for 20 minutes, stirring occasionally.

9. Add the chicken, olives, and salt. Cook uncovered for about 10 minutes, or until the sauce thickens.

10. Add the lemon juice. Taste and adjust the seasoning.

11. Serve hot with rice on the side.

FREEKEH WITH CHICKEN
Freek bi-Dajaj

SERVES 4
PREPARATION TIME: 15–20 MINUTES
COOKING TIME: 1½ HOURS

Freekeh is common in Southeastern Turkey, Syria, Jordan, and Lebanon, and is delicious with chicken, but if you can't find it, coarse bulgar is a good substitute. Serve this dish with yogurt or a salad. Desert truffles make an excellent companion to freekeh, the crowning glory of a kingly dish.

1 whole chicken (3 lb/1.5 kg),
    quartered
1 lb/450 g chicken wings
6 tablespoons/90 ml vegetable oil
5–6 cups/1.2–1.5 liters hot water
1 cup/5 oz/150 g finely chopped onion
2 cups/12 oz/350 g freekeh (do not
    wash unless necessary—water
    will diminish the smoky flavor)
1 teaspoon salt, or to taste
⅔–1 lb/300–500 g chopped,
    cooked desert truffles (*see* p. 17;
    optional)

For the spice mix

2 teaspoons allspice
2 teaspoons cinnamon
½–¾ teaspoon ground black pepper
½ teaspoon salt, or to taste

Aromatics

1 very small onion (3 oz/85 g),
    quartered
1 small carrot, chopped
4 white peppercorns
4 cloves
1 cinnamon stick

To garnish

¼ cup/1½ oz/40 g pine nuts
¼ cup/¾ oz/20 g sliced almonds
¼ cup/60 ml vegetable oil

1. Clean and wash the chicken pieces and wings and dry with a paper towel. Prepare the spice mix and sprinkle the chicken with half of it.

2. Fry the chicken pieces and wings in 3 tablespoons of the vegetable oil until golden, then discard the oil.

3. In a large stockpot, cover the chicken pieces with the hot water and bring to a boil, skimming any foam that forms on the surface. Add the aromatics, cover the pot, and simmer gently over low heat for 45 minutes.

4. Using a slotted spoon, remove the chicken pieces and the wings. Reserve the wings for another use, and set the chicken pieces aside, keeping them warm.

5. Strain the stock and return it to the pot. Boil, uncovered, until it has reduced to about 4 cups/1 liter.

6. In a large pot, heat the rest of the oil over medium to low heat and fry the onions, stirring, until light golden in color. Add the freekeh and the rest of the spice mix and continue to stir for 30 seconds more.

7. Pour the stock over the onion-freekeh mixture and bring to a boil. Add the salt. Lower the heat, cover, and cook for 45 minutes–1 hour. After 20 minutes of cooking, stir a few times and add the desert truffles, if using.

8. Test the freekeh—if it requires more cooking time, stir in ¼ cup/60 ml more hot stock or water and simmer, covered, for 10 minutes then test again. Repeat as necessary. Taste and adjust the seasoning, if necessary.

9. For the garnish, fry the nuts in the oil, stirring constantly, until they begin to color (*see* p. 23).

10. Spoon the freekeh onto a platter, top with the chicken pieces, and garnish with the nuts. Serve hot.

MLOUKHIYEH WITH CHICKEN
Mloukhiyeh bi-Dajaj

SERVES 6
PREPARATION TIME: 15–20 MINUTES
COOKING TIME: 50 MINUTES–1 HOUR

Mloukhiyeh, or Jew's mallow, is an annual herb cultivated in Syria, Lebanon, and Egypt. It is also the name of a well-known dish in these countries, though the Egpytians claim its origins. The dish is prepared with chicken or meat, and sometimes with a mixture of the two. It is served with toasted flatbread, rice, and a sauce of chopped onion in vinegar or lemon juice.

This recipe uses chicken and fresh *mloukhiyeh* leaves, but many households and restaurants in Aleppo use dried leaves (*see* p. 261). In other parts of the world, it is easier to find frozen. When chopped, the herb produces a slimy secretion that can be avoided by carefully separating the leaves from the stalks (*see* p. 19). Another trick is to add lemon juice to the boiling stock just before adding the leaves.

1 whole chicken (3 lb/1.5 kg),
    quartered
¼ cup/60 ml oil or butter
9 garlic cloves (1¼ oz/40 g), crushed
¼ cup/¾ oz/20 g ground coriander
1 cup/2 oz/60 g finely chopped
    cilantro
2 teaspoons salt, or to taste
¼ cup/60 ml lemon juice
10 cups/8 oz/250 g fresh *mloukhiyeh*
    (Jew's mallow) leaves, or
    8 oz/250 g frozen, finely sliced

For the stock

2 cinnamon sticks
2 cardamom pods (optional)
5 allspice berries
2 bay leaves
1 garlic clove (4g; optional)
1 small carrot, chopped
2 parsley stems
1 very small onion (3 oz/85 g)

To serve

1 small onion (4 oz/115 g), chopped
⅓ cup/75 ml red wine vinegar
1 loaf Arabic flatbread
2 cups/14 oz/400 g short-grain rice,
    cooked (*see* p. 30)

1. Place the chicken in a large pot with water to cover. Bring to a boil, skimming off any foam that forms. Lower the heat, add the stock ingredients, cover, and simmer over medium to low heat for 40–50 minutes, or until the chicken is tender.

2. Remove the chicken pieces and discard the skin and bones (if you are making this dish ahead, store the chicken in a small pot with a little of the stock).

3. Measure and strain the stock: you should have 5 cups/ 1.2 liters (add water or boil rapidly to achieve the correct measure). Return the stock to the pot and bring to a boil.

4. Meanwhile, place the oil or butter in a skillet and fry the garlic for a few seconds. Add the coriander, cilantro, and ¼ teaspoon of the salt, and stir for a further 30 seconds. Add this mixture to the boiling stock, lower the heat, and simmer for a few seconds. Add the lemon juice and adjust the seasoning, if necessary. (The recipe can be prepared to this step a few hours before serving.)

5. Just before serving, add the *mloukhiyeh*, simmer for a few seconds (1 minute if frozen), and pour into a serving bowl. Reheat the chicken pieces, if necessary.

To serve

6. Mix the onion and vinegar, season with salt, and set aside.

7. Open the Arabic flatbread, toast it until browned all over, and break it into bite-size pieces.

8. Serve hot. The dish is typically eaten layered in a bowl, starting with a few pieces of bread, a layer of rice, some chicken pieces, a ladleful of *mloukhiyeh*, then a few spoonfuls of onion-vinegar sauce.

MEAT

LEG OF LAMB IN VINEGAR WITH BULGAR
Fakhdeh Dobo

SERVES 12
PREPARATION TIME: 20 MINUTES
COOKING TIME: 3½ HOURS

The name for this dish, *dobo*, comes from the Italian *addobbo*, "to decorate," referring to ingredients that enhance the flavor or appearance of a dish. As odd as it may seem, the star of this ancient Aleppian recipe is vinegar. The meat is cooked in diluted vinegar and spices, resulting in a delicious stock that is used to cook the bulgar. If you like the taste of vinegar, you can increase the ratio of vinegar to water as high as one-third.

2 teaspoons Aleppo spice mix or
    seven-spice powder
2 teaspoons allspice
1 teaspoon cinnamon
1 tablespoon salt
15 garlic cloves (2 oz/60 g), peeled
    and cut in half if large
Whole leg of lamb on the bone
    (about 7 lb/3 kg)
1½ cups/350 ml red wine vinegar
1 cup/240 ml red wine (optional)

Aromatics

20 cloves
15 cardamom pods
1–1½ in/3–4 cm piece of ginger
20 black peppercorns
6 bay leaves
1 nutmeg, broken to pieces

1. Preheat the oven to 475°F/240°C.

2. Mix the Aleppo spice mix or seven-spice powder with the allspice, cinnamon, and 1½ teaspoons of the salt. Combine half of this mixture with the peeled garlic.

3. Using the tip of a knife blade, make deep incisions in the meat at intervals, and fill each one with a piece of spiced garlic. Sprinkle the leg with the rest of the spice mix.

4. Place the lamb on an oiled rack in a baking tray and bake for 20 minutes.

5. Transfer the lamb to a large pot or slow cooker and add the vinegar, wine, the remaining 1½ teaspoons salt, and 10 cups/2.5 liters water. Bring to a simmer, skimming off any foam that forms on the surface.

6. Add the aromatics, cover, and cook on very low heat (the surface of the liquid should be just trembling) for 6 hours, until the flesh falls easily from the bone. (A slow cooker is excellent for this.)

7. Remove the leg and set aside, partially covered, to keep it hot. Strain the stock through a fine strainer or cheesecloth and discard the aromatics.

8. Boil the stock, uncovered, until it has reduced to 6 cups/ 1.5 liters. Taste and adjust seasoning. Set aside 2 cups/ 480 ml of the stock to serve with the leg. (I usually refrigerate the stock until the fat collects as a solid mass at the top, then remove and discard the fat.)

continued overleaf

For the bulgar

2¾ cups/1 lb/450 g coarse
    white bulgar
½ cup/120 ml olive or vegetable oil
    or 1 stick/4 oz/115 g butter
1 small onion (4 oz/115 g),
    finely chopped
4 cups/1 liter reserved cooking stock
Salt, to taste

To serve (optional)

⅓ cup/1¾ oz/50 g pine nuts
¼ cup/1 oz/30 g pistachios
½ cup/1½ oz/40 g sliced almonds
½ cup/120 ml vegetable oil
Plain yogurt

To prepare the bulgar

9. Wash the bulgar in a strainer and set aside to drain.

10. In a medium-size pot, heat the oil or butter over medium to low heat and fry the onion, stirring well, until it starts to color. Add the bulgar and continue to fry for a few seconds.

11. Pour in the rest of the reserved stock and bring the mixture to a boil. Taste and add salt, if needed.

12. Lower the heat, cover the pot, and cook on very low heat for 20 minutes. Remove from the heat.

13. Without removing the lid, set the bulgar aside in a warm place for 15 minutes, allowing the grains to swell and absorb all the moisture (*see* Notes). Stir with a fork and replace the lid until serving.

To serve

14. Transfer the lamb to a chopping board. Remove and discard the bones. Separate the meat into large chunks and place in a pot with the 2 cups/480 ml of reserved stock. Bring to a boil then lower the heat to medium and simmer uncovered for about 10 minutes, or until the meat is hot and the sauce has thickened slightly.

15. If using, fry the nuts in the oil (*see* p. 23).

16. Place the bulgar on a serving platter with the meat pieces on the side or on top and garnish with fried nuts, if using. Place the thickened meat stock and yogurt in separate bowls to be served on the side.

NOTES

As a general rule, 1½ cups/360 ml of liquid are needed to cook 1 cup/6 oz/170 g of coarse bulgar. In this case, less liquid is needed because of the vinegar; however some kinds of bulgar may need more liquid and more cooking time. If necessary, add about ¼ cup/60 ml boiling water to the cooked bulgar and continue to cook until the desired tenderness.

LEG OF LAMB WITH FREEKEH
Fakhdeh bi-Freek

SERVES 12
PREPARATION TIME: 25 MINUTES
COOKING TIME: 4 HOURS
RESTING TIME: 30 MINUTES

Field-roasted green wheat (freekeh) is paired with the most popular lamb cut to produce a festive dish that is much loved in Aleppo. It is superb to feed a large group and can be stored in the freezer for up to one month (freeze the lamb, freekeh, and 1 cup/240 ml stock seperately, and reheat the lamb in the stock, serving-side down). A slow cooker works very well for this type of dish.

For the lamb

7 lb/3 kg leg of lamb on the bone

Vegetable oil

20 cloves

15 cardamom pods

1–1½ in/3–4 cm piece of ginger

20 black peppercorns

6 bay leaves

1 nutmeg, broken into pieces

1 tablespoon salt, or to taste

For the freekeh

½ cup/120 ml olive or vegetable oil

1 large onion (8 oz/225 g),
    finely chopped

2 teaspoons Aleppo spice mix or
    seven-spice powder

2 teaspoons allspice

2 teaspoons cinnamon

1 teaspoon ground black pepper

6 cups/2 lb/1 kg medium-grain
    freekeh, picked through

1–1½ lb/500–800 g cooked desert
    truffles (optional; *see* p. 17)

Salt, if needed

To serve (optional)

⅓ cup/1¾ oz/50 g pine nuts

¼ cup/1 oz/30 g pistachios

½ cup/1½ oz/40 g flaked almonds

½ cup/120 ml vegetable oil

Plain yogurt

1. Preheat the oven to 475°F/240°C. Place the lamb on an oiled rack in a roasting pan and bake for 20 minutes, until colored.

2. Place the lamb in a large stockpot or slow cooker and cover with water. Bring to a boil, skimming any foam that forms.

3. Add the spices and salt, cover, and cook at a very low simmer for about 6 hours, replenishing the stock or water as necessary, until the meat falls easily from the bone. Remove the lamb. Strain the stock, discarding the whole spices. Set the lamb aside in about 1 cup/240 ml of the stock.

4. Boil the remaining stock, uncovered, or add more water to make 11 cups/2.6 liters. Taste and adjust the seasoning, and skim the fat, if desired (I usually refrigerate the stock until the fat collects at the top, making it easier to remove).

To prepare the freekeh

5. In a large pot, heat the oil over low heat and fry the onion until golden. Add the spices and freekeh and continue frying, stirring constantly, for about one more minute.

6. Pour in the reserved 11 cups/2.6 liters of stock and bring to a boil. Lower the heat, cover the pot, and cook for about one hour, stirring a few times after 20 minutes of cooking. If using, add the desert truffles towards the end of cooking.

7. Remove from the heat and check the freekeh is cooked (simmer with a little more water, if not). Add salt, if needed. Wrap the lid in a thick dish towel before covering the pot, and set aside for 30 minutes.

To serve

8. If using, fry the nuts in the oil (*see* p. 23).

9. Spoon the freekeh onto a large platter and top with the leg of lamb and fried nuts, if using. Serve hot, with yogurt on the side.

STUFFED LAMB ROLLS
Barzowlat Malfoofeh

SERVES 6
PREPARATION TIME: 15–25 MINUTES
COOKING TIME: 1 HOUR

"What's in a name? That which we call a rose by any other name would smell as sweet." These words from Shakespeare's *Romeo and Juliet* came to mind while I was writing this recipe. *Barzowlat Malfoofeh* has many names taken from different languages. In Aleppo it is known as *Barzowlat*, a derivative of the Italian word *bresaola*, in French *alouettes sans tête*, and in Arabic *sharhat malfoofeh*, meaning rolled slices.

The dish has origins in ancient Venice, and came with the Italian Levantine travelers who settled in Aleppo in the second half of the last millennium. Italian *bresaola* is air-dried meat, while the Aleppian *barzowlat* uses fresh meat and various other local ingredients.

In this dish, thinly pounded steaks (called *bismashkat* in Aleppo) are stuffed, fried, and cooked in tomato sauce. It is usually served with rice, and you can substitute beefsteaks for the lamb. You will need toothpicks to secure the rolls.

For the rolls

2 lb/1 kg lamb steak, very
    thinly sliced
½ teaspoons salt, plus more to taste
½ teaspoon ground black pepper,
    plus more to taste
3–4 carrots (14 oz/400 g), peeled
15 garlic cloves (2 oz/60 g), peeled
    and coarsely chopped
1½ teaspoons Aleppo spice mix or
    seven-spice powder
½ teaspoon ground allspice
⅓ cup/1½ oz/40 g all-purpose flour
6 tablespoons/90 ml olive oil

For the tomato sauce

¼ cup/60 ml olive oil or butter
1 small onion (4 oz/115 g),
    finely chopped
2 lb/1 kg fresh tomatoes, skinned,
    seeded, and puréed, or
      28 oz/800 g can tomato purée
1 teaspoon ground allspice
1 teaspoon salt, or to taste

1. Place each slice of meat between sheets of plastic wrap or wax paper and pound with a meat mallet until it is very thin. Season lightly with salt and black pepper.

2. Cut the carrots into batons a little longer than the short side of the meat slices.

3. Mix the chopped garlic with the Aleppo spice mix or seven-spice powder, allspice, ½ teaspoon black pepper, and ½ teaspoon salt.

4. Place a carrot baton on the short end of a slice of meat, add some of the garlic mixture, and roll tightly, securing with a toothpick. Repeat with the rest of the meat slices.

5. Place the flour on a shallow plate and dip each meat roll in flour to lightly coat.

6. In a large pan, heat the oil over high heat and brown the rolls in batches.

7. Next make the sauce: In a medium-large pot, heat the oil or butter and sauté the onion over low heat, stirring until tender. Add the tomato purée, allspice, and salt. If using canned tomatoes, add ½ cup/120 ml water.

8. Add the meat rolls to the sauce and bring the mixture to a boil over medium to high heat. Lower the heat, cover the pan, and simmer for 1 hour, or until the meat is tender and the sauce has thickened (add a little water if the sauce is too thick).

9. Taste and adjust the seasoning and serve hot.

STUFFED LAMB NECK
Raqbeh Mahshiyeh

SERVES 6
PREPARATION TIME: 30 MINUTES
COOKING TIME: 3½ HOURS

Lamb meat from the shoulder or neck has the most succulent flavor and responds particularly well to braising. Here, lamb neck is stuffed with a flavorful meat and rice stuffing and cooked in an aromatic stock.

To increase the number of portions, you can increase the amount of stuffing and sew thin lamb steaks to the neck at the opening, enlarging the cavity. Some prefer to cook the stuffing separately, but stuffing cooked inside the neck is richer in flavor. You can serve this dish with your choice of yogurt, a salad of sliced radish or watercress, fried potatoes, or cooked desert truffles (if used in the stuffing). You will need butcher's twine and a trussing needle, or several small skewers.

For the lamb

2 tablespoons olive oil or melted
    butter, plus more for oiling
2–3 lb/1–1.5 kg boneless lamb neck,
    cut open
1 teaspoon Aleppo spice mix or
    seven-spice powder mixed with
    1 teaspoon salt
2 tablespoons pine nuts
3 tablespoons/1 oz/30 g unsalted
    pistachios, peeled
¼ cup/1 oz/30g flaked almonds
¼ cup/60 ml vegetable oil
Lamb stock or water to cover
    (about 12–16 cups/3–4 liters)

For the stuffing

¼ cup/1¾ oz/50 g short-grain rice,
    preferably Egyptian
2–3 desert truffles (1¾ oz/50 g;
    optional)
7 oz/200 g lean ground lamb
1 teaspoon Aleppo spice mix or
    seven-spice powder
1 teaspoon salt, or to taste
½ teaspoon allspice
¼ teaspoon cinnamon
¼ teaspoon ground black pepper

1. Preheat the oven to 400°F/200°C and oil the rack of a large roasting pan.

2. Sprinkle the lamb inside and out with the spice mix and salt. Rub with the olive oil or melted butter. Place on the prepared rack and bake for 15 minutes.

3. Fry the nuts in the vegetable oil until they just begin to turn golden (*see* p. 23). Transfer to paper towels to drain.

To stuff the neck

4. Wash and drain the rice. Clean and finely chop the desert truffles, if using (*see* p. 17).

5. Mix all the stuffing ingredients with 2 tablespoons water and about a third of the fried nuts.

6. Loosely fill the cavity of the lamb neck with the stuffing and close the opening with a trussing needle and butcher's twine or with skewers.

To cook the neck

7. Place the stuffed neck in a large pot with enough water or stock to cover. Bring to a slow simmer over low heat. Simmer for 10 minutes, skimming off any foam that forms on the surface.

8. Reduce the heat until the water is just trembling. Add the aromatics, cover the pot, and cook for 3 hours, replenishing hot water as needed.

continued overleaf

Aromatics

3 cinnamon sticks

5 cardamom pods (optional)

1 very small onion (3 oz/85 g),
    studded with 10 cloves

10 allspice berries

5 bay leaves

1 small carrot, chopped

2 parsley stems

1 celery stick (optional)

9. Remove the neck from the stock and set aside, loosely covered to keep it warm. Strain the stock well and return it to the pot. Boil rapidly over high heat to reduce the stock by about a third, or until the sauce is your preferred thickness. Season to taste.

To serve

10. Remove the twine or skewers, sprinkle the remaining nuts over the dish, and serve hot with the sauce on the side.

NOTES

To serve, you may choose to remove the stuffing from the neck, arrange it on a serving platter, and shred the meat, serving it on top of the stuffing. If preferred, you can double the stuffing ingredients and cook the stuffing separately from the meat.

MINTED PATTIES
Aqras Na'na'

MAKES 3 LARGE OR 12 SMALL PATTIES
PREPARATION TIME: 15 MINUTES
COOKING TIME: 3–5 MINUTES

This is a delicious and refreshing hot appetizer of ground meat patties flavored with mint and spices and grilled over charcoal or fried. Some like to serve it in a garlicky lemon sauce (*mtaffayeh*), adding another dimension to this elegant dish. The meat can be served as a main dish accompanied by potatoes and a salad, or it makes an excellent sandwich filler.

1 lb/450 g lean ground lamb or beef

½ small onion (2 oz/60 g), grated

2½ tablespoons coarse dried mint or 1½ tablespoons fine dried mint

½ teaspoon Aleppo spice mix or seven-spice powder

¼ teaspoon cinnamon

¼ teaspoon ground black pepper

¼ teaspoon ground chili pepper

1½ teaspoons salt, or to taste

Olive or vegetable oil

For the sauce (optional)

4 garlic cloves (½ oz/15 g), crushed

⅓ cup/75 ml lemon juice

½ teaspoon salt, or to taste

A splash of olive oil (optional)

1. In the bowl of a food processor, combine the meat with the grated onion, mint, Aleppo spice mix, cinnamon, black pepper, chili, and salt, and pulse until well mixed.

2. Form the paste into 3 large patties (around 6 in/15 cm in diameter) or into 12 smaller ones. Brush a rolling pin with olive oil and roll the patties until they are quite thin. Grill over charcoal, broil in the oven, or fry over high heat in vegetable oil, until golden and cooked through.

3. If using, mix the sauce ingredients and pour over the patties while still hot.

4. Serve hot or warm.

CHILI AND GARLIC KEBAB
Kabab Khashkhash

MAKES 10 SKEWERS
PREPARATION TIME: 20 MINUTES
COOKING TIME: 15–20 MINUTES

This kebab is for spice lovers. It is typically served on a bed of grilled and crushed tomatoes, with Biwaz Bread (p. 275) on the side. The dish reheats very well and makes an excellent sandwich or a heartier meal if served with rice.

The name *khashkhash* means noisy, originally describing the clanking sound produced by swords locking in battle. The recipe is a derivative of an old Aleppian recipe in which kebab is rolled in Arabic flatbread with a spread of tomatoes and garlic and grilled. The crisp bread produced a crunch sound when eaten. If it was not noisy, eaters would return the roll to the grill until it had crisped enough to produce the desired sound.

For the kebab

1 lb/450 g ground lamb

4 garlic cloves (½ oz/15 g),
    crushed or finely chopped

1–2 hot red chilies, seeds removed,
    finely chopped

¼ cup/½ oz/15 g finely
    chopped parsley

2 teaspoons Aleppo pepper
    or paprika

1 tablespoon Aleppo spice mix
    or seven-spice powder

½ teaspoon cinnamon

1½ teaspoons salt, or to taste

To serve

8 small tomatoes (1¾ lb/800 g),
    peeled and crushed

¾ teaspoon salt, or to taste

Biwaz Bread (p. 275) or
    Arabic flatbread (optional)

1. Combine all of the kebab ingredients in a bowl and mix well. Transfer to a clean surface and knead for 30 seconds (like you would bread dough).

2. With moistened hands, divide the meat into 10 portions, each about the size of a prune (2 oz/60 g) and form into balls.

3. Insert a wide, flat skewer through the center of the meatball; mold the meat around the skewer to a length of about 5 in/14 cm. Suspend the finished kebab over a deep baking dish, resting the skewers on each side, while you finish the rest.

4. Preheat the grill (preferably charcoal); when it is glowing, grill the tomatoes and the kebabs, turning them frequently until cooked to your liking (if preferred, you can broil them in the oven, turning them once). If serving with Biwaz Bread, grill it for few seconds to heat through, and cut into triangles.

5. Mix the crushed tomatoes with salt to taste and arrange them on a serving platter. Top the tomatoes with the kebab (either with the skewers or you can remove them). Serve with the bread.

ALEPPO KEBAB
Kabab Halabi

MAKES 10 SKEWERS
PREPARATION TIME: 15 MINUTES
COOKING TIME: 10–15 MINUTES

This is the simplest of all kebabs, with a distinctive taste of lamb and Aleppo spice mix. Kebabs are best grilled on a charcoal flame and are usually served with grilled vegetables and Biwaz Bread (p. 275). There are many regional variations of this dish; see below.

For the kebab

1 lb/450 g finely ground lamb

2 tablespoons Aleppo spice mix or
    seven-spice powder

½ teaspoon cinnamon

2 teaspoons Aleppo pepper or
    paprika

1½ teaspoons salt, or to taste

To serve (optional)

Grilled vegetables, such as peppers
    and onions

Biwaz Bread (p. 275)

1. Combine all of the kebab ingredients in a bowl and mix well. Transfer to a clean surface and knead for 30 seconds (like you would bread dough).

2. With moistened hands, divide the meat into 10 portions, each about the size of a prune (2 oz/60 g) and form into balls.

3. Insert a wide, flat skewer through the center of the meatball; mold the meat around the skewer to a length of about 5 in/14 cm. Suspend the finished kebab over a deep baking dish, resting the skewers on each side, while you finish the rest.

4. Preheat the grill (preferably charcoal); when it is glowing, grill the kebab, turning them frequently until cooked to your liking (if preferred, you can broil them in the oven, turning them once).

5. If serving with Biwaz Bread, grill it for few seconds to heat through and cut into triangles. Serve the kebab on the skewers, or remove from the skewers to a platter with the grilled vegetables and bread.

VARIATIONS

- You can add 1 tablespoon red pepper paste or a handful of shelled pistachios or pine nuts to the mixture above.
- For Kebab with Desert Truffles: Boil 7–8 small desert truffles in salted water for about 5 minutes, drain, finely chop, and add to the kebab mixture.
- For Kebab as in Gaziantep: Add finely chopped chili peppers to the kebab mixture.
- For Kebab as in Izmir: Add chopped mushrooms and chopped fresh white cheese to the kebab mixture.

GRILLED KEBAB WITH ARTICHOKE HEARTS
Kabab Shawki

SERVES 6 AS AN APPETIZER OR 4 AS A MAIN DISH
PREPARATION TIME: 20 MINUTES
COOKING TIME: 20–25 MINUTES

This dish is best early in the season when artichokes are fresh and tender. Good quality frozen artichoke hearts can be used when artichokes are not in season. The kebabs can be grilled, cooked in the oven, or fried. If frying, try adding pine nuts to the kebab mixture. Serve as an appetizer, or with rice as a main dish.

For the kebab

8 oz/225 g finely ground lamb

1 tablespoon Aleppo spice mix or
    seven-spice powder

¼ teaspoon cinnamon

¼ teaspoon ground black pepper

¾ teaspoon salt, or to taste

For the artichoke hearts

6 tablespoons/90 ml olive or
    vegetable oil

8 artichoke hearts (1 lb/450 g;
    see p. 14 to prepare from fresh),
    quartered if large

¼ teaspoon ground coriander

¼ teaspoon allspice

¼ teaspoon ground white pepper

½–1 cup/120–240 ml low-sodium
    beef stock or water (¼ cup/60 ml
    more if to be served with rice)

½ teaspoon salt, if using water

To serve (**optional**)

Saj bread or Arabic flatbread
    (*see* p. 338)

Cooked rice

To prepare the kebab

1. Mix the ground meat with the rest of the ingredients. Knead the mixture for 30 seconds (as you would bread dough).

2. With moistened hands, divide the mixture into about 15 portions and form into balls.

3. If grilling, thread the kebab balls onto long skewers, leaving room at the edges. Suspend the kebabs over a baking dish, resting the skewers on the sides of the dish, until they are ready to be grilled.

4. Barbecue the kebabs over glowing coals, turning them frequently until the meat is cooked. Alternatively, you can grill them under a hot broiler or fry them on the stovetop. Set aside, keeping them warm.

To prepare the artichoke hearts

5. Heat the oil in a large pot and fry the artichoke hearts over low heat for about 8 minutes, stirring frequently.

6. Add the coriander, allspice, and white pepper and fry for 1 minute more. Raise heat to medium and pour in ½ cup/ 120 ml meat stock or water and salt, to taste. Bring to a simmer, cover, and cook for about 15 minutes, adding a few tablespoons of liquid if it looks dry. You should have a reduced sauce with a concentrated flavor that is a perfect marriage with the kebab.

To serve

7. Pull the kebab off the skewers and mix them with the artichoke hearts and sauce. Spoon everything into a dish and serve hot with rice. Alternatively, serve over pieces of bread as in Meatballs in Sour Cherry Sauce (p. 158). Or, you can serve in a bread bowl: Brush *saj* bread or any other thin flatbread with oil on both sides and place between 2 nonstick pans of roughly the same size. Bake until crisp. Remove the pans and bake for a few minutes more until golden.

KEBAB AND VEGETABLE STEW FROM URFA
Kabab Urfali

SERVES 6
PREPARATION TIME: 25 MINUTES
RESTING TIME: 1 HOUR OR OVERNIGHT
COOKING TIME: 2 HOURS

This is a tasty dish of kebab and mixed vegetables, grilled over charcoal flame and then stewed until tender. It is a summer dish that originated in Urfa, a town across the Turkish border north of Aleppo. In the old days this dish was prepared from leftover grilled meat, kebab, and vegetables, which were layered and cooked in the oven, producing the best flavor, but I have included a quicker variation, if preferred.

For the kebab and eggplant

1 lb/450 g finely ground lamb (chop by hand to achieve a fine texture)
2 tablespoons Aleppo spice mix or seven-spice powder
½ teaspoon cinnamon
2 teaspoons Aleppo pepper or paprika
1½ teaspoons salt, or to taste
1 lb/450 g long eggplants (preferably the same size)

For the vegetables

3 lb/1.5 kg tomatoes (about 6 large)
4 medium sweet green peppers (1 lb/450 g)
1 teaspoon Aleppo spice mix or seven-spice powder
½ cup/120 ml olive oil, plus more for basting

For the stew

1 teaspoon salt, or to taste
½ teaspoon ground black pepper
2 tablespoons/1 oz/30 g cold butter

To serve (optional)

Arabic flatbread (*see* p. 338), cut into triangles
Cooked rice

To prepare the kebab and eggplant

1. Using the listed ingredients, follow the method for Grilled Kebab and Eggplant (p. 150) until step 6. Carefully remove the skewers.

To prepare the vegetables

2. Place the tomatoes and sweet peppers in a bowl. Mix with the Aleppo spice mix or seven-spice powder and olive oil, and marinate for 30 minutes.

3. Grill tomatoes and sweet peppers over a charcoal fire or under the broiler, basting them with the marinade, until the skin is charred.

4. Peel the tomatoes and cut them into rounds. Peel the green peppers, remove the seeds, and cut them into large pieces.

To prepare the stew

5. In a large pot or ovenproof dish, arrange in layers: first layer half of the tomatoes, all of the green peppers, all of the kebab and eggplant, and then the rest of the tomatoes, sprinkling each layer with some of the salt and pepper. Cut the butter into small pieces and evenly sprinkle over the top layer.

6. Cover the pot or ovenproof dish with aluminum foil and place over low heat on top of the stove, over a charcoal fire, or in an oven preheated to 350°F/180°C for about 1½ hours.

7. Carefully flip the stew onto a platter and serve hot with Arabic flatbread or rice on the side.

VARIATION: A QUICKER METHOD

Prepare the kebab and egplant as above. Slice the tomatoes and peppers. Layer the ingredients and cook the dish as per steps 5–7.

GRILLED KEBAB AND EGGPLANT
Kabab Banjane

SERVES 4–6
PREPARATION TIME: 20 MINUTES
COOKING TIME: 30–35 MINUTES

This dish is considered a *tamliha* (derived from the word *milih*, meaning salt), a small snack served at the end of a light meal or in combination with other dishes like Baba Ghanouj with Pomegranate Molasses (p. 42), Hummus (p. 39), Bulgar and Yogurt Dip (p. 38), and Aleppian Batersh (p. 60).

It is an elegantly presented dish, but it can also be served in Arabic fatbread or with Biwaz Bread (p. 275) and grilled and crushed tomatoes (*see* Chili and Garlic Kebab p. 145). This dish also forms the basis of Kebab and Vegetable Stew from Urfa (p. 149). You will need skewers.

For the kebab

1 lb/450 g ground lamb

2 tablespoons Aleppo spice mix or
seven-spice powder

½ teaspoon cinnamon

2 teaspoons Aleppo pepper
or paprika

2½ teaspoons salt, or to taste

1 lb/450 g long, thin eggplants
(preferably of similar size)

¼ cup/60 ml vegetable oil

To serve (optional)

1 large sweet red pepper
(6 oz/170 g), sliced

1 large sweet green pepper
(6 oz/170 g), sliced

Parsley leaves

1. In a large bowl, mix the lamb, spices, and 1½ teaspoons of the salt. Knead the mixture for 30 seconds (as you would dough).

2. With moistened hands, divide the meat into 20 portions and form into balls.

3. Cut the stems off the eggplants; peel each eggplant lengthwise, leaving ½ in/1 cm strips of skin at intervals. Cut crosswise into ¾ in/2 cm slices.

4. Thread the eggplant pieces onto the skewers, alternating them with meatballs, making sure each skewer begins and ends with a piece of eggplant. Suspend the finished kebabs over a deep baking dish resting the skewers on each side.

5. Preheat the grill (preferably charcoal); when it is glowing, grill the kebabs, turning them frequently, until the meat is almost cooked (the eggplants will be charred but not cooked). Alternatively, you can do this under a preheated broiler.

6. Place the skewers in the bottom of a wide pot or pan (or you can carefully remove the eggplant and meat from the skewers and arrange them in a smaller pot, close together so they hold their shape). Pour in ½ cup/240 ml water, the oil, and the remaining 1 teaspoon salt.

7. Place the pot over a high heat and bring to a boil. Lower the heat, cover, and simmer for 20 minutes, or until the eggplants are cooked and only a little liquid remains. (Alternatively, this can be done in an oven preheated to 350°F/180°.)

8. Turn off the heat, carefully remove the kebab and eggplant, and place on a platter. Garnish as desired and serve hot.

NOTES

Above is the traditional and best way to make this dish. However, if preferred, you can oven-bake the skewers instead of boiling: After step 3, arrange the eggplant and kebab pieces in an ovenproof dish with ½ cup/240 ml water, the oil, and 1 teaspoon salt, and bake, uncovered, in a 350°F/180°C oven for around 20 minutes, basting frequently with the cooking liquid.

GRILLED LAMB OR BEEF
Lahem Mashwi

SERVES 4
PREPARATION TIME: 20 MINUTES
RESTING TIME: 1 HOUR OR OVERNIGHT
COOKING TIME: 15–20 MINUTES

Though grilling over a charcoal flame is not as convenient as grilling over a gas flame, the dry heat of charcoal sears meat quickly, creating a caramelized exterior and smoky flavor unparalleled by any other grilling technique. Here the meat is marinated in a red wine-vinegar sauce. This recipe traditionally uses boneless lamb loin (ask for *smeiskat* if you can find a Middle Eastern butcher shop), but it also works well with beef.

2 medium sweet red peppers
    (8 oz/225 g)
2 medium sweet green peppers
    (8 oz/225 g)
15 pearl onions (9 oz/250 g)
1 eggplant (10 oz/300 g; optional)
4 tender lamb or beef steaks (about
    1 lb 5 oz/600 g in total),
    cut into bite-size pieces
1 lb/250 g sheep's tail fat, cubed
    (optional)

For the marinade

¼ cup/60 ml red wine
1 tablespoon red wine vinegar
½ cup/120 ml olive oil
1 bay leaf
1 stick celery, chopped
2 teaspoons Aleppo spice mix or
    seven-spice powder
¼ teaspoon ground black pepper
1 tablespoon salt, or to taste

1. Cut the peppers into halves or quarters and remove the seeds and membranes. Press gently with your palm to flatten.

2. Blanch the onions, plunging them immediately into cold water. Drain and peel, leaving the root area (the part that holds the layers together) intact.

3. If using eggplant, cut off the green caps and stems, peel, and cut into 1½ in/4 cm cubes (they will shrink when grilled).

4. Mix marinade ingredients in a nonreactive bowl (like glass). Add the meat, sheep's tail fat (if using), sweet peppers, onions, and eggplant (if using), and mix well to coat. Cover with plastic wrap and set aside for 1 hour or refrigerate overnight. Bring to room temperature before grilling.

5. Thread the meat onto skewers, alternating it with tail fat (if using). Thread the onions and eggplant pieces onto separate skewers. Skewer the peppers or place them in a grill basket.

6. Grill the vegetables first, and then grill the meat until cooked to your liking.

7. Serve meat and vegetables on the skewers, or removed from the skewers and arranged on a platter.

VARIATIONS

- You can add other vegetables, in addition to or instead of those listed above, such as firm red tomatoes and hot chili peppers (brush these with oil before grilling).
- You can roll each piece of meat in a vine leaf (*see* p. 31) before grilling; this adds a special flavor to the meat.
- For Grilled Meat with Desert Truffles: Wash and cube the desert truffles (*see* p. 17), soak them in oil, and thread them onto the skewers with the meat and sheep tail before grilling.
- The above recipe may be prepared with tomato marinade, see Grilled Lamb Chops, p. 153).

GRILLED LAMB CHOPS
Kastaletta Mashwiyeh

SERVES 4
PREPARATION TIME: 5 MINUTES
RESTING TIME: 1 HOUR OR OVERNIGHT
COOKING TIME: 10–15 MINUTES

What better way to delight the appetite than tender cutlets of lamb marinated in spiced tomato sauce and grilled over glowing charcoal flame! The chops can also be cooked under the broiler to achieve a delicious result, but the much-coveted smoky taste will not be there. Serve them with potatoes of your choosing for a substantial meal.

8 lamb chops (about 1½ lb/700 g)

For the marinade

⅓ cup/75 ml tomato purée
1 tablespoon tomato paste
1 tablespoon red pepper paste
¼ cup/60 ml olive oil
1 tablespoon ground coriander
1 teaspoon Aleppo pepper or paprika
1 teaspoon Aleppo spice mix or
    seven-spice powder
¼ teaspoon ground black pepper
    (or more if you like it hot)
1½ teaspoons salt, or to taste

1. Mix the marinade ingredients in a nonreactive bowl (like glass). Add the lamb chops and coat well with the marinade. Cover with plastic wrap and set aside for 1 hour or refrigerate overnight.

2. Preheat the grill (preferably charcoal) and bring the lamb to room temperature.

3. Place the lamb chops on an oiled grill rack over the glowing coals and grill for a few minutes on each side until cooked to your liking (alternatively, you can cook them under a hot broiler).

4. Serve hot.

VARIATIONS: GRILLED LAMB CHOP STEW

One of my pleasures is to create a new dish from leftovers. Since lamb chops dry up when reheated, place the leftovers in a pot with beef stock or water and some more of the marinade ingredients. Bring to a boil, cover, and cook on low heat for about 45 minutes, or until the chops are very tender and the quantity of sauce has reduced. Serve with boiled potatoes or rice and a simple salad. Voilà, you have a new dish for the day.

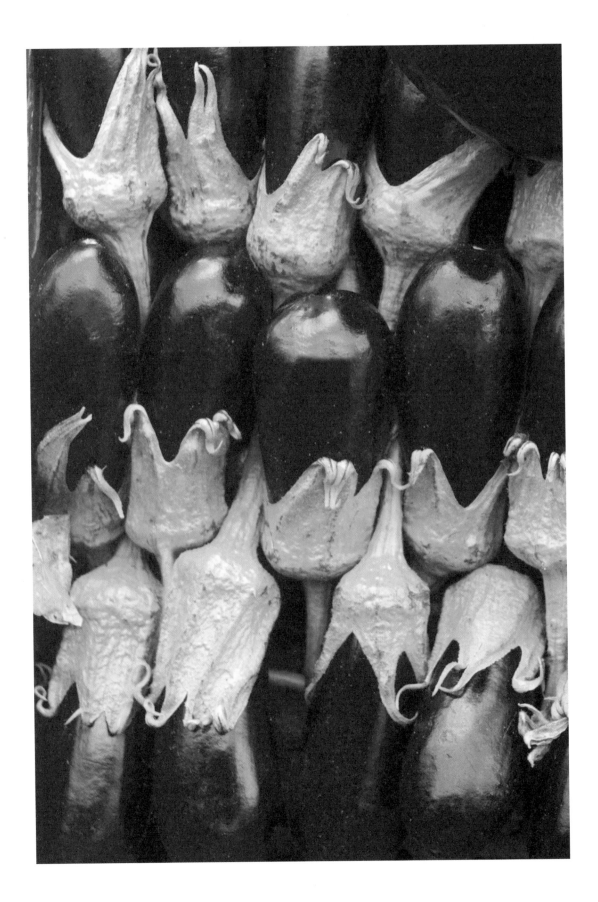

KEBAB-WRAPPED EGGPLANTS IN TOMATO SAUCE
Armoot Kabab

SERVES 4
PREPARATION TIME: 20 MINUTES
COOKING TIME: 15–25 MINUTES

In this artistic dish, small eggplants are encased in kebab meat and cooked in tomato sauce. The name *armoot* (meaning "pear" in Arabic) refers to the way the eggplant looks with its stem protruding from the kebab-meat covering. This dish is a beautiful addition to a buffet and a satisfying family meal served with rice (I like to serve it with turmeric rice: add ¼ teaspoon turmeric per cup of rice to the cooking water).

1 lb/450 g baby eggplants (about 12)

Peanut or vegetable oil,
    for deep-frying

1 lb/450 g extra lean ground lamb
    or beef (pulse in a food processor
    to achieve a fine texture)

1 medium egg

1 tablespoon breadcrumbs

1 tablespoon Aleppo spice mix or
    seven-spice powder

¾ teaspoon ground black pepper

1½ teaspoons salt, or to taste

1 tablespoon pine nuts, to garnish

2 medium sweet red peppers
    (8 oz/225 g), cubed

2½ cups/600 ml water or
    lamb or beef stock

¼ cup/60 ml tomato paste

1 teaspoon sugar

1 tablespoon lemon juice

¼ cup/½ oz/15 g coarsely chopped
    parsley leaves, to garnish

1. Remove the leaves from the tops of the eggplants, leaving the stems intact. Peel the eggplants and stems.

2. In a large frying pan, heat the oil over medium heat and deep-fry the eggplants whole for about 1 minute, removing them before they begin to color. Place on paper towels to cool. Reserve the oil.

3. Mix the ground meat with the egg, breadcrumbs, spice mix, ½ teaspoon of the black pepper, and 1 teaspoon of the salt. Divide into portions equal to the number of eggplants you have and roll into balls.

4. With moistened hands, place a meatball on the thick end of an eggplant. Pressing on it, squeeze and push the meat mixture up and around the eggplant until it reaches the stem. It should cover the whole eggplant, with just the stem protruding. Repeat until you have covered all the eggplants.

5. Fry the pine nuts in reserved oil and use a slotted spoon to transfer to a strainer or a plate lined with a paper towel.

6. Deep-fry the meat-encased eggplants in the same hot oil for 1 minute, or until the meat has browned.

7. Place the peppers into a large pot and top with the fried eggplants.

8. Mix the water or stock, tomato paste, sugar, lemon juice, and the rest of the black pepper and salt, and pour over the eggplants in the pot.

9. Bring the mixture to a boil, cover, and cook over low heat for about 15 minutes. Uncover and cook for a few more minutes, or until the sauce has thickened slightly.

10. Garnish with fried pine nuts and chopped parsley. Serve hot.

PASTA CAKE WITH KEBAB
Qaleb Ma'karoneh

SERVES 6
PREPARATION TIME: 30 MINUTES
COOKING TIME: 1 HOUR
RESTING TIME: 15 MINUTES

Although pasta is generally identified with Italy, pasta dishes are made all over the world. In Aleppo, this beautiful pasta cake is prepared with Aleppian ingredients: meat, Aleppian spices, and red pepper paste, creating an interesting variation of conventional spaghetti with tomato sauce. Traditionally, this dish was prepared with sheep's offal instead of kebab and with boiled eggs placed between layers of pasta. You will need a 5½ cup/1.3 liters ovenproof charlotte pan or deep cake pan with the same capacity.

For the tomato sauce

3 tablespoons olive oil

½ small onion (2 oz/60 g), finely chopped

3 garlic cloves (⅓ oz/12 g), crushed

1½ teaspoons Aleppo spice mix or seven-spice powder

½ teaspoon ground black pepper

1 tablespoon tomato paste (if using fresh tomatoes)

1 lb/450 g ripe tomatoes, peeled and puréed, or 14 oz/400 g can tomato purée, mixed with ½ cup/120 ml water

2 tablespoons red pepper paste

1 teaspoon sugar

1½ teaspoons salt, or to taste

2 eggs, beaten with 2 tablespoons water, ¼ teaspoon cinnamon, and 1 teaspoon salt (if needed)

For the pasta cake

¾ lb/350 g ground lamb

2 tablespoons breadcrumbs

2 teaspoons Aleppo spice mix

3 tablespoons vegetable oil

2 tablespoons pine nuts

8 oz/225 g spaghetti, cooked al dente

7 oz/200 g grated white cheese

Butter, for greasing

1 teaspoon salt, or to taste

To prepare the tomato sauce

1. Place the oil in a medium pot over medium heat and fry the onion until tender. Add the garlic, Aleppo spice mix or seven-spice powder, black pepper, and tomato paste (if using) and fry briefly.

2. Pour the tomato purée over the onion mixture and stir in the red pepper paste, sugar, and salt.

3. Bring the sauce mixture to a boil. Lower the heat and simmer uncovered for about 5 minutes, or until the sauce thickens slightly. Remove from the heat. Cool to warm.

4. Strain the egg mixture into the sauce and mix well.

To make the pasta cake

5. Mix the meat with 2 tablespoons of the breadcrumbs, the Aleppo spice mix, and about ½ teaspoon of salt. With moistened palms, form the meat into small balls (about 50).

6. Heat the oil in a large pan and fry the pine nuts until golden. Using a slotted spoon, transfer them to absorbent paper towels. Fry the meatballs in batches in the same oil.

7. In a large bowl, combine the pasta with the tomato sauce and mix well, adding the grated cheese in batches. Mix in the pine nuts, meatballs, and salt, if needed.

8. Preheat the oven to 350°F/180°C and generously butter a 5½ cup/1.3 liters ovenproof charlotte or cake pan.

9. Spoon the pasta into the buttered pan in 3 batches, firmly pressing on each batch, keeping the meatballs away from the sides of the pan. Sprinkle the remaining breadcrumbs on top.

10. Cover the pan with foil and bake for 45 minutes. Let rest 15 minutes before carefully flipping onto a serving platter.

KEBAB WITH YOGURT AND EGGS
Kabab bi-Baid wa-Laban

SERVES 4–5
PREPARATION TIME: 20–25 MINUTES
COOKING TIME 20 MINUTES

I have always told visitors to Aleppo not to miss the small eatery in the souq that makes a festive occasion out of this dish. You can watch how they make it, and take photographs too. The kebab is grilled over charcoal while cubes of sheep's tail fat are added to the pan. The meatballs are then fried in the melting tail fat along with eggs. In another large pot, sheep's milk yogurt is cooked with crushed garlic. A large round platter is covered with triangles of Arabic flatbread, on top of which the meatballs and eggs are arranged. The hot yogurt sauce is poured on top. Eaters are supplied with spoons, but no plates to share this fantastic communal dish, which can serve twelve. Visitors dine in groups of at least six, as the cook will not prepare the dish with less than 2 lb (1 kg) of lamb! Though perhaps less theatrical, the recipe below is an easier and healthier version of this dish.

10 oz/300 g ground lamb

2 tablespoons breadcrumbs
(optional)

1 teaspoon Aleppo spice mix or
seven-spice powder

1¾ teaspoons salt, or to taste

¼ cup/60 ml olive oil (if frying)

2 cups/1 lb/450 g plain yogurt

2 garlic cloves (¼ oz/8 g), crushed

1 tablespoon cornstarch
(if using cow's milk yogurt)

4 medium eggs

Dash of cinnamon

¼ teaspoon allspice

1 loaf Arabic flatbread, cut into
triangles

2 tablespoons pine nuts,
fried or toasted

1 tablespoon chopped parsley

1. In a large bowl, combine the ground meat, breadcrumbs (if using), Aleppo spice mix or seven-spice powder, and ½ teaspoon of the salt and mix well. Transfer to a clean surface and knead for 30 seconds (like you would bread dough).

2. With moistened hands, divide the meat into 22 small portions and form into balls.

3. Thread the balls onto skewers and grill over charcoal or fry in the oil in a nonstick skillet over medium heat. (The recipe can be prepared to this step one day in advance. Reheat the kebab by rolling in hot oil in a skillet before proceeding.)

4. Whisk the yogurt until smooth and pass through a strainer into a pot. Place over medium heat and stir until it slowly comes to a boil. Add the crushed garlic.

5. Mix the cornstarch (if using) with 1 tablespoon water, and pour it into the yogurt along with 1 teaspoon of the salt, or to taste. Bring to a boil again, stirring constantly. Remove from the heat.

6. Crack the eggs onto a plate and sprinkle with the cinnamon, ¼ teaspoon allspice, and the remaining ¼ teaspoon salt.

7. Slip the eggs into a nonstick skillet placed over medium heat. Stir a few times with a wooden spoon, mixing the yellow of the egg with the white (for a marbled effect), separating the mixture into bite-size pieces as it cooks.

8. Arrange the bread triangles onto a serving platter. Pour the hot yogurt over the bread, and scatter kebab and fried eggs on top. Garnish with pine nuts and parsley. Serve immediately.

MEATBALLS IN SOUR CHERRY SAUCE
Kabab Karaz

SERVES 5–6
PREPARATION TIME: 20–25 MINUTES
COOKING TIME: 10 MINUTES

This may well be Aleppo's most famous dish, and it is considered the crown jewel of Aleppian main dishes. It combines what Aleppo is known for: kebab and crimson sour cherries (*washneh*). It is a stew-like dish of spiced meatballs in a sweet-and-sour sauce.

Washneh are small sour cherries grown in cherry orchards of Ariha, located in the southwestern part of Aleppo. In the West, they are known as Saint Lucie's cherries (*Prunus mahaleb*). The cherries are collected in June during the cherry season and frozen so they can be enjoyed throughout the year. They can be found in the freezer section of Syrian and Armenian shops. The cherries are small and sour and a must for this recipe, though fresh or canned Morello cherries (*griottes*) can be substituted.

1 lb 5 oz/600 g ground lamb

½ teaspoon ground black pepper

1½ teaspoons Aleppo spice mix or
    seven-spice powder

1 tablespoon cinnamon

2½ teaspoons salt, or to taste

3 tablespoons olive or vegetable oil
    (if frying)

2 lb/1 kg pitted frozen sour cherries,
    or fresh if in season

½ cup/3½ oz/100 g sugar

1 loaf Arabic flatbread

To garnish

3 tablespoons pine nuts,
    grilled or fried (*see* p. 23)

1 tablespoon chopped parsley leaves

1 teaspoon cinnamon, to taste

1. In a bowl, combine the meat, black pepper, spice mix, 1½ teaspoons of the cinnamon, and about 1½ teaspoons of the salt; mix well. Transfer to a clean surface and knead for 30 seconds (like you would bread dough). With moistened hands, divide the meat into 36 portions and form into balls.

2. Thread the balls onto skewers and grill over charcoal, or fry in oil in a nonstick skillet over medium heat until almost cooked through.

3. Remove 7 oz/200 g of the cherries and set aside. Purée the rest in a food processor or blender. Strain the processed cherries over a bowl, pressing on them to extract the juice (you should end up with about 2 cups/480 ml juice).

4. In a medium pot, combine the juice, sugar, the remaining cinnamon, and about ½ teaspoon salt. Place over medium heat and stir well. Bring the mixture to a boil, lower the heat, and simmer, uncovered, for about 7 minutes, or until syrupy. (The recipe can be prepared to this step one day in advance.)

5. Add the meatballs and the reserved whole cherries to the simmering sauce and continue to cook until the meatballs are heated through. Taste and adjust seasoning.

6. Cut the bread into triangles and use half to line the base of a serving platter and the rest around the edges.

7. Spoon the meatballs and sauce onto the bread, garnish with pine nuts, parsley, and a sprinkle of cinnamon, and serve hot.

VARIATIONS

You can stuff the center of each meatball with fried or toasted pine nuts before cooking.

KIBBEH

BASIC KIBBEH PASTE

MAKES ABOUT 25 STUFFED KIBBEH, EACH 1½ IN/4 CM
PREPARATION TIME: 15–20 MINUTES
RESTING TIME: 10–20 MINUTES

Follow these steps for the best modern method to prepare kibbeh paste. Use this method for the recipes in this chapter.

Generous 1 cup/7 oz/200 g
    fine bulgar
8 oz/225 g extra lean ground
    lamb or beef, chilled
1 teaspoon salt, or to taste
Crushed ice and/or ice-cold water,
    if necessary
½ small onion (2 oz/60 g),
    coarsely chopped
¼ teaspoon ground black pepper
1 teaspoon Aleppo spice mix or
    seven-spice powder

1. Wash the bulgar in a few changes of water. Soak in cold water for 10 minutes (8 minutes if using white and not dark bulgar), drain, squeeze dry, and set aside.

2. Pulse the meat in a food processor with a little of the salt and one crushed ice cube until a smooth paste has formed (you may need to do this in batches). Transfer the paste to a bowl and refrigerate.

3. Add the chopped onion to the food processor with a little more of the salt and pulse a few times. Add a few tablespoons of the soaked and squeezed bulgar, and pulse until a fine paste has formed. Set aside.

4. Add the chilled meat, spices, and the rest of the salt and bulgar, and process until it forms a firm, dough-like paste. (If it is too stiff, add 1 ice cube or a few tablespoons of ice-cold water until it is supple.)

5. Transfer the paste to a wide bowl (traditionally, an earthenware bowl called *gdara*) and knead for 1 minute, adding a few more teaspoons of ice-cold water if needed. Alternatively, if you have a meat grinder, refrigerate the paste for 30 minutes (if soft) and pass twice through the feed tube using the finest setting, or pulse again in the food processor.

6. Divide the paste into portions as specified in the recipe. Or, if you would like to use one of the basic stuffings on p. 165, divide the paste into 25 walnut-size pieces (each just over ¾ oz/20 g) and stuff according to the method on p.163. You can also roll them into unstuffed balls for use in one of the recipes in this chapter.

BASIC METHOD FOR STUFFING KIBBEH

This is the basic method for preparing and stuffing kibbeh shells.

1. Moisten your hands with cold water, briefly knead each portion, and form into balls (if the paste is too moist and difficult to shape, refrigerate for 20 minutes).

2. Holding a ball in your left hand, burrow into it with the index finger of your right hand. Keeping your hands moistened, work the index finger in turning motions, patting the paste around the left hand, rotating the ball to widen the opening so as to form a thin, hollow shell. Try to form the closed end into an egg shape or ball.

3. Fill shell with the stuffing, gently pressing it in with your finger.

4. Moistening your fingers with ice-cold water, close the open end of the kibbeh to form into a ball or egg shape.

5. If cooking kibbeh in a stock or sauce, or before freezing, place the balls on a lightly oiled baking pan and bake in a 400°F/200°C oven for about 5 minutes, shaking the pan halfway through, to seal the outside. Otherwise, cook as per recipe.

NOTES

- If freezing, cool and freeze in one layer, transferring to sealed plastic bags once they are frozen.
- You can form hollow kibbeh without any stuffing for dishes cooked in stock, such as Kibbeh in Pomegranate Stock (p. 195) or Kibbeh and Chicken in Yogurt Sauce (p. 200). They are more difficult to shape when empty.
- The thickness of the kibbeh shells determines the size and number of balls prepared from the ingredients listed here; it may take some practice to achieve thin enough shells to make 25 at the dimensions specified.

BASIC MEAT STUFFING

TO STUFF ABOUT 25 KIBBEH BALLS
PREPARATION TIME: 2 MINUTES
COOKING TIME: 8 MINUTES

Use these basic stuffings as specified in the following recipes, or you can use them to stuff Basic Kibbeh Paste (p. 162).

3 tablespoons pine nuts or
    ½ cup/1¾ oz/50 g walnut halves,
    chopped, or a mixture of both
1–2 tablespoons vegetable oil
8 oz/225 g lean ground lamb or beef
½ teaspoon Aleppo spice mix or
    seven-spice powder
½ teaspoon ground allspice
¼ teaspoon ground black pepper
¼ teaspoon cinnamon
½ teaspoon salt, or to taste

1. If using the pine nuts, fry them in 1 tablespoon of the oil until golden. Leave the walnuts raw.

2. In a skillet or medium pot, heat the remaining oil over high heat until the oil is moderately hot.

3. Add the ground meat and all of the spices and season with the salt. Fry, stirring with a wooden spoon to break up any lumps. Continue stirring until the meat is cooked and has lost its pink color (without allowing the meat to dry out).

4. Taste and adjust seasoning, add the nuts, and allow to cool.

VARIATIONS

- You can use a mixture of nuts, such as walnuts, pine nuts, and unsalted, shelled pistachios.
- To save time, you can fry the pine nuts with the meat but the method above gives a better flavor.

BASIC BUTTER STUFFING

TO STUFF ABOUT 25 KIBBEH BALLS
PREPARATION TIME: 5 MINUTES

1 stick butter (½ cup/4 oz/115 g),
    chilled
¾ teaspoon Aleppo spice mix or
    seven-spice powder
Pinch dried mint

1. Cut the butter into 25 squares (for round kibbeh balls) or rectangles (for egg-shaped kibbeh balls) and place them on a large plate.

2. Sprinkle with the Aleppo spice mix or seven-spice powder and the dried mint. Refrigerate until needed.

3. Follow the method on p. 163 to stuff each kibbeh ball with one piece of butter.

FRIED KIBBEH
Kibbeh Maqliyeh

MAKES 12 PIECES; SERVES 4–6
PREPARATION TIME: 50 MINUTES–1 HOUR
COOKING TIME: 15 MINUTES

These egg-shaped kibbeh, with a crisp exterior and a moist stuffing, can be made ahead and are very handy to cook upon the arrival of unexpected guests. Serve them as part of a mezze (allowing 1 or 2 per person) or as an appetizer or light meal with a salad and a bowl of yogurt (3 to 4 per person). They are also good for buffet lunches or dinners (*see* Variations to oven-bake). You can double this recipe, if desired.

1 recipe Basic Meat Stuffing (p. 165)
2 tablespoons chopped parsley
1 recipe Basic Kibbeh Paste (p. 162;
   increase the bulgar to
   2 cups/12 oz/ 350 g)
Vegetable oil, for deep-frying

1. Mix the parsley into the prepared stuffing and divide into about 12 pieces.

2. Divide the kibbeh paste into about 12 pieces. Knead each briefly, hollow out into an egg shape about 3 in/8 cm long, and stuff according to the Basic Method for Stuffing Kibbeh (p. 163). You can freeze the balls at this stage, if desired.

3. Deep-fry the kibbeh in hot oil (directly from the freezer, if frozen) until golden, about 1–2 minutes per batch, and transfer to a strainer. Serve hot or warm.

VARIATIONS: OVEN-BAKED KIBBEH

Preheat the oven to 350°F/180°C and generously oil a baking tray. Place the stuffed kibbeh balls (directly from the freezer, if frozen) on the tray and brush the tops with oil. Bake for 30 minutes, shaking the pan a few times to coat the balls with oil.

LADY'S BRACELET KIBBEH
Kibbeh Siwar al-Sit

MAKES 21 PIECES; SERVES 5–7 AS A MAIN COURSE
PREPARATION TIME: 35–40 MINUTES
COOKING TIME: 20 MINUTES

Lady's Bracelet Kibbeh is a charming name for this enticing kibbeh, which resembles a bracelet studded with emerald gems, triggering in the gourmet an irresistible desire to devour it. It is best served with plain yogurt and a green salad or vegetable dish.

For the stuffing

1 recipe Basic Meat Stuffing (p. 165;
use a combination of pine nuts
and walnuts for this recipe)

For the kibbeh paste

1 recipe Basic Kibbeh Paste (p. 162;
increase the bulgar to
1½ cups/9 oz/250 g)

To bake and serve

⅓ cup/75 ml vegetable oil
¼ cup/1 oz/30 g pistachios,
finely chopped
1 tablespoon/½ oz/15 g butter,
melted

1. Set the stuffing aside to cool, then divide it into about 21 portions.

2. Divide the paste into 21 pieces (each about 1 oz/28 g). Briefly knead each piece and form into a ball.

3. Use the Basic Method for Stuffing Kibbeh (p. 163) to stuff the kibbeh and smooth into balls.

4. Flatten each ball slightly and make an indentation at the top with your thumb to fill later with the pistachios. (At this stage, the kibbeh can be frozen for later use; bake directly from frozen.)

5. Preheat the oven to 350°F/180°C.

6. Coat the bottom of a baking pan with the vegetable oil and arrange the kibbeh balls on it in a single layer. Bake for 15 minutes (20 minutes from frozen), brushing them with the oil as needed.

7. Mix the pistachios and melted butter. Remove the pan from the oven, distribute the pistachio mixture among the indentations, and bake for 5 more minutes, taking care not to brown the pistachios. Serve hot or warm.

GRILLED KIBBEH WITH MINT
Kibbeh Mashwiyeh bi-Na'na'

MAKES 50 BITE-SIZE PIECES; SERVES 8 AS AN APPETIZER
PREPARATION TIME: 40–55 MINUTES
COOKING TIME: 30 MINUTES IF GRILLING; 10 MINUTES IF BAKING

Grilled kibbeh is a staple dish all over Syria, but each city has its own version. In Damascus it is stuffed with ground meat and pomegranate molasses, while in Aleppo it is stuffed with butter and mint.

The recipe below stands out as one of the best. Each kibbeh is the size of a small prune, filled with butter, mint, and spices, grilled over charcoal, then rolled in melted ghee or butter and served hot. It is best not to use a fork, or the butter will ooze out. Place a whole kibbeh in your mouth (I use my hands!) and sink your teeth gently into it, releasing a burst of flavor beyond belief. Then you will agree with me that it is the best grilled kibbeh you have ever had!

Charcoal grilling imparts a wonderful smoky flavor not achieved by baking (you will need a fine grate so they don't fall through), but I have included both methods. A caution to eaters: The butter filling can get very hot, so make sure the kibbeh has cooled enough to eat without burning your tongue. The balls must be bite-sized, since biting into the kibbeh may cause the filling to splatter.

For kibbeh paste

1 lb/450 g extra lean ground
    lamb or beef
2 teaspoons salt, or to taste
Crushed ice and/or ice-cold water,
    if necessary
1½ cups/9 oz/250 g fine bulgar
1 small onion (4 oz/115 g),
    coarsely chopped
½ teaspoon ground black pepper
1 teaspoon Aleppo spice mix or
    seven-spice powder

For the stuffing

1¾ sticks butter (scant 1 cup/
    7 oz/200 g), chilled
1½ tablespoons coarse dried mint
1½ teaspoons Aleppo spice mix or
    seven-spice powder

To bake, reheat, or for the finishing touch (optional)

Vegetable oil or melted butter

1. Prepare the kibbeh paste: Follow the method for Basic Kibbeh Paste (p. 162) using the kibbeh ingredients listed here. Divide into about 50 equal pieces, each weighing just over ¾ oz/20 g, and form into rougly 1 inch/3 cm balls using moistened hands.

2. Prepare the stuffing: Cut the cold butter into 50 small cubes and arrange on a plate. Sprinkle with the dried mint and spice mix, and refrigerate until needed.

3. To form the kibbeh balls: Make an indentation in each kibbeh ball and fill it with a square of spiced butter. Close the paste around the filling to form a ball.

To cook the kibbeh

4. Preheat the barbecue (preferably charcoal) and grill the kibbeh, turning them frequently until fully cooked and the butter stuffing has melted. Alternatively, bake in the oven: Preheat the oven to 400°F/200°C. Roll raw kibbeh balls in melted butter or vegetable oil and bake uncovered for 10 minutes, shaking the pan a few times until they are cooked and the butter inside has melted (test one).

To give shine to kibbeh or to reheat (optional)

5. Heat the butter or oil in a wide skillet over medium heat (do not overheat or the butter will separate). Lightly fry the kibbeh a few at a time, shaking the pan and turning them so they are covered completely with the fat.

6. Serve warm and enjoy the unbelievable flavor of these kibbeh!

BUTCHER'S KIBBEH WITH VEGETABLES
Kibbeh Qassabiyeh

MAKES 36 PIECES; SERVES 4–6
PREPARATION TIME: 15 MINUTES
RESTING TIME: 10 MINUTES
COOKING TIME: 10 MINUTES FOR KIBBEH; 15 MINUTES FOR VEGETABLES

Here is a brilliant way to prepare kibbeh in a hurry, or for those who cannot master the art of hollowing kibbeh shells. These kibbeh are made by mixing kibbeh paste and ground meat, rather than stuffing the one with the other. Serve Butcher's Kibbeh as a main dish with vegetables (see below), or as part of a hot mezze spread. For beginners: these easy-to-prepare kibbeh balls may be used in place of other varieties of kibbeh in dishes like Kibbeh with Quince (p. 198) or Kibbeh in Sumac Stock (p. 196).

½ cup/3 oz/85 g fine white bulgar,
    soaked in water for 10 minutes
    and squeezed dry

8 oz/225 g extra lean ground lamb
    or beef

8 oz/225 g lean ground lamb or beef

1 very small onion (3 oz/85 g),
    grated

1½ teaspoons ground cumin

1½ teaspoons Aleppo spice mix or
    seven-spice powder

1 tablespoon coarse dried mint or
    1 teaspoon fine dried mint

2 teaspoons Aleppo pepper
    or paprika

1 teaspoon salt, or to taste

¼ cup/1½ oz/40 g pine nuts

¼ cup/60 ml vegetable oil

For the vegetables (optional)

2 tablespoons vegetable oil

1 small sweet green pepper (2½ oz/
    75 g), seeds removed, sliced

1 small sweet red pepper (2½ oz/
    75 g), seeds removed, sliced

1 small onion (4 oz/115 g),
    sliced into half-moons

½ teaspoon Aleppo spice mix or
    seven-spice powder

½ teaspoon Aleppo pepper or paprika

½ teaspoon salt, or to taste

1. Pulse the extra lean ground meat to a paste in a food processor, and add it to the bulgar in a large bowl.

2. Mix in all the other ingredients except the pine nuts and oil, and knead by hand for 30 seconds, adding a few tablespoons of ice-cold water if the mixture is too stiff.

3. Fry the pine nuts in 2 tablespoons of the oil until golden then remove to a strainer. Cool and mix half the pine nuts into the meat mixture.

4. Moistening your hands with cold water, divide the kibbeh into about 36 walnut-sized pieces (about ¾ oz/20 g each). Briefly knead each piece and form it into a ball, keeping your hands moistened to obtain a smooth surface.

5. To grill: Thread the balls onto skewers and grill over charcoal, basting with the rest of the oil. To oven-bake: Preheat the oven to 400°F/200°C, generously oil a baking dish, and bake for 10 minutes, or until fully cooked, shaking the dish halfway through to make sure the kibbeh are coated in oil.

6. Prepare the vegetables, if using: In a large skillet, heat the oil over high heat. Sauté the green pepper, red pepper, and onion for 1 minute, stirring. Add the spice mix, Aleppo pepper or paprika, and salt. Stir for a few minutes more, taking care not to overcook the vegetables.

7. Garnish with the remaining pine nuts and serve with the vegetable accompaniment, if desired.

NOTES

To reheat the kibbeh: Heat a little oil in a skillet over medium heat and roll the kibbeh balls in the oil until heated through.

EGG KIBBEH
Kibbet Baid

MAKES 7 PIECES
PREPARATION TIME: 30 MINUTES
RESTING TIME: 1 HOUR
COOKING TIME: 7 MINUTES

Egg Kibbeh is similar to Scotch eggs, a popular British snack in which eggs are wrapped in sausage meat and fried. The famous London department store Fortnum & Mason claims to have invented Scotch eggs in 1738, but they may have been inspired by the Moghul dish *nargisi kofta*. But who knows whether this dish was prepared before or after the British one!

This recipe consists simply of peeled boiled eggs, wrapped in kibbeh paste and boiled. It used to be made when extra paste was available from the preparation of Pan-Baked Kibbeh; peeled, boiled eggs were a quick, easy stuffing for kibbeh paste, and so a new dish was born. You can use the paste given below, or use leftover paste from other recipes. Egg Kibbeh can be served warm with salad as a light meal. Served cold, they make excellent appetizers or snacks.

7 large eggs at room temperature
   (very fresh eggs are more
   difficult to peel)
1 teaspoon salt
A few drops of white vinegar
1 recipe Basic Kibbeh Paste (p. 162)

For the stock

2 cinnamon sticks
10 white peppercorns
1 tablespoon salt, or to taste

1. Boil the eggs: Place the eggs in a pot with water to cover. Add 1 teaspoon salt and a few drops of white vinegar. Bring to a boil, lower the heat, and simmer gently for 9 minutes. Remove eggs to cold water. Drain and peel while still warm. Cool.

To prepare the kibbeh

2. With moistened hands, divide the paste into 7 equal pieces, and form each piece into a ball. Hollow each ball into a shell with an opening at one end and an egg-sized cavity (*see* Basic Method for Stuffing Kibbeh, p. 163). Or, for an easier method, roll the paste to a wide strip and tightly wrap around the egg, sealing the ends together.

3. Insert the eggs into the kibbeh balls, pressing well to remove any air that remains between the egg and the paste. With moistened fingers, seal the opening around the egg and smooth. Refrigerate for 1 hour.

To cook and serve

4. In a large pot that can hold the kibbeh in one layer, combine 8 cups/2 liters water with the stock ingredients and bring to a boil over high heat.

5. Lower the heat to medium and place the balls in the simmering liquid. When the mixture comes to a boil again, simmer for 7 minutes; then transfer the kibbeh balls to a strainer.

6. Slice into rounds or quarters and serve warm or cold.

KIBBEH WITH WALNUT STUFFING
Kibbeh Sajiyeh

MAKES ABOUT 15 KIBBEH PATTIES; SERVES 5–7 AS A MAIN COURSE
PREPARATION TIME: 45 MINUTES–1 HOUR
COOKING TIME: 15–20 MINUTES

Among the many kibbeh recipes in Aleppo, this one is a classic. It is prepared at homes, in restaurants, and sold in street stalls to be eaten out of napkins that collect the oil. Originally, this dish was prepared as a large disc filled with ground suet (the fat found around sheep kidneys) and grilled over a charcoal flame. Nowadays, smaller sizes are prepared with meat or butter stuffing to be served buffet-style. Two or three pieces of the kibbeh below make a main dish, best accompanied by Armenian Salad (p. 93), Cucumber and Garlic Yogurt (p. 98), Baba Ghanouj with Pomegranate Molasses (p. 42), or Red Pepper and Walnut Spread (p. 44).

For the kibbeh paste

1 lb/450 g extra lean ground lamb
    or beef
1 teaspoon salt, or to taste
Crushed ice and/or ice-cold water,
    if necessary
1½ cups/9 oz/250 g fine bulgar
½ small onion (2 oz/60 g),
    coarsely chopped
1 tablespoon red pepper paste
2 tablespoons ground cumin
¾ teaspoon Aleppo spice mix or
    seven-spice powder
½ teaspoon cinnamon
Pinch ground allspice
½ teaspoon ground black pepper

For the stuffing

1 stick butter (½ cup/4 oz/115 g),
    at room temperature
¾ cup/3 oz/85 g finely chopped
    walnuts
1 tablespoon ground cumin
1 teaspoon Aleppo spice mix or
    seven-spice powder
½ teaspoon ground allspice
Pinch ground black pepper
Pinch salt, or to taste

Vegetable oil

1. Prepare the paste: Follow the method for Basic Kibbeh Paste (p. 162), using the ingredients listed here. Divide the paste into about 30 pieces (each weighing around 1 oz/30 g).

2. Prepare the stuffing: Mix the stuffing ingredients and set aside at room temperature.

To stuff the kibbeh

3. Turn 2 medium-size dessert plates upside down on your work surface and lay a square of plastic wrap over each one (the inside rim of the bottom of your plate will determine the diameter of your kibbeh disc; the one I use is 4 in/11 cm). Moisten the plastic wrap with cold water.

4. Moisten your hands with ice-cold water. Place one piece of kibbeh in the center of your plate. Flatten the paste to fill the indentation in your plate in a thin layer, creating a disc.

5. Spread about 2 teaspoons of stuffing on the disc, leaving a border of ½ in/1 cm at the edges.

6. Make a second disc of kibbeh paste using the second plate; then use the plastic wrap to peel off the disc and arrange it on top of the stuffed disc, pressing the edges together to seal it. Peel off the plastic wrap to reveal a stuffed patty.

7. Repeat with the rest of the paste and stuffing.

To cook and serve the kibbeh

8. To fry: Heat a tablespoon or two of vegetable oil in a nonstick skillet over medium heat. Fry the patties in batches until lightly golden on both sides, about 2–3 minutes per batch. Alternatively, you can oven-bake: Lightly oil a baking tray and preheat the oven to 350°F/180°C. Arrange the patties on the tray, brush them with vegetable oil, and bake until lightly golden, about 15–20 minutes, turning them over halfway through cooking. Serve hot or warm.

NOTES: ALTERNATIVE METHODS, STUFFINGS, AND TO FREEZE

- If preferred, you can prepare the discs by rolling the kibbeh paste between moistened sheets of plastic wrap or wax paper, and cutting the discs to the desired size, but the above method produces neater results.
- Some use meat stuffing in this dish, but it is not the authentic version. Lately, disc-shaped kibbeh is available with a variety of fillings, including finely chopped desert truffles, so feel free to fill with your preferred stuffing.
- After step 5, you can freeze the patties on baking trays (transfer to plastic bags or containers once frozen). To cook from frozen, fry as above, only over a lower heat setting, or bake for about 18–25 minutes.

SPRING KIBBEH
Kibbeh Rabi'iyeh

MAKES ABOUT 22 PATTIES; SERVES 5–7 AS A LIGHT MAIN COURSE
PREPARATION TIME: 40 MINUTES
COOKING TIME: 20–25 MINUTES

This is a very old recipe for kibbeh patties filled with cheese. They are excellent to freeze and fry or bake when needed. I have opted for small-size patties but patties of various sizes can be prepared as desired.

For the kibbeh paste

8 oz/225 g extra lean ground lamb
    or beef, chilled
1 teaspoon salt, or to taste
2 tablespoons ice-cold water
1¼ cups/7½ oz/215 g fine white
    bulgar
½ small onion (2 oz/60 g),
    coarsely chopped
1½ teaspoons ground cumin
¾ teaspoon Aleppo spice mix or
    seven-spice powder
½ teaspoon cinnamon
½ teaspoon ground allspice

For the stuffing

10 oz/300 g baladi cheese (*jibneh
    khadra*), Halloumi, or any salty
    firm white cheese
1 teaspoon Aleppo pepper or paprika
Pinch ground white pepper
2 tablespoons finely chopped parsley
Salt, if needed

¼ cup/60 ml vegetable oil
    or melted butter

1. Prepare the paste: Follow the method for Basic Kibbeh Paste (p. 162), using the ingredients listed here. Divide the paste into 44 pieces (about ¾ oz/20 g each).

2. Prepare the stuffing: Coarsely grate the cheese. If it is too salty, soak the cheese in cold water for 1 hour, changing the water 3 times or as needed, and squeeze dry. Mix with the rest of the ingredients and form into 22 balls and flatten into rounds.

To stuff and cook the kibbeh

3. Preheat the oven to 350°F/180°C.

4. Using a plate with 3 in/8 cm indentation, follow steps 3 to 7 for Kibbeh with Walnut Stuffing (p. 172) to stuff each patty with a round of cheese stuffing.

5. Place half of the butter or oil in a large baking pan and heat in the oven for a few minutes until hot.

6. Arrange the patties in the pan in one layer and dot the top with the rest of the oil or butter. Bake for 20–25 minutes, or until the patties are puffed up and golden. Serve hot.

NOTES: FREEZING

Follow the steps above but bake for only 10 minutes. Cool and freeze in sealed containers. Bake directly from frozen: Dip each patty in oil or melted butter and place in a baking pan in one layer. Cover tightly with aluminum foil and bake at 350°F/180°C for about 20 minutes.

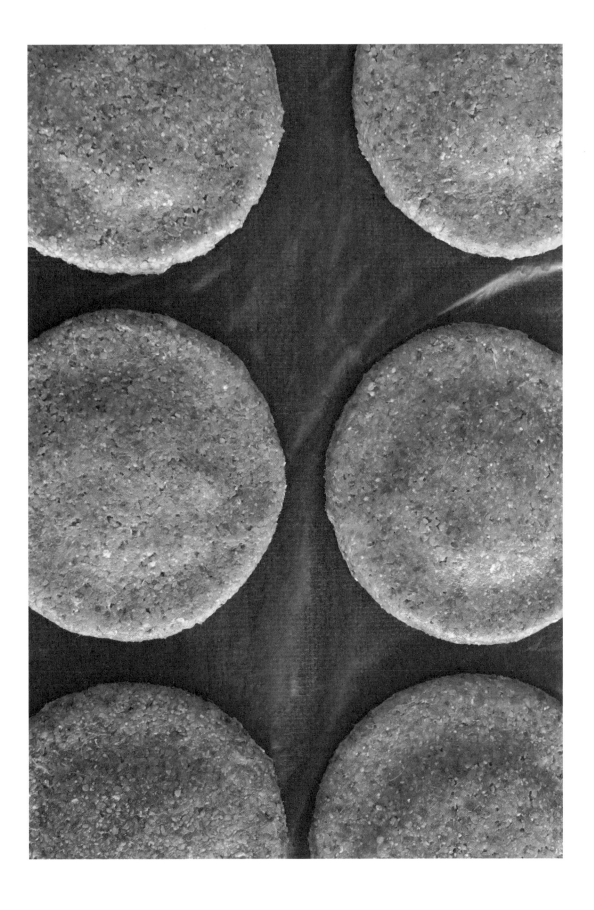

KIBBEH ROLLS
Kibbeh Mabroomeh

MAKES 2 ROLLS
PREPARATION TIME: 30 MINUTES
COOKING TIME: 30 MINUTES

Here is a beautiful and different way to present the classic kibbeh dish, forming it into rolls stuffed with ground meat and pistachios (walnuts can be added to the stuffing, if desired). The dish is suitable for a buffet, or it can be prepared in thinner rolls to serve as finger food. The rolls freeze very well after baking. One roll can be cut into up to 20 slices and serves up to 10 as part of a mezze.

1 recipe Basic Kibbeh Paste (p. 162)

For the stuffing

1½ tablespoons olive oil,
    plus more for oiling
½ small onion (2 oz/60 g),
    finely chopped
1 teaspoon salt, or to taste
7 oz/200 g lean finely ground lamb
    or beef (pulse in a food processor
    to achieve a fine texture)
2 tablespoons pine nuts
½ teaspoon Aleppo spice mix or
    seven-spice powder
¼ teaspoon ground black pepper
¼ teaspoon cinnamon
1 teaspoon ground cumin
Scant 1 cup/3½ oz/100 g shelled,
    unsalted pistachios
1 tablespoon pomegranate molasses
    or sumac

To prepare the stuffing

1. In a pan, heat the oil over low heat and add the onions and a little salt. Fry gently until tender and starting to color. Turn the heat up to high and add half of the ground meat and the pine nuts and spices, stirring until the meat browns. Mix in the pistachios, pomegranate molasses or sumac, and the rest of the ground meat. Set aside to cool.

To prepare the kibbeh rolls

2. Prepare the paste: Follow the method for Basic Kibbeh Paste (p. 162), dividing the paste into halves. Knead one half and shape it into a 12 x 5 in/30 x 12 cm rectangle on a length of plastic wrap moistened with water.

3. Place half of the stuffing in the center, along the length of the rectangle, and press it into the paste.

4. Tightly roll the paste rectangle over the stuffing with the aid of the plastic wrap, making sure all the stuffing is enclosed. Close the seams with wet fingers and smooth to form a seamless roll. Discard the plastic wrap.

5. Wrap the kibbeh roll in oiled aluminum foil and twist the ends.

6. Repeat with the rest of the kibbeh paste and stuffing to form 2 rolls. (The recipe can be prepared a day ahead up to this step.)

7. Preheat the oven to 350°F/180°C. Bake the rolls in their foil for 30 minutes; then remove the foil and bake for 15 more minutes or until golden, turning the rolls once.

8. Allow to cool for about 30 minutes before cutting the rolls into ½ in/1 cm slices. Serve hot or warm.

PAN-BAKED KIBBEH
Kibbeh bi-Furon

SERVES 8
PREPARATION TIME: 40–50 MINUTES
COOKING TIME: 20–25 MINUTES

Kibbeh is an important dish in many parts of the Arab world, but it is a staple in Syria. This is the most popular variety and one of the easiest to make. It consists of a stuffing of ground meat, nuts, and spices, sandwiched between two layers of kibbeh paste. In other regions, onion is added to the stuffing and the nuts vary; Armenians prepare this dish with a mixture of bulgar and semolina (in this recipe, you can use 1¾ cups/10 oz/300 g fine bulgar and ½ cup/3 oz/85 g fine semolina in place of the bulgar). The size of the pan is crucial: a smaller pan makes a thick kibbeh and a larger pan makes a thinner one. Typical accompaniments are plain yogurt and a salad. In Aleppo, this dish is sometimes served with Mloukhiyeh (p. 133).

For the kibbeh paste

2¼ cups/13½ oz/380 g fine bulgar
1¼ lb/600 g extra lean ground lamb
   or beef
1 small onion (4 oz/115 g), chopped
1 teaspoon Aleppo spice mix or
   seven-spice powder
1 teaspoon ground allspice
½ teaspoon ground black pepper
½ teaspoon cinnamon
2 teaspoons salt, or to taste

For the stuffing

¼ cup/60 ml vegetable oil
⅓ cup/1¾ oz/50 g pine nuts or
   1 cup/3½ oz/100 g walnut
   halves, or a mixture of both
1 lb/450 g lean ground lamb or beef
1 teaspoon Aleppo spice mix or
   seven-spice powder
1 teaspoon ground allspice
½ teaspoon ground black pepper
¼ teaspoon cinnamon
1½ teaspoons salt, or to taste
Handful shelled pistachios (optional)

½ cup/120 ml vegetable oil or
   melted butter

1. Using the method for Basic Kibbeh Paste (p. 162), prepare the paste using the ingredients listed here. Divide in half.

2. Using the method for Basic Meat Stuffing (p. 165), prepare the stuffing using the ingredients listed here. If using, mix the pistachios into the stuffing.

3. Grease a 13 in/33 cm round cake pan with some of the butter or vegetable oil.

4. Flatten one piece of kibbeh paste between two sheets of wax paper and roll with a rolling pin until you have a disc just larger than your baking pan. Remove the top layer of paper and flip the paste into the base of the pan; then peel off the other layer. Smooth the paste with cold water-moistened fingers. (Alternatively, press the paste directly into the pan with moistened hands, patting it to make a thin, even layer.)

5. Spread the stuffing on the layer of paste, leaving a small rim of exposed paste at the edges. Pat the stuffing down.

6. Roll the remaining paste to fit over the stuffing in the pan. With moistened hands, seal the edges together and press the top firmly to level it and join the two layers with the stuffing.

7. Preheat the oven to 400°F/200°C.

8. Wet the blade of a knife and pass it between the kibbeh and the sides of the pan. With your thumb, make an indentation in the center, all the way to the base. Score into squares or diamonds, only allowing the knife to reach the middle layer.

9. Pour the remaining oil or melted butter over the surface of the kibbeh and bake for 20–25 minutes. Remove from the oven and immediately sprinkle with about 3 tablespoons of water, to retain suppleness. Cut into slices and serve hot.

KIBBEH TARTARE
Kibbeh Nayyeh

SERVES 8 AS PART OF A MEZZE
PREPARATION TIME: 15 MINUTES
RESTING TIME: 30 MINUTES

This is the beloved national dish of Lebanon and Syria. I have tasted this raw kibbeh dish in restaurants throughout the region and I assure you that *Kibbeh Nayyeh* in Aleppo surpasses all. Chopped vegetables and ground red pepper are added to the meat to give it zest, depth of flavor, and a vibrant red color.

⅓ cup/2 oz/60 g fine bulgar
    (preferably the soft, white variety)
1 small sweet red pepper (2½ oz/
    75 g), seeds removed, chopped
¼ cup/½ oz/15 g chopped parsley
1 small onion (4 oz/115 g),
    finely chopped
1 lb/450 g best-quality extra lean
    ground lamb or beef (*see* Notes)
Crushed ice
1 teaspoon ground cumin
½ teaspoon cinnamon
¼ teaspoon ground allspice
2 teaspoons Aleppo pepper or
    paprika
¼ teaspoon ground chili pepper
    (optional)
1¼ teaspoons salt, or to taste
½ cup/120 ml olive oil

To garnish (optional)

Red and green pepper slices
Mint sprigs
Chopped walnuts

To serve

Arabic flatbread
Chopped scallions or white onion
Mint leaves

1. Wash the bulgar and soak in water to cover for 10 minutes. Squeeze out the bulgar and place in a food processor with the red pepper, parsley, and onion. Process until a coarse paste has formed and set aside for 20 minutes.

2. Pulse the meat in a food processor with a little of the salt and one crushed ice cube just until a smooth paste has formed (you may need to do this in batches). Transfer to a bowl.

3. Drag the blade of a knife through the meat to collect any small white ligaments. Wipe the blade and repeat.

4. Add the bulgar mixture to the meat in the bowl, along with the cumin, cinnamon, allspice, Aleppo pepper, chili (if using), salt, and 2 tablespoons of the olive oil. Knead the mixture for 1 minute. Taste and add salt.

5. With hands dipped in olive oil, form the kibbeh paste into balls the size of walnuts. Elongate the balls slightly, then squeeze each gently, with the fingers of one hand, to form indents at the sides (or *see* Notes).

6. Arrange the kibbeh on a platter and garnish as desired. Drizzle the remaining olive oil on top and serve cold with Arabic flatbread, scallions or onion, and mint on the side.

NOTES

- The chefs in Aleppo pride themselves in the creative presentation of this dish. The photo shows the presentation typical of the famous Aleppo Club.
- The meat must be lean, very high quality, very fresh, and free of ligaments and fat. If you can't find ground leg, buy a whole piece of meat, chop it, and grind it in a food processor. Putting the meat in the freezer until it just begins to freeze helps with this.
- Note that consuming raw or undercooked meat may increase your risk of foodborne illness.
- Kibbeh Tartare must be served the same day it is prepared. You can shape any leftovers into patties and fry them.

RICE KIBBEH
Kibbet Roz

MAKES 32 PIECES; SERVES 8 AS AN APPETIZER OR 4 AS A MAIN COURSE
PREPARATION TIME: 45 MINUTES
RESTING TIME: 4 HOURS OR OVERNIGHT
COOKING TIME: 30–40 MINUTES

This is one of my favorite dishes among the many delicious kinds of kibbeh prepared in Aleppo. I will never forget the delight of consuming these heavenly bites at the Aleppo Club (*Nadi Halab*). They have a crisp exterior and a tender and meaty interior that bursts in your mouth.

For the rice shell

2⅓ cups/1 lb 2½ oz/525 g short-grain rice, preferably Egyptian, rinsed and drained

3 teaspoons salt, or to taste

1 very small onion (3 oz/85 g), grated

⅓ cup/¾ oz/20 g breadcrumbs

3 tablespoons olive oil

1 tablespoon red pepper paste

½ teaspoon ground white pepper

For the stuffing

14 oz/400 g lean finely ground lamb or beef (pulse in a food processor to achieve a fine texture)

1 tablespoon Aleppo spice mix or seven-spice powder

½ teaspoon ground nutmeg

½ teaspoon ground cardamom

1 teaspoon ground black pepper

½ teaspoon cinnamon

1 teaspoon salt, or to taste

½ cup/1¾ oz/50 g peeled, flaked almonds, fried in oil (*see* p. 23)

¼ cup/1½ oz/40 g pine nuts, fried in oil (*see* p. 23)

Peanut or vegetable oil, for deep-frying

To prepare the rice

1. In a medium pot, bring 3 cups/700 ml water to a boil over high heat and add 2½ teaspoons of the salt. Add the rice, lower the heat to very low, cover, and cook for 15 minutes.

2. Remove the pot from the heat and cool for 10 minutes. Fluff the rice with a fork, cover, and set aside for 10 more minutes.

3. Spread the rice on an oiled tray to cool, and refrigerate for 4 hours or overnight.

To prepare the stuffing

4. Dry-fry the meat, spices, and salt in a nonstick skillet over medium heat, stirring well. Mix in the fried nuts and remove the pan from the heat. Cool.

To prepare the shell

5. Mix the cold rice with the rest of the shell ingredients and combine in a food processor. Pulse to a fine, doughlike paste. Flatten the paste on a tray and refrigerate for one hour.

To stuff and fry the kibbeh

6. Divide the paste into 32 pieces, each about 1½ oz/40 g. Dip your hands in vegetable oil, knead each piece, and hollow it into an egg shape 3 in/8 cm long. Fill with the stuffing, pressing on it gently (*see* p. 163 for further instructions).

7. It is best to freeze the rice kibbeh before frying: Freeze the kibbeh in one layer on trays lined with wax paper (You can transfer them to a sealed container for longer-term storage).

8. Just before serving, heat the peanut or vegetable oil over medium heat until hot. Deep-fry the kibbeh until slightly colored. Lower the temperature slightly and continue frying to give them a crisp exterior. Using a slotted spoon, transfer to a dish lined with paper towels. Serve immediately. (They will stay crisp for up to two hours.)

FRIED VEGETABLE PATTIES
Kibbeh Zangliyeh

MAKES ABOUT 15 PATTIES; SERVES 5 AS AN APPETIZER
PREPARATION TIME: 15 MINUTES
RESTING TIME: 1 HOUR
COOKING TIME: 10 MINUTES

The name *Zangliyeh* is a derivative of *zongol*, a word of Persian origin that refers to a flour paste fried in oil. In Aleppo, these are thin vegetable patties made with spinach, chickpeas, onion, bulgar, and spices, fried in oil, and served with grape molasses. The Christian community often makes them on Fridays during lent, particularly on Holy Friday. I devour these patties the minute they are removed from the hot oil. They are, at that moment, at their best, with a seductive crust and a soft center.

1 lb/450 kg spinach, roots and tough stems removed (10 oz/300 g spinach leaves)

1½ cups/9 oz/250 g cooked or canned chickpeas (*see* Notes), coarsely chopped

1½ cups/6½ oz/185 g all-purpose flour

½ cup/1 oz/30 g coarsely chopped parsley

⅓ cup/1½ oz/40 g finely chopped scallions

1 tablespoon fine bulgar, washed

1½ tablespoons ground coriander

Heaped tablespoon ground cumin

1½ teaspoons Aleppo pepper or paprika

½ teaspoon salt, or to taste

¼ cup/60 ml olive oil

To serve

¼ cup/60 ml thick grape molasses (or you can use honey)

1. Wash the spinach leaves and dry in a salad spinner, then coarsely chop and place in a large bowl. Add the chickpeas. Mix in the flour, followed by the rest of the ingredients, except for the oil. Gradually add about ¼ cup/60 ml water, mixing well with your hands.

2. Knead the mixture for about 5 minutes, allowing the spinach to give out its moisture. Cover the bowl and set aside for one hour. (The spinach will wilt more because of the salt.)

3. Add 1 teaspoon water, or a little more until you have a moist but quite stiff paste. (The recipe can be prepared ahead and frozen in small batches at this point; thaw before frying.)

4. In a large skillet, heat the olive oil over medium heat (the oil should cover the base of the pan to a depth of ¼ inch/½ cm).

5. Fill a small bowl with water and keep it on hand. With moistened hands, take about ¼ cup of the spinach paste, pat between your palms into a rectangle about 4 x 3 in/11 x 8 cm and ½ in/1 cm thick, and place in the hot oil.

6. Fry the patties in batches until underside and sides are golden; then flip and fry the other side. Transfer cooked patties to a serving platter and serve hot with grape molasses.

NOTES

See p. 16 to cook your own chickpeas. (One part dried yields 2½ parts cooked and drained chickpeas.) In Aleppo, you can buy a small variety of chickpeas that do not need to be chopped.

VEGETARIAN POTATO KIBBEH
Kibbeh Hileh

MAKES 18 PIECES; SERVES 4–6 AS A MAIN DISH
PREPARATION TIME: 20–25 MINUTES
COOKING TIME: 5–10 MINUTES

Here is a delicious and satisfying vegetarian kibbeh with a tasty stuffing of onions, walnuts, and pomegranate molasses. In Aleppo it is the dish of the day during the Christian Lent period.

The dish is also known by the name *Kibbet al-Arba'ine Shaheed*, meaning the "kibbeh of the forty martyrs." The name refers to the forty Armenian martyrs who suffered in the year 320 AD for disobeying the emperor. Their gruesome fate was to be whipped, then forced into ice ponds before being burned alive.

This versatile kibbeh may be fried or boiled and served with salad, or used in kibbeh stew dishes like Kibbeh in Pomegranate Stock (p. 195) or Kibbeh and Chicken in Yogurt Sauce (p. 200), or it can be served with jarred tomato sauce or the red pepper and walnut sauce on p. 137.

For the stuffing

2 medium onions (1 lb/450 g),
    finely chopped
⅓ cup/75 ml olive oil
⅓ cup/1½ oz/40 g chopped walnuts
¼ cup/60 ml pomegranate molasses
1 cup/2 oz/60 g chopped parsley
1 teaspoon salt, or to taste

For the kibbeh paste

1 medium potato (7 oz/200 g),
    boiled, peeled, and cooled
2¼ cups/13½ oz/380 g fine bulgar
2 cups/9 oz/250 g all-purpose flour
3 tablespoons ground coriander
1 very small onion (3 oz/85 g),
    grated
2 teaspoons salt, or to taste

Peanut or vegetable oil, for deep-
    frying (optional)

To prepare the stuffing

1. In a large pot, fry the onions in the olive oil over medium heat until tender and just starting to color. Remove the pot from the heat and mix in the rest of the stuffing ingredients. Taste and adjust the seasoning, if necessary. Cool.

To prepare the kibbeh paste

2. Coarsely grate the potato.

3. Rinse the bulgar, drain, and squeeze dry. Mix with the grated potatoes and add the flour, ground coriander, grated onion, and salt.

4. Gradually mix in about 1 cup/240 ml water to form a stiff dough (but be careful not to over-mix).

To stuff and cook

5. Divide the paste into 18 portions (about 1 oz/30 g each). Follow the method on p. 163 to shape and stuff the kibbeh, making the walls a little thicker than ¼ in/½ cm. Seal the paste around the stuffing and reshape, if necessary, into a 3 in/8 cm oblong.

6. Refrigerate for 1 hour or freeze for 30 minutes. Cook the balls in boiling, salted water for 5 minutes, or until cooked through, or deep-fry over medium heat in the peanut or vegetable oil (*see* p. 166). Remove with a slotted spoon, drain, and cool before serving. (Kibbeh can be frozen at this stage; defrost by boiling for a few minutes or rolling in vegetable oil in a hot frying pan.)

7. Serve warm or cold or use as a replacement for meat kibbeh.

VEGETARIAN KIBBEH WITH SPINACH
Kibbeh Hileh bi-Sabanekh

MAKES 17 PIECES; SERVES 4–6 AS A MAIN DISH
PREPARATION TIME: 30–45 MINUTES
RESTING TIME: 20 MINUTES
COOKING TIME: 5 MINUTES

This is also one of my favorite kibbeh dishes due to its unusual mixture of flavors. It is meatless (the name *hileh* means counterfeit), and served with a sauce that is all at once spicy, sweet-and-sour, and nutty.

These vegetarian kibbeh offer the kibbeh lover a different texture; not as crunchy as Fried Kibbeh, nor as soft as the kibbeh used in stews like Kibbeh and Chicken in Yogurt Sauce (p. 200). It is rather a cross between the two. It is also known by the name *Kibbet Sabanekh*, meaning spinach kibbeh, or *Kibbeh Harra*, meaning hot kibbeh.

Another advantage to this kibbeh is that the shell is a little thick, making it easier to hollow and stuff. Keep them in the freezer, and it is a matter of minutes to prepare the sauce and serve this seductive dish.

For the stuffing

1½ lb/700 g spinach or 10 oz/300 g
    spinach leaves
1 teaspoon salt, or to taste
1 small onion (4 oz/115 g), grated
½ cup/2 oz/60 g finely chopped
    walnuts
3 tablespoons pomegranate
    molasses
¼ teaspoon ground black pepper

For the shells

Generous 1 cup/6½ oz/185 g
    fine bulgar (preferably brown
    hard wheat bulgar)
1½ cups/6½ oz/185 g all-purpose
    flour
½ cup/3 oz/85 g fine semolina
1 small onion (4 oz/115 g), grated
2½ tablespoons ground coriander
¼ teaspoon ground black pepper
1½ teaspoons salt, or to taste
½ cup/120 ml ice-cold water,
    or more if needed

To prepare the stuffing

1. Wash and drain the spinach leaves.

2. Mix the still-wet leaves with the salt and place in a pot over low heat. Cook, stirring, until the leaves are tender, reduced considerably in size, and no liquid remains.

3. Remove the pot from the heat. Squeeze the spinach well and finely chop. Mix with the rest of the stuffing ingredients. Taste and adjust the seasoning. Cool. (Stuffing can be made 1 day ahead and refrigerated until use.)

To prepare and stuff the shells

4. Rinse the bulgar under cold running water and soak in cold water for 10 minutes. Squeeze dry and set aside for 10 minutes.

5. In a bowl, mix the bulgar with the rest of the shell ingredients, except the water.

6. Gradually pour in the ice-cold water, mixing and kneading until you have a smooth, firm paste (add a few more tablespoons of water if needed).

7. Divide the paste into 17 pieces. Knead each piece, and form into an egg-shape.

8. Use the method on p. 163 to form and stuff the shells (the shell should be about ½ in/1 cm thick), and seal the paste around the filling. (Kibbeh balls can be frozen at this stage to be boiled when needed.)

continued overleaf

For the sauce

3 tablespoons red pepper paste

¼ cup/60 ml lemon juice

2 tablespoons pomegranate
   molasses

5 garlic cloves (¾ oz/20 g), crushed

½ cup/2 oz/60 g grated walnuts
   (I use a cheese grater)

½ cup/120 ml olive oil

1 teaspoon salt, or to taste

To make the sauce

1. Mix all the ingredients and keep at room tempertature.
    (Sauce can be made 1 day ahead and stored in the refrigera-
    tor. Bring to room temperature before use.)

To cook and serve

2. In batches, boil the kibbeh in salted water for about 5
    minutes (the kibbeh will rise to the top when cooked), and
    transfer finished kibbeh to a strainer to remove excess water.

3. Roll the hot kibbeh balls in the sauce and place on a serving
    platter.

4. Serve the kibbeh hot or at room temperature with the rest of
    the sauce on the side.

LENTIL KIBBEH
Kibbet Adess

SERVES 6
PREPARATION TIME: 15 MINUTES
COOKING TIME: 20–25 MINUTES

This beautiful and healthy vegetarian dish is laden with protein, iron, and fiber. Red split lentils are combined with bulgar, onions, and spices and served with a colorful chopped salad. It makes a beautiful summer appetizer, or it can be served as a main dish alongside meat kibbeh or other meat or chicken dishes. It is excellent for a buffet, since it can be prepared ahead (*see* Notes).

For the kibbeh

1½ cups/10 oz/300 g split red lentils

½ cup/3 oz/90 g fine white bulgar

1 teaspoon salt, or to taste

2 tablespoons/1 oz/30 g butter

¼ cup/60 ml olive oil or vegetable oil

1 small onion (4 oz/115 g),
     finely chopped

2 teaspoons ground cumin

½ teaspoon ground white pepper

¼ teaspoon Aleppo pepper or
     paprika, to garnish

For the salad

3 small tomatoes (10 oz/300 g),
     finely chopped

1 cup/2 oz/60 g finely chopped
     parsley

½ small onion (2 oz/60 g),
     finely chopped

6 tablespoons/90 ml lemon juice

6 tablespoons/90 ml olive oil

½ teaspoon ground cumin

1 teaspoon salt, or to taste

1. Pick over, wash, and drain the lentils. Place them in a medium-size pot with 3 cups/700 ml water over high heat and bring to a boil. Lower the heat, cover the pot, and simmer for 10 minutes, or until the lentils are mushy and only a little bit of cooking liquid remains in the pan.

2. Wash and drain the bulgar and add it to the lentils with a little salt. Simmer, covered, for a further 3 minutes, stirring a few times, until the bulgar absorbs the remaining liquid.

3. In a skillet, heat the butter with the olive oil and sauté the onions over very low heat until tender, without allowing them to color, 8–10 minutes. Add ¼ cup/60 ml water and the cumin and white pepper. Simmer until the water has been absorbed.

4. Add the onions to the lentils and mix well. Taste and adjust seasoning, if necessary.

5. When the mixture has cooled to room temperature, mix well with moistened hands and form into balls. Roll each ball between your fingers to form a pointed egg shape, leaving the indents created by your fingers.

6. Place the kibbeh around the edges of a serving platter and sprinkle with Aleppo pepper. Mix the salad ingredients and place the salad in a bowl in the center.

NOTES

- If preferred, you can pulse the salad ingredients in a food processor to serve as a salsa. Serve it separately, as above, or pour it on top of the kibbeh.
- To prepare ahead: Lentil Kibbeh can be prepared and formed a day in advance. Cover and refrigerate until serving. After refrigeration overnight, the salad will become more liquidized and saucelike, which is also nice with the kibbeh.

FISH KIBBEH
Kibbet Samak

MAKES ABOUT 24 KIBBEH, EACH 4 IN/10 CM
PREPARATION TIME: 30–40 MINUTES
COOKING TIME: 30 MINUTES

This dish is particularly popular with the Christian community during Lent, when meat is forbidden. The stuffing of nuts and onions is flavored with a delicate, interesting mixture of spices, accentuated by the sweet-and-sour flavors of pomegranate molasses and raisins. The shells are formed very thinly (if you are not an expert at forming very thin kibbeh shells, you may end up with extra filling). Fish Kibbeh is usually followed by Milk Pudding (p. 307).

For the stuffing

⅓ cup/75 ml olive oil

1½ lb/680 g onions, coarsely chopped

2½ teaspoons salt, or to taste

1 teaspoon cinnamon

2 teaspoons ground cumin

2 teaspoons ground allspice

1 tablespoon ground coriander

½ cup/2½ oz/75 g pine nuts

1¼ cups/5 oz/150 g chopped walnuts

3 tablespoons pomegranate molasses

1 tablespoon grated orange zest

¾ cup/3 oz/100 g raisins

1 teaspoon safflower threads
  (or use saffron)

½ teaspoon ground black pepper

½ cup/1 oz/30 g chopped parsley
  or cilantro

For the kibbeh paste

1½ lb/700 g skinless, boneless
  white fish fillet

2 teaspoons salt, or to taste

1½ cups/9 oz/250 g fine bulgar

1 very small onion (3 oz/85 g),
  coarsely chopped

½ teaspoon ground allspice

½ teaspoon cinnamon

½ teaspoon ground black pepper

Peanut or vegetable oil, for
  deep-frying

To prepare the stuffing

1. In a large pan, heat the olive oil and sauté the onions over low heat until they soften and are starting to color, about 15–20 minutes.

2. Add the rest of the stuffing ingredients, except for the parsley or cilantro, and continue to fry for about 5 more minutes.

3. Remove from heat and add the chopped herbs. Taste and adjust the seasoning, if needed. Cool.

To prepare and stuff the kibbeh

4. Cut the fish fillet into large cubes, then pulse once or twice in a food processor with ½–1 teaspoon of salt. Transfer the fish paste to your work surface. Pass the blade of a knife through the paste several times to remove the thin white sinews that collect on the blade.

5. Follow the method for Basic Kibbeh Paste (p. 162), using the ingredients listed here (skip step 2, since you have already ground the fish).

6. With moistened hands, divide the paste into 24 pieces and form each piece into an egg shape about 4 in/10 cm long. Use the Basic Method for Stuffing Kibbeh (p. 163) to stuff and seal the kibbeh. (The recipe can be prepared in advance to this step; freeze the kibbeh and fry directly from frozen.)

To cook and serve

7. Heat the oil in a large pot or deep-fryer. Fry the kibbeh in batches for 2 to 3 minutes until golden brown.

8. Serve hot or warm.

KIBBEH AND CARROT STEW
Kibbeh Jazariyeh

SERVES 6
PREPARATION TIME: 1 HOUR–1 HOUR AND 30 MINUTES
COOKING TIME: 45 MINUTES

In this dish, carrots and kibbeh are cooked in a sweet-and-sour pomegranate molasses stock. You can use the more available orange carrots here, but the dish is best prepared with black carrots if you can find them.

1 recipe Basic Kibbeh Paste (p. 162), stuffed with 1 recipe Basic Meat Stuffing or Basic Butter Stuffing (p. 165), or left hollow, formed into balls

4 cups/1 liter Basic Meat Stock, including meat (p. 20), or any lamb or beef stock

¼ cup/60 ml olive oil

1 small onion (4 oz/115 g), finely chopped

2 lb/1 kg carrots, peeled and chopped

2 tablespoons tomato paste

2 tablespoons pomegranate molasses

¼ cup/60 ml lemon juice

1 tablespoon sugar

1½ teaspoons Aleppo spice mix or seven-spice powder

¾ teaspoon ground black pepper

2½ teaspoons salt, or to taste

1. In a large pot, heat the oil and fry the onions on low heat until translucent (8–10 minutes).

2. Raise the heat to high, add the carrots, and fry for 1 minute. Pour in the stock and the rest of the ingredients, except the kibbeh balls and the meat from the stock, if using. Stir to mix.

3. Bring the mixture to a boil, lower the heat, and simmer, covered, for 30 minutes, or until the carrots are tender.

4. Add the kibbeh balls and meat (if using) and simmer for a further 2–3 minutes, or until the kibbeh is cooked. Taste and adjust the seasoning. Serve hot.

KIBBEH AND SPINACH STEW
Kibbeh Sabankhiyeh

SERVES 6
PREPARATION TIME: 1 HOUR–1 HOUR AND 30 MINUTES
COOKING TIME: 40 MINUTES

In this colorful dish, kibbeh, spinach, garlic, and cilantro are cooked in a meat stock thickened with rice and bulgar. It is full of vitamins and nutrients. You can make it as below, or serve the fried garlic and cilantro on the side, to be added individually.

1 recipe Basic Kibbeh Paste (p. 162), stuffed with 1 recipe Basic Meat Stuffing or Basic Butter Stuffing (p. 165), or left hollow, formed into balls

3½ cups/830 ml Basic Meat Stock, including meat (p. 20), or any lamb or beef stock

3 lb/1.5 kg spinach, stems removed, or 1½ lb/700 g spinach leaves, washed

1 very small onion (3 oz/85 g), finely chopped

½ cup/120 ml olive oil

1½ tablespoons ground coriander

Heaped ¼ cup/2 oz/60 g short-grain rice, preferably Egyptian

¼ cup/1½ oz/45 g coarse bulgar

5 garlic cloves (¾ oz/20 g), crushed

½ teaspoon ground black pepper

1 teaspoon salt, or to taste

2 cups/4 oz/115 g finely chopped cilantro

Lemon juice, to serve

1. Coarsely chop the spinach leaves and finely chop the tender stems.

2. In a large pot, fry the onion in 2 tablespoons of the oil over medium to low heat until tender. Add the ground coriander and fry for a few more seconds.

3. Add 2 cups of water, the rice, and bulgar. Bring the mixture to a boil, cover the pot, and simmer for 15 minutes, stirring a few times. Remove from the heat and set aside, covered, for 10 minutes.

4. Meanwhile, heat the rest of the oil in a skillet over low heat and fry the crushed garlic for a few seconds. Stir in the black pepper, ½ teaspoon of the salt, and the cilantro. Fry for a few more seconds; then remove from the heat and set aside.

5. Remove the lid from the bulgar-rice mixture, and whip it with a hand whisk for about 5 minutes; the rice will disintegrate, thickening the mixture, while the bulgar will stay whole.

6. Add the stock and bring to a boil over medium heat. Add the spinach and simmer for 2 minutes.

7. Add the kibbeh balls and the meat from the stock, if using, and cook for 2 more minutes.

8. Finally, add the garlic mixture. Taste and adjust the seasoning, if necessary.

9. Remove the pot from the heat and spoon into a large tureen or individual bowls. Serve hot with lemon juice on the side.

KIBBEH IN POMEGRANATE STOCK
Kibbeh Rimmaniyeh

SERVES 6
PREPARATION TIME: 1 HOUR–1 HOUR AND 30 MINUTES
COOKING TIME: 20 MINUTES

This is a welcome dish on cold winter days and when fresh pomegranate juice is available, but it is appealing all year round. The dish is rich with vegetables, meat, and kibbeh, cooked in a sweet-and-sour sauce with a slight kick. When pomegranate juice is not available, pomegranate molasses or unsweetened bottled pomegranate juice are good substitutes (*see* Notes). You can make this dish vegetarian by using vegetable stock and replacing the kibbeh with Vegetarian Potato Kibbeh (p. 183).

1 recipe Basic Kibbeh Paste (p. 162), stuffed with 1 recipe Basic Meat Stuffing or Basic Butter Stuffing (p. 165), or left hollow, formed into balls

2 cups/480 ml Basic Meat Stock, including meat (p. 20), or any meat or vegetable stock

2 celery sticks

1 medium onion (8 oz/225 g)

1½ cups/350 ml pomegranate juice

14 oz/400 g small zucchini, skin grooved with the tines of a fork, cut into bite-size pieces

14 oz/400 g small eggplants cut into bite-size pieces

1½ lb/700 g tomatoes (about 4 large), peeled, seeded, and chopped

8 garlic cloves (1 oz/30 g), crushed

2 tablespoons pomegranate molasses

2 tablespoons lemon juice

1 tablespoon sugar

¼–½ teaspoon ground black pepper

2½ tablespoons salt, or to taste

¼ cup/¾ oz/10 g finely chopped celery leaves

1 tablespoon dried mint

1. Cut the celery sticks into ¾ in/2 cm pieces. Peel and quarter the onions and separate them into layers.

2. Place the stock in a pot over high heat and bring to a boil. Add the pomegranate juice, onion, and chopped celery stems. Lower the heat to medium and simmer for about 4 minutes.

3. Add the zucchini and eggplants. Cover and simmer for a further 4 minutes.

4. Add the tomatoes, crushed garlic, pomegranate molasses, lemon juice, sugar, black pepper, salt, and kibbeh balls. Simmer for a further 3 minutes (the broth should cover the ingredients; add more stock or hot water as needed).

5. Add the celery leaves, dried mint, and meat from the stock, if using. Bring to a boil and simmer for 1 minute. Taste and adjust seasoning, if necessary.

6. Pour into a large bowl or individual bowls and serve hot.

NOTES

If fresh pomegranate juice is not available, increase the stock by 1 cup/240 ml, the pomegranate molasses by 2–3 tablespoons, and the lemon juice by 2–3 tablespoons.

KIBBEH IN SUMAC STOCK
Kibbeh Summaqiyeh

SERVES 6
PREPARATION TIME: 1 HOUR AND 15 MINUTES–1 HOUR AND 45 MINUTES
COOKING TIME: 20 MINUTES
RESTING TIME: 30 MINUTES

This dish is named for sumac; the sour, dark-red seasoning that is used to add a piquant flavor to various dishes in the Middle East. In this special stew, kibbeh and eggplants are cooked in a meat stock and flavored with sour sumac berries. You can also make a delicious version using artichoke bottoms instead of eggplants. This dish is best served with rice.

1 recipe Basic Kibbeh Paste (p. 162), stuffed with 1 recipe Basic Meat Stuffing or Basic Butter Stuffing (p. 165), or left hollow, formed into balls

2¼ cups/550 ml Basic Meat Stock, including meat (p. 20), or any meat stock

¾ cup/2½ oz/70 g whole sumac berries (or use ground)

3 tablespoons olive or vegetable oil

4 garlic cloves (½ oz/15 g), crushed

3 tablespoons tomato paste

½ teaspoon ground allspice

¼ teaspoon ground black pepper

2 teaspoons salt, or to taste

1 lb/450 g small, long eggplants, left unpeeled, chopped

1 tablespoon dried mint

1. In a small pot, combine the sumac with 1¼ cups/300 ml water and bring to a boil over high heat. Lower the heat and simmer, covered, for 2 minutes. Set aside for 30 minutes; then strain the liquid and discard the sumac berries. (Alternatively, steep the ground sumac in the boiling water in a small muslin bag.)

2. Heat the oil in a medium-size pot over medium heat and fry the garlic for a few seconds. Add the tomato paste, allspice, and black pepper, and fry for a few more seconds, stirring well.

3. Pour in the stock, sumac-infused water, and salt. Bring the mixture to a boil, lower the heat to medium, and simmer, covered, for 2 minutes.

4. Add the eggplants and simmer for 2 minutes, or until they are almost tender.

5. Turn the heat to low and add the kibbeh balls, meat from the stock (if using), and dried mint, and simmer for 2 more minutes. Taste and adjust the seasoning, if necessary.

6. Serve hot.

KIBBEH STEW WITH CARAMELIZED ONION
Kibbeh bi-Hamis

SERVES 4–6
PREPARATION TIME: 40–50 MINUTES
COOKING TIME: 50 MINUTES–1 HOUR

Hamis is a word of Syriac origin that means "to tenderize." Kibbeh and tender lamb meat are cooked in a hearty meat stock enriched with caramelized onion to form this vibrant dish. It is usually prepared in early spring when the lambs are young and served on its own, or over rice or bulgar with a delicious garlic sauce.

1 recipe Basic Kibbeh Paste (p. 162), stuffed with 1 recipe Basic Meat Stuffing or Basic Butter Stuffing (p. 165), or left hollow, formed into balls

3½ cups/830 ml Basic Lamb Stock, including meat (p. 20), or any good quality lamb stock

3 tablespoons olive or vegetable oil

2 cups/10 oz/300 g thinly sliced onions

2 tablespoons all-purpose flour

½ teaspoon ground cumin

½ teaspoon cinnamon

¼ teaspoon ground black pepper

1 tablespoon pomegranate molasses (optional)

Cooked rice or bulgar, to serve (optional)

For the garlic sauce garnish (optional)

3 garlic cloves (⅓ oz/12 g), minced

2 tablespoons red wine vinegar

1 tablespoon chopped parsley

½ teaspoon salt, or to taste

1. In a large pot, heat the oil over medium heat and sauté the onions, stirring, until golden and caramelized. Add the flour, cumin, cinnamon, and black pepper and fry for a further 30 seconds.

2. Pour the stock over the onion mixture and bring to a boil, stirring continuously. Cover the pot and simmer for 10 minutes, or until the onions are tender.

3. Here, I like to purée the broth until smooth using an immersion blender or food processor, which gives the broth a nice light-brown color, but you can skip this step for a more rustic texture.

4. Mix in the pomegranate molasses, if using; then taste and adjust seasoning, if necessary.

5. Add the kibbeh balls to the stock and simmer for 2 minutes, or until cooked. Add the meat from the stock, if using, and simmer to heat through.

6. Make the garlic sauce: Combine the garlic sauce ingredients and add 2 tablespoons of water, mixing well.

7. Serve hot over rice or bulgar and drizzled with garlic sauce (if using).

VARIATIONS

Cooked desert truffles may be added to the dish in step 5 (*see* p. 17 to clean and cook desert truffles).

KIBBEH WITH QUINCE
Kibbeh Safarjaliyeh

SERVES 8–9
PREPARATION TIME: 40–50 MINUTES
COOKING TIME: 45 MINUTES–1 HOUR AND 15 MINUTES

Kibbeh with Quince is an ancient dish; the recipe was even found in a cookbook from the twelfth century. Quince arrives in the markets in the fall, when there is a rush to buy it fresh. Many Aleppians freeze it to prepare Kibbeh with Quince all year round (*see* p. 27). In this dish, kibbeh is cooked in a meat stock with pomegranate juice and quince, which impart a delightfully sharp flavor and a pink color to the dish.

1 recipe Basic Kibbeh Paste (p. 162), stuffed with 1 recipe Basic Meat Stuffing or Basic Butter Stuffing (p. 165), or left hollow, formed into balls

5½ cups/1.3 liters Basic Meat Stock, including meat (p. 20), or any lamb or beef stock

2 cups/480 ml pomegranate juice

¾ cup/180 ml lemon juice, or to taste

3 tablespoons sugar

20 garlic cloves (3 oz/80 g), crushed

2 teaspoons salt, or to taste

2 lb/1 kg quince, to make 1¾ lb/800 g cored

¼ cup/60 ml vegetable oil or 4 tablespoons/2 oz/60 g butter, cubed

2 tablespoons dried mint

1. In a large pot, combine the stock with the pomegranate juice, lemon juice, sugar, crushed garlic, and salt. Bring to a boil over high heat; then lower the heat to medium and simmer for 5 minutes.

2. Chop the quince, with the skin, into ¾–1 in/2–3 cm cubes and add them to the pot. Simmer until the quince is tender; then remove with a slotted spoon and set aside.

3. Using a fork, mash 6 or 7 pieces of the quince to make about ½ cup/120 ml pulp, and return it to the pot to thicken the stock. Continue to simmer for a further 5 minutes.

4. Taste the sauce and adjust the seasoning by adding more lemon juice, sugar, or salt, as needed.

5. Add the kibbeh balls and meat (if using) and simmer for a further 2 minutes, or until the kibbeh is cooked. Return the quince to the pot and add the oil or butter and mint. Bring to a boil, then remove from the heat.

6. Serve hot.

VARIATIONS

- If you can't find fresh pomegranate juice, increase the stock to 6 cups/1.5 liters, add 1 cup/240 ml water, and more lemon juice and sugar to taste.
- You can add 3–5 tablespoons/45–75 ml tomato paste in step 1.

KIBBEH AND CHICKEN IN YOGURT SAUCE
Kibbeh Labaniyeh

SERVES 6
PREPARATION TIME: 55 MINUTES–1 HOUR
COOKING TIME: 40–45 MINUTES

The Aleppians consider Kibbeh and Chicken in Yogurt Sauce to be one of their most exceptional dishes, especially in winter; it is warming, filling, and soothing. This dish is made as special treat at the onset of the New Year, followed by the dessert Milk Pudding (p. 307), because it is believed that serving white dishes on the first day of the year will bring good luck and purity to the coming year.

This dish is typically made with chicken, lamb, or beef, but it is also good as a vegetarian dish (using vegetable stock and Vegetarian Potato Kibbeh, p. 183). You can also save time by omitting the chicken and using pre-made chicken stock.

3 whole chicken legs with bone and
    skin (about 1½ lb/700 g)
½ teaspoon salt, or to taste

Aromatics

1 cinnamon stick
1 bay leaf
1 small carrot, chopped
2 parsley stems
½ small onion (2 oz/60 g), halved

For the kibbeh

1 recipe Basic Kibbeh Paste (p. 162),
    stuffed with 1 recipe Basic Meat
    Stuffing or Basic Butter Stuffing
    (p. 165), or left hollow, formed
    into balls

For the yogurt sauce

4 cups/2 lb/1 kg plain cow's, sheep's,
    or goat's milk yogurt
1½ tablespoons or ⅓ cup/1½ oz/40 g
    cornstarch, depending on the kind
    of yogurt used (*see* Notes)
1 teaspoon salt, or to taste

To prepare the chicken

1. Place the chicken in a large pot, cover with cold water, and bring to a boil, skimming the foam that forms on the top. Add the aromatics and the salt, and bring to a boil. Cover, lower the heat, and simmer on very low heat for 40–50 minutes, or until the chicken is tender and falling off the bones.

2. Remove the chicken from the stock and discard the skin and bones. Shred the meat into bite-size pieces and set aside.

3. Strain the stock through a fine strainer or cheesecloth into a clean pot. Bring to a boil and boil rapidly, without stirring, to reduce the liquid to 1¾ cups/415 ml (or add water if the quantity needs to be increased).

To make the sauce and kibbeh

4. Place the yogurt in a bowl and whisk to mix well.

5. Mix ¼ cup/60 ml water into the cornstarch and stir into the yogurt.

6. Pass the mixture through a strainer into a medium-size pot. Add the reserved chicken stock.

7. Place the pot over medium heat, stirring continuously with a wooden spoon and always in the same direction, until the mixture comes to a boil. Taste and add the salt, if needed.

8. Add the kibbeh balls and simmer for 1 minute over low heat, until the kibbeh is cooked; then add the chicken pieces. (Recipe may be prepared a day in advance up to this step.)

For the garnish

8 garlic cloves (1 oz/30 g), crushed

6 tablespoons/90 ml olive oil

2 tablespoons dried mint

4 teaspoons Aleppo pepper or
   paprika

To serve

1. Prepare the garnishes: Fry the garlic briefly in the olive oil over medium to low heat; add 2 teaspoons of the dried mint and sauté for a few more seconds. Transfer to a small bowl. Place the rest of the dried mint and the Aleppo pepper in separate small bowls.

2. Spoon the stew into a serving bowl or individual bowls, garnish as desired, and serve hot, with the bowls of pepper, mint, and garlic on the side.

NOTES: THICKENING YOGURT WITH CORNSTARCH

- Use 1½ tablespoons cornstarch to thicken the chicken stock if using sheep's milk yogurt or goat's milk yogurt. Use ⅓ cup/1¾ oz/50 g cornstarch if using cow's milk yogurt (or see below).
- Alternatively, if using cow's milk yogurt, you can use 3 egg whites or 2 eggs as a thickening agent instead of cornstarch (using whole eggs gives a richer sauce than egg whites): Mix the eggs or whites into the yogurt after step 4. (Whipping yolks for 3 minutes before adding them to the yogurt will keep the yogurt sauce white.)

VARIATIONS

- Fresh cilantro can be used in place of the dried mint. Sauté ¾ cup/1¾ oz/50 g finely chopped cilantro with the crushed garlic.
- You can also stir the crushed fried garlic and dried mint (or chopped cilantro) with the frying oil into the yogurt sauce at the end of cooking, rather than serving on the side. Do so if your family likes garlic.
- You can also add 3–4 tablespoons of cooked rice to the dish.

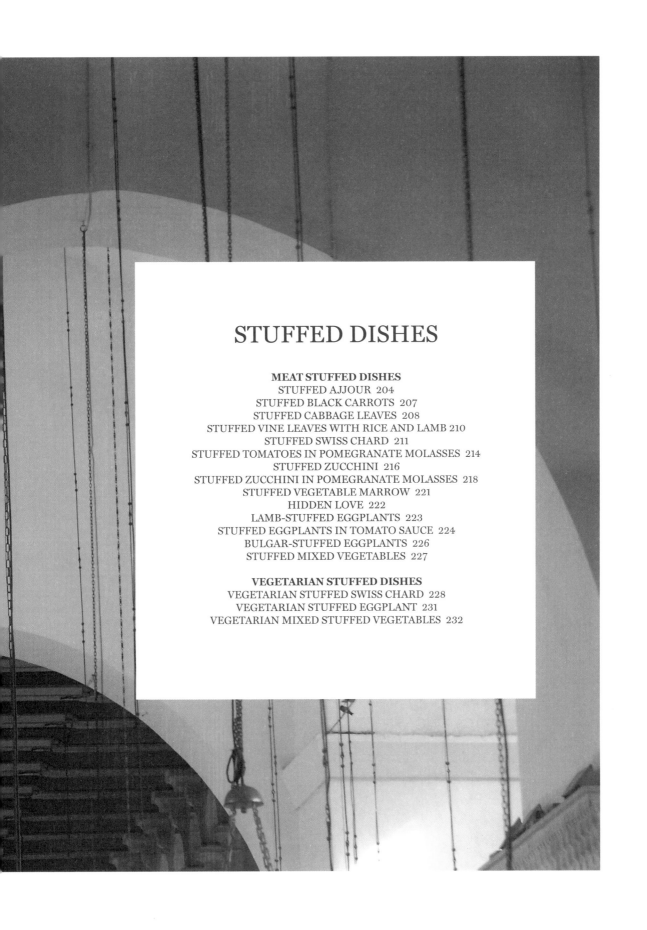

STUFFED DISHES

STUFFED AJJOUR
Ajjour Mahshi

SERVES 4–6
PREPARATION TIME: 20–25 MINUTES
COOKING TIME: 1 HOUR

Ajjour (the young fruit of the ivy gourd, or *Coccinia grandis*) is a squash-type vegetable with distinctive ribs and a superb flavor between that of a zucchini and a cucumber. A rounded variety comes from the Qamishli district, in the northeast of Syria, while a slender variety comes from Aleppo.

The recipe below uses a stuffing of ground meat and rice; however, it is also common to use freekeh or coarse bulgar instead (*see* Variations). The dish is an old one and much favored, to the extent that there is a saying in Aleppo, "*Al ajjoura bil joora,*" which basically means, "The ajjour is in the pot, so everything is okay."

Ajjour is at its best at the beginning of the season; they tend to be bitter later on, so taste them before using. Look out for them in South Asian, East Asian, and Middle Eastern grocery stores, or substitute pickling cucumbers. This dish can be prepared 1 day in advance.

3 lb/1.5 kg ajjour, (about 11, each 2–3 in/6–7 cm long)

¾ cup/5 oz/150 g short-grain rice, preferably Egyptian, rinsed and drained

10 oz/300 g lean ground lamb or beef

3 tablespoons/1½ oz/40 g butter or vegetable oil

½ teaspoon cinnamon

2 teaspoons Aleppo spice mix or seven-spice powder

1 teaspoon ground allspice

Lamb or beef bones (optional), soaked in ice-cold water for 30 minutes and drained

1½ teaspoons salt, or to taste

For the yogurt mint sauce

2 cups/1 lb/450 g plain yogurt

2 teaspoons dried mint, or 2 tablespoons chopped fresh mint

2 garlic cloves (¼ oz/8 g), crushed

1¼ teaspoons salt, or to taste

1. Wash the ajjour and cut off the ends. Core the ajjour, leaving a ¼ in/½ cm thick shell.

2. Mix the rice with the ground meat, butter or oil, and spices.

3. Fill the ajjour a little more than halfway, without forcing the stuffing; it will expand during cooking.

4. Place the lamb bones, if using, in the base of a small to medium pot. Arrange the stuffed ajjour tightly on top in one layer.

5. Cover with water, add 1½ teaspoons salt, and bring to a boil over high heat. Lower the heat, cover the pot, and simmer for one hour, or until the ajjour is tender.

6. Meanwhile, make the sauce: Mix all the sauce ingredients and set aside at room temperature.

7. Remove the ajjour from the pot and discard the bones (if using) and the cooking liquid (or reserve for reheating leftovers). Serve hot with yogurt-mint sauce on the side.

VARIATIONS: FREEKEH OR BULGAR STUFFING

Replace the rice with ¾ cup/4½ oz/130 g freekeh or ¾ cup/4½ oz/130 g coarse bulgar. Heat the wheat with the butter or oil and 6 tablespoons/90 ml water, stirring until the water evaporates. Cool, then mix in the rest of the stuffing ingredients. You can also add 2 tablespoons red pepper paste and ¼ cup/60 ml tomato paste, if desired.

STUFFED BLACK CARROTS
Jazar Aswad Mahshi

SERVES 4–6
PREPARATION TIME: 25–30 MINUTES
COOKING TIME: 1–2 HOURS

Black carrots are grown mainly in Turkey, the Middle East, and the Far East. In Aleppo they are plentiful during the winter season and are the main ingredient in the dish below and in Carrot Stew (p. 248).

Black carrots are very hard, and it is just about impossible to core them with an ordinary vegetable corer. In Aleppo, they are available in the market already cored by means of an electric drill. A clever and willing carpenter may do the job for you, but if you use orange carrots, buy them thick and bring them to room temperature before coring.

2 lb/1 kg black, purple, or orange
    carrots, peeled and cored

For the stuffing

⅓ cup/2½ oz/70 g short-grain rice,
    preferably Egyptian, soaked in
    water for 30 minutes, drained
1 small onion, finely chopped
    (2 oz/60 g)
2 tablespoons pomegranate
    molasses
2 teaspoons tomato paste
7 oz/200 g lean ground lamb or beef
2 teaspoons Aleppo spice mix or
    seven-spice powder
¼ teaspoon ground nutmeg
1 teaspoon salt, or to taste

For the cooking liquid

1 lb/450 g ripe tomatoes
⅓ cup/75 ml pomegranate molasses
2 teaspoons sugar, or to taste
1½ teaspoons salt, or to taste
4 garlic cloves (½ oz/15 g), crushed
2 teaspoons dried mint
1 tablespoon lemon juice, if needed

1. Combine the stuffing ingredients and mix in 3 tablespoons water.

2. Stuff the carrots, pushing gently on the stuffing with your finger, but leaving ½ in/2 cm empty at the opening.

3. Arrange the stuffed carrots tightly in a pot.

4. Prepare the cooking liquid: Quarter the tomatoes and blend them in a food processor in 2 batches. Transfer to a vegetable mill placed over a bowl and turn the handle to collect the sauce (I find this an easy method to get thick tomato juice free of skin and seeds). If you don't have a mill, skin the tomatoes, remove the seeds, then purée them in a food processor.

5. Mix the tomato pulp with 2½ cups/600 ml water, the pomegranate molasses, sugar, and salt. Pour over the carrots in the pot.

6. Bring to a boil over high heat; then lower the heat, cover the pan, and simmer for 2 hours, or until the carrots are tender and the sauce thickens slightly.

7. Mix the garlic and mint and add it to the pot. Simmer for a few more minutes. Taste and add the lemon juice, if needed.

8. Transfer the carrots and sauce to a serving bowl and serve hot.

VARIATIONS

Some like to cook Stuffed Cabbage Leaves (p. 208) with Stuffed Black Carrots, giving the cabbage leaves a lovely color.

STUFFED CABBAGE LEAVES
Malfoof Mahshi

SERVES 8–9
PREPARATION TIME: 30–40 MINUTES
COOKING TIME: 1½ HOURS
RESTING TIME: 10 MINUTES

This is a warming and comforting dish to share with family and friends. It is time-consuming, but you can prepare it ahead and refrigerate it for a few days until you need to serve it (*see* Notes).

     Stuffed cabbage is a popular dish throughout the Levant, as well as in Greece, Iran, Turkey, and southern Europe. The Aleppian addition of pomegranate molasses gives the dish a beautiful color and a complexity of flavor, but you can substitute lime juice (*see* Variations).

1–2 white cabbages (about 6½ lb/
    3 kg), at room temperature
Salt, to taste
12 garlic cloves (1¾ oz/50 g), peeled
6 tablespoons/90 ml olive or
    vegetable oil

For the stuffing

1 lb/450 g lean ground lamb or beef
1½ cups/10 oz/300 g short-grain
    rice, preferably Egyptian,
    washed and drained
6 garlic cloves (⅓ oz/25 g), crushed
6 tablespoons/90 ml olive oil
1 teaspoon Aleppo spice mix or
    seven-spice powder
1 teaspoon ground allspice
1 teaspoon cinnamon
½ teaspoon ground black pepper
1 teaspoon salt, or to taste

For the cooking liquid

2 tablespoons tomato paste
About ½ cup/120 ml pomegranate
    molasses (*see* Variations
    for other options)
1 tablespoon sugar
1½ teaspoons salt, or to taste

To prepare cabbage leaves

1. Cut each leaf near the core then gently remove (they are fragile). You will use only the large outer leaves (about 33, weighing about 4 lb/2 kg). (I use the leftover smaller inner leaves to make a salad.)

2. Bring a large pot of salted water to a boil over high heat. Carefully push the cabbage leaves into the water, in batches, and boil just until soft and easily pliable (about 30 seconds). Transfer to a colander to cool.

3. Place each leaf on a cutting board, cut away and reserve the thick spine, and cut each leaf into 2 or 3 large pieces.

To stuff the leaves

4. Combine the stuffing ingredients and mix in ½ cup/120 ml water.

5. Line the base of a pot with the reserved cabbage spines, and top with the oil.

6. Place one cut leaf on your work surface, shiny-side down. Place about 1½ tablespoons of the stuffing along the length of the thin rib nearest to you, and roll loosely into a thin cigar shape, trimming off any extra, if needed. Place in the pot, on top of the spines, seam-side down.

7. Continue with the rest of the leaves, arranging them side-by-side in the pot, along with the 12 peeled garlic cloves. Place any leftover stuffing in a gauze bag and place on top, along with any unused leaves.

To cook and serve

8. Mix the cooking liquid ingredients and pour into the pot with 4 cups/1 liter water. Cover with an upturned plate and place a heavy weight on top.

9. Bring to a boil over high heat, then lower the heat, cover, and simmer slowly for about 1½ hours. Taste and adjust seasoning.

10. Remove the pot from heat and set aside for 10 minutes. Remove the weighted plate, carefully remove the cabbage rolls one by one (I use my hands, I think they are the best utensils!), and arrange on a serving dish. Pour the sauce on top, or place it in a separate bowl. Roll the cabbage spines and place them on top of the rolls. Serve hot.

NOTES

If preparing ahead, drain the sauce and store the rolls and sauce seperately. Refrigerate until needed. To serve: Pour the sauce over the stuffed cabbage and reheat, covered, over low heat.

VARIATIONS

- About ½ cup/120 ml lemon juice and 1 tablespoon dried crushed mint leaves can be used in the cooking liquid in place of the pomegranate molasses.
- You can use green varieties of cabbage instead, the best of which is Savoy: keep the leaves whole, fill them with extra stuffing, and fold them like a packet (as for Vegetarian Stuffed Swiss Chard, p. 211) rather than a cigar-shape.
- Some like to cook Stuffed Cabbage Leaves with Stuffed Black Carrots (p. 207), because the carrots impart their beautiful color.

STUFFED VINE LEAVES WITH RICE AND LAMB
Yabraq

SERVES 10–12
PREPARATION TIME: 1 HOUR
COOKING TIME: 4 HOURS

Many poems have been written in honor of this much-loved dish. It is nicknamed *Asabeh al Janneh*, meaning "fingers of paradise." The dish is prepared in many Arab countries, as well as in Turkey, Cyprus, and Greece where it is called *dolma*. The stuffing is always based on rice and ground meat, but there are slight regional variations. In Aleppo it is sometimes cooked with artichokes, and usually with plenty of garlic.

Time and patience are needed to prepare this delicious and nourishing dish, which is ideal for a crowd. The saying goes in Aleppo, *"ma as'ab laffo wa ma ahwan saffo,"* meaning, how difficult to roll and how quickly it is eaten. The result, however, is very rewarding. Some steps may be taken to simplify the job, such as preparing the whole dish up to 3 days before cooking, or preparing it in stages over three days. The dish does not freeze well, but can be refrigerated for 5 days to be reheated when needed, or you can halve this recipe, as desired. In Aleppo, during the sour prune (*janarek*) season, it is customary to place some of the fruits at the base of the pot, giving the dish an extraordinary tart flavor.

1½ lb/700 g vine leaves (canned, frozen, or *see* p. 31 to prepare from fresh)

1 lb/450 g artichoke bottoms (about 7; *see* page 14; optional)

1–2 heads garlic, cloves separated and peeled (optional)

¾ cup/180 ml olive oil

1 tablespoon salt, or to taste

¾ cup/180 ml lemon juice or verjuice (sour grape juice), or a mixture of both

For the stuffing

2 lb/1 kg lean ground lamb or beef

2¼ cups/15 oz/425 g short-grain rice, preferably Egyptian

4 garlic cloves (½ oz/15 g), crushed

2 tablespoons Aleppo spice mix or seven-spice powder

1 tablespoon cinnamon

1 tablespoon ground allspice

1 tablespoon black pepper

½ cup/120 ml olive oil

1 tablespoon salt, or to taste

1. Combine the stuffing ingredients.

2. Rinse and drain the vine leaves and remove the stalks. Cut any very large leaves in half. Place one leaf (or half) on your work surface, shiny-side down, and put about 1 teaspoon of the stuffing along the stem end. Fold the sides over the ends of the stuffing, and roll like a cigarette toward the top of the leaf, folding in the sides as you go (*see* Photo on p. 212). Continue with the rest of the leaves and stuffing.

3. Line the base of a large pot with the artichoke bottoms, if using. Tightly arrange the stuffed vine leaves on top in circular rows, with garlic cloves tucked in between. Spoon the oil on top.

4. Pour 3½ cups/830 ml water and the salt into the pot and bring to a boil over high heat. Lower the heat to very low and place an upturned plate directly on top of the stuffed vine leaves in the pot. Place a weight on top of the plate. Cover the pot and cook for 2 hours on very low heat (if you have one, place a heat diffuser between the burner and the pot).

5. Remove the lid and pour the lemon juice on top, then replace the lid and continue cooking on very low heat for a further two hours. Taste and adjust the seasoning. There should be just a little liquid left.

6. Remove the pot from the heat and set aside, covered with the lid and a thick towel, for about 15 minutes, then flip gently onto a serving platter. Carefully remove the pot and serve hot.

STUFFED SWISS CHARD
Siliq Mahshi

SERVES 6–8
PREPARATION TIME: 40 MINUTES
COOKING TIME: 1 HOUR AND 10 MINUTES
RESTING TIME: 15 MINUTES

Here is another stuffed vegetable dish that Aleppians are proud of. The dish is simple, but the faint bitterness of the Swiss chard gives this dish an exquisite flavor, subtly distinguishing it from the better-known stuffed vine leaves. Stuffed Swiss Chard is typically served hot with Garlic Yogurt (p. 98). Some like to serve it with the cooking liquid on the side to use as a sauce.

4 lb/2 kg Swiss chard
    (choose large leaves)
12 oz/350 g stewing lamb of beef,
    cut into pieces (optional)
3 tablespoons/1½ oz/45 g butter
    or olive oil
3 cups/700 ml reduced-sodium
    lamb or beef stock or water
1½ teaspoons salt, or to taste

For the stuffing

1 cup/7 oz/200 g short-grain rice,
    preferably Egyptian
14 oz/400 g lean ground lamb
    or beef
1 teaspoon ground allspice
¼ teaspoon ground black pepper
2 teaspoons salt, or to taste
Garlic Yogurt (p. 98), to serve
    (optional)

1. Cut the stems and central ribs out of the large Swiss chard leaves, leaving you with lengthwise halves (you can use the removed stems in a salad, p. 106). Cut the coarse stems off any smaller leaves, leaving the leaves whole, and gently pound the central ribs to flatten.

2. Blanch the leaves in boiling salted water and drain.

3. Prepare the stuffing: Wash the rice, soak it in cold water for 10 minutes, and drain. Mix in the rest of the stuffing ingredients and ¼ cup/60 ml water.

4. To stuff the leaves: Place one leaf half on your work surface horizontally, shiny-side down. Place 1 tablespoon of stuffing along the long side nearest to you, fold the sides over the ends of the filling, and then roll like a cigarette. For small whole leaves, place the stuffing along the widest end and proceed as above. (The leaves can also be rolled without folding in the sides, *see* Stuffed Cabbage Leaves, p. 208).

5. If using, place the pieces of stewing meat on the bottom of a large, shallow pot (a 10 cup/2½ liter capacity pot is best) and tightly arrange the stuffed rolls in a circular fashion. Top with the butter or oil, if desired.

6. Pour the stock or water over the rolls, add the salt, and bring to a boil over high heat. Lower the heat to very low, cover the leaves with an upturned plate to hold them in place, and put a weight on top of the plate. Cover and cook for 70 minutes.

7. Remove from the heat. If you would like to serve the cooking liquid as a sauce, carefully pour it into a bowl and set aside, otherwise set the pot aside, covered, for about 15 minutes.

8. Remove the weight and plate and invert a large serving platter over the pot. Holding the two together, flip the pot over onto the platter, and set aside for 5 minutes to allow the stuffing to settle. Carefully lift off the pot, leaving a cake of stuffed leaves. Serve hot with Garlic Yogurt on the side.

STUFFED TOMATOES IN POMEGRANATE MOLASSES
Banadoora Mahshiyeh

SERVES 4
PREPARATION TIME: 35 MINUTES
COOKING TIME: 45 MINUTES

Aleppo is the city of kibbeh and stuffed vegetables. Every kind of vegetable and many fruits are stuffed, including beautiful red tomatoes. This is a summer dish, made when tomatoes are at their peak, sun-drenched and juicy. There is a significant difference in flavor between good ripe tomatoes in season and the tasteless tomatoes that are available out of season.

8 small firm tomatoes (about
    1¾ lb/800 g)

For the stuffing

¼ cup/60 ml olive oil

⅓ cup/1¾ oz/50 g pine nuts

½ small onion (2 oz/60 g),
    finely chopped

12 oz/350 g finely ground lamb or
    beef (pulse in a food processor
    to achieve a fine texture)

1½ teaspoons Aleppo spice mix or
    seven-spice powder

½–¾ teaspoon ground black pepper

½ teaspoon cinnamon

2 teaspoons salt, or to taste

2 tablespoons breadcrumbs

½ cup/1 oz/30 g coarsely chopped
    parsley

To prepare the tomatoes

1. Cut 1 in/2 cm off the tops of the tomatoes and set aside to be used later as "lids."

2. Using a small spoon, scoop out the seeds. Sprinkle the cavities with salt and place the tomatoes on paper towels, cut-side down. Set aside for 30 minutes.

To prepare the stuffing

3. In a skillet, heat 2 tablespoons of the oil over medium heat and fry the pine nuts, stirring frequently, until golden. Remove with a slotted spoon and set aside.

4. Lower the heat and fry the onions in the same oil until tender. Raise the heat to medium and add the rest of the oil, ground meat, and spices. Fry, stirring, until the meat is almost cooked but not dry. Remove from the heat. Mix in the pine nuts, parsley, and breadcrumbs.

To prepare the sauce

5. If using fresh tomatoes, peel and de-seed them and purée them in a blender or food procoessor. If using canned tomato purée, mix with ¼ cup/60 ml water.

6. In a medium pot, heat the oil over medium to low heat and fry the onions until translucent (8–10 minutes). Add the garlic and black pepper and fry for a few seconds.

7. Pour the tomato sauce over the onion mixture, stir in the tomato paste (if using), pomegranate molasses, sugar, ¾ cup/320 ml water, and salt.

8. Bring the sauce to a boil over high heat and pour into an ovenproof baking dish. (Recipe may be prepared to this step 1 day in advance.)

For the sauce

3 small ripe tomatoes (10 oz/
   300 g), or 1¼ cups/300 ml
   canned tomato purée
2 tablespoons olive or vegetable oil
½ small onion (2 oz/60 g),
   finely chopped
3 garlic cloves (⅓ oz/12 g), crushed
¼–½ teaspoon ground black pepper
1 tablespoon tomato paste (if using
   fresh tomatoes)
3 tablespoons pomegranate
   molasses
1 teaspoon sugar
1½ teaspoons salt, or to taste

To cook and serve

1. Preheat the oven to 400°F/200°C.

2. Fill the tomatoes with the stuffing, pressing gently on it.
    Cover with the reserved tomato "lids."

3. Arrange the stuffed tomatoes in the sauce, and cover the
    dish with aluminum foil.

4. Bake for 25 minutes, covered, then remove the foil and bake
    uncovered for a further 20 minutes, adding a little water to
    the sauce if needed.

5. Spoon a teaspoon of the tomato sauce into each stuffed
    tomato and serve hot with rice on the side.

VARIATIONS

You can add one egg to the stuffing to make it more compact.

STUFFED ZUCCHINI
Koosa Mahshi

SERVES 4–6
PREPARATION TIME: 25–30 MINUTES
COOKING TIME: 30 MINUTES

Serve this delicious dish with Garlic Yogurt with Mint (p. 98). You can use the inner flesh in Zucchini and Garlic in Olive Oil (p. 46), or Zucchini Omelets (p. 65).

2 lb/1 kg small zucchini (about 9),
    at room temperature

A few lamb or beef bones (optional)

1 teaspoon salt, or to taste

2 tablespoons olive oil

For the stuffing

⅓ cup/2½ oz/70 g short-grain rice,
    preferably Egyptian

7 oz/200 g lean ground lamb or beef

¼ cup/60 ml olive oil or
    melted butter

1 teaspoon Aleppo spice mix or
    seven-spice powder

½ teaspoon ground allspice

¼ teaspoon ground black pepper

1 teaspoon salt, or to taste

1. Using the tines of a fork, make thin grooves along the length of the zucchini (optional). Cut off the stem.

2. Hollow the inside with the help of a corer, leaving a thin shell.

3. Prepare the stuffing: Wash and drain the rice, then mix in the rest of the stuffing ingredients.

4. Fill the zucchini with the stuffing, pressing lightly and leaving ½ in/1 cm empty at the opening to allow the rice to expand.

5. Place the bones (if using) in a large pot. Arrange the stuffed zucchini on top and cover with water. Add the salt and oil.

6. Place an upturned plate on top of the stuffed zucchini in the pot, and place a weight on top of the plate. Bring to a boil, lower the heat, and simmer for 30 minutes until the zucchini is tender and the rice is cooked.

7. Transfer the stuffed zucchini to a serving platter, reserving the cooking liquid for reheating any leftovers. (Stuffed Zucchini can be made 1 day ahead and stored in the refrigerator.)

STUFFED ZUCCHINI IN POMEGRANATE MOLASSES
Koosa Sheikh al-Mahshi

SERVES 4–6
PREPARATION TIME: 30–35 MINUTES
COOKING TIME: 30 MINUTES

This is a dish for meat lovers: an all-meat stuffing gives it a distinctive flavor. It makes a wonderful family dinner, served with rice or bulgar. If you can't find pomegranate molasses, see the variation on p. 26. You can use the leftover zucchini cores to make Zucchini and Garlic in Olive Oil (p. 46) or Zucchini Omelets (p. 65).

2½ lb/1 kg baby zucchini (13–14),
    at room temperature
½ cup/120 ml olive or vegetable oil

For the stuffing

6 tablespoons/90 ml olive oil
⅓ cup/2¼ oz/60 g pine nuts
½ small onion (2 oz/60 g),
    finely chopped
12 oz/350 g lean finely ground lamb
    or beef (pulse in a food processor
    to achieve a fine texture)
1 tablespoon Aleppo spice mix or
    seven-spice powder
½–¾ teaspoon ground black pepper
½ teaspoon cinnamon
2 teaspoons salt, or to taste
½ cup/1 oz/30 g coarsely chopped
    parsley

For the cooking liquid

1½ tablespoons tomato paste
⅓ cup/75 ml pomegranate molasses
1½ teaspoons sugar
1½ teaspoons salt, or to taste

To serve (optional)

Rice Pilaf with Vermicelli (p. 110),
    or plain rice or bulgar

1. Using the tines of a fork, make thin grooves along the length of the zucchini (optional). Cut off the stems. Hollow the insides with the help of a corer or the pointed end of a peeler, leaving a thin shell.

To prepare the stuffing

2. In a skillet, heat the olive oil over medium heat and fry the pine nuts, stirring frequently, until they begin to color. Remove them with a slotted spoon and set aside.

3. Lower the heat and sauté the onions in the same oil until tender (8–10 minutes). Raise the heat to medium and add the meat, spices, and salt. Cook, stirring frequently until the meat is almost cooked but not dry. Remove from the heat. Stir in the pine nuts and parsley.

4. Fill the zucchini with the stuffing, pushing it in well, and leaving ½ in/1 cm empty at the opening.

To cook and serve

5. In batches, fry the zucchini in the olive or vegetable oil until golden, turning them a few times.

6. Pour the cooking liquid ingredients into a pot with 2½ cups/600 ml water. Add the zucchini and bring to a boil.

7. Cover the pot and simmer over low heat for about 30 minutes, or until tender.

8. Serve hot with rice or bulgar pilaf.

VARIATIONS

You can add one egg to the stuffing to make it more compact.

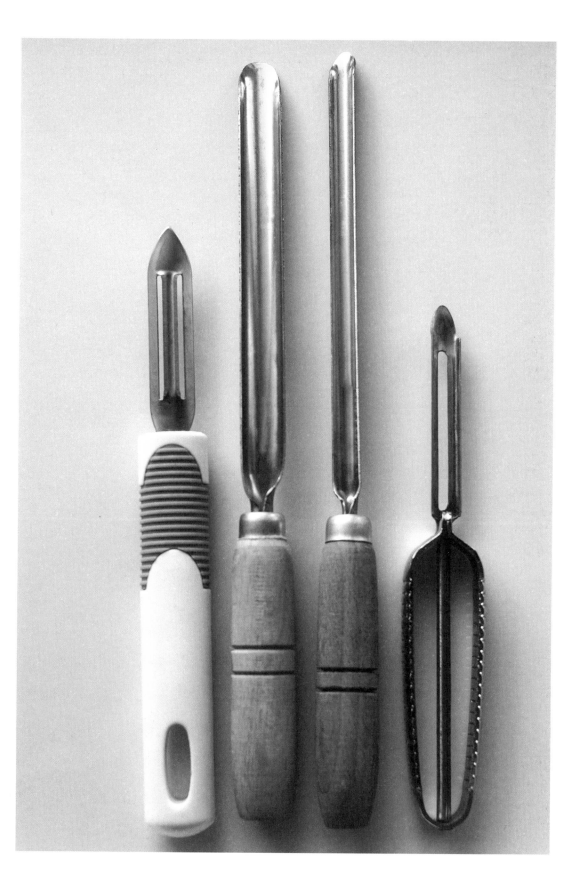

STUFFED VEGETABLE MARROW
Qare' Mahshi

SERVES 4–6
PREPARATION TIME: 30 MINUTES
COOKING TIME: 50 MINUTES

Vegetable marrow is a slim, pale-green gourd related to cucuzza squash, bottle gourd, or calabash, harvested young for use as a vegetable. This is a dish of delectable flavor. Small stuffed vegetable marrows are served with a stock of verjuice (sour grape juice), garlic, and mint. In Aleppo, you can find vegetable marrows fresh or dried. If you are unable to find them, you can substitute zucchini or small summer squash.

12 small vegetable marrows
   (2 lb/1 kg), at room temperature
   (make sure none are bitter)
A few lamb or beef bones (optional)
3 medium sweet red or green
   peppers (12 oz/350 g)

For the stuffing

¾ cup/5 oz/150 g short-grain rice,
   preferably Egyptian
10 oz/300 g lean ground lamb or beef
1 teaspoon ground allspice
1 teaspoon cinnamon
½ teaspoon ground black pepper
1 medium tomato (4½ oz/125 g),
   grated
4 tablespoons/2 oz/60 g butter,
   melted and cooled
1 teaspoon salt, or to taste

For the cooking liquid

2 cups/480 ml water and 1 cup/
   240 ml beef stock, or 3 cups/
   700 ml water
1 cup/240 ml verjuice
   (sour grape juice)
1½ teaspoons salt, or to taste
4 garlic cloves (½ oz/15 g), crushed
1 tablespoon dried mint

1. Using a small sharp knife, scrape the skin off the marrows. (it can be thinly peeled, but scraping gives them a better appearance). Cut off and discard the stem and about 1 in/2 cm off the bottoms (you can taste the flesh for any bitterness). Place the marrows in a bowl of cold water.

2. Scrape or peel the marrows again to ensure all of the green skin has been removed. Using a long corer, core each marrow, starting from the thick bottom. Return to the cold water.

3. Prepare the stuffing: Mix all the stuffing ingredients.

4. Prepare the cooking liquid: Mix all the ingredients except for the garlic and mint.

5. Place the bones (if using) in the bottom of a pot large enough to hold the vegetables.

6. Fill the cavities of the marrows with stuffing, pressing gently on the stuffing and leaving about ½ in/1 cm open to allow the rice to expand. Arrange the stuffed marrows on top of the bones in the pot.

7. Cut the tops off the sweet peppers and remove the seeds and inner membranes. Fill them with the remaining stuffing and arrange them on top of the stuffed marrows.

8. Pour the prepared sauce mixture over the stuffed vegetables and bring to a boil over high heat. Lower the heat to simmer, cover the pot, and cook for 30 minutes.

9. Remove the lid and add the crushed garlic and mint to the sauce. Simmer for a further 10 minutes, then taste and adjust seasoning.

10. Remove the peppers and continue cooking for a further 10 minutes, or until the marrow is tender and the cooking liquid has reduced to a sauce.

11. Transfer to a platter and serve hot with sauce on the side.

HIDDEN LOVE
Hibb al-Ib

SERVES 4–6
PREPARATION TIME: 30–35 MINUTES
COOKING TIME: 1 HOUR

There is a romantic story behind this traditional Aleppian dish of stuffed zucchini or eggplant with green beans. It is the story of two lovers who were forbidden to see each other, so they used to hide in the fields, one pretending to collect green beans, and the other zucchini (some say eggplant). One day the lovers could not be found. Their clothes were discovered in two bundles; one filled with zucchini and the other with green beans. To this day, the mystery of the lovers has not been solved and the people of Aleppo continue to cook this dish. The two vegetables are cooked together in tomato sauce, signifying the closeness that is shared between lovers.

I like to serve this dish with rice, fresh radishes, raw green peppers, and yogurt on the side.

1 lb/450 g Romano beans
    (or any wide, flat green beans)
¼ cup/60 ml vegetable oil
1 small onion (4 oz/115 g),
    finely chopped
4 garlic cloves (½ oz/15 g), minced
7 oz/200 g lean ground lamb or beef
½ teaspoon ground black pepper
1 teaspoon cinnamon
1 tablespoon ground coriander
    (optional)
1 teaspoon salt, or to taste

For the zucchini

1 lb/450 g baby zucchini (about 10;
    or use baby eggplants)
⅓ cup/2½ oz/70 g short-grain rice,
    washed and drained
3½ oz/100 g lean ground lamb or beef
2 tablespoons tomato paste
¼ teaspoon cinnamon
½ teaspoon salt, or to taste

For the cooking liquid

1 lb/450 g ripe tomatoes, grated
4 tablespoons/60 ml tomato paste
1 tablespoon lemon juice if needed
2 teaspoons sugar
2 cups/480 ml hot water
1 teaspoon salt, or to taste

1. Trim the ends of the green beans, remove the strings, if any, and cut each into 3 or 4 pieces.

2. In a large pot, heat the oil over medium heat and sauté the onion. Add the garlic, meat, spices, and salt and cook, stirring well, until the meat browns but does not dry out. Raise the heat, add the green beans, and sauté for 1 minute, stirring.

To prepare the zucchini

3. Using the tines of a fork, make thin grooves along the length of the zucchini (or skip this step). Cut off the stems. Hollow the inside with the help of a corer or peeler, leaving a thin shell.

4. Prepare the stuffing: mix the rice, ground meat, tomato paste, cinnamon, salt, and 2 tablespoons of water.

5. Fill the zucchini with the stuffing, pressing lightly, leaving ½ in/1 cm empty at the opening to allow the rice to expand.

6. Arrange the stuffed zucchini over the green beans in the pot.

To cook and serve

7. Combine the cooking liquid ingredients, pour into the pot, and bring to a boil. Lower the heat, partially cover the pot, and simmer for 1 hour, or until the green beans are soft and the sauce thickens. Taste and adjust the seasoning.

8. Spoon into a large serving dish and serve hot.

VARIATIONS

You can replace the 7 oz/200 g ground meat with 1 lb/450 g cubed stewing meat.

LAMB-STUFFED EGGPLANTS
Banjane Mahshi

SERVES 4–6
PREPARATION TIME: 30–35 MINUTES
COOKING TIME: 1 HOUR

This excellent dish is prepared with simple ingredients: ground meat, rice, eggplants, and tomatoes, illustrating what can be achieved with the addition of spices and a careful balance of flavors.

2 lb/1 kg small eggplants (about 12)
5 garlic cloves (¾ oz/20 g), crushed
2 teaspoons dried mint

For the stuffing

¾ cup/5 oz/150 g short-grain rice,
    preferably Egyptian, washed
    and drained
10 oz/300 g lean ground lamb
    (or use beef)
1 large tomato (7 oz/200 g), grated
1 tablespoon tomato paste
1 tablespoon red pepper paste
3 tablespoons pomegranate
    molasses
1 tablespoon olive oil
½ teaspoon ground allspice
¼ teaspoon ground black pepper
¼ teaspoon cinnamon
1½ teaspoons salt, or to taste

For the cooking liquid

2 large tomatoes (14 oz/200 g),
    peeled and finely chopped
¼ cup/60 ml lemon juice
1½ teaspoons salt, or to taste

1. Cut off the green caps and stems off the eggplants and cut off a ¼ in/½ cm slice from the narrow end of each eggplant to use as a "lid" to cover the opening (optional).

2. Core the eggplants, leaving a thin shell, and place them in a bowl filled with cold water.

3. Mix all the stuffing ingredients in a large bowl.

4. Remove the eggplants one at a time, drain, and fill loosely with the stuffing, leaving ½ in/1 cm empty at the opening. If using, place the eggplant "lids" in the openings, covering the stuffing. Arrange the stuffed eggplants closely in a pot.

5. Mix the cooking liquid ingredients with 3½ cups/830 ml water and pour on top of the eggplants.

6. Place an upturned plate into the pot to cover the eggplants and hold them in place, and place a heavy weight on top, before covering the pot.

7. Bring to a boil over high heat, then lower the heat, cover the pot, and cook for about 45 minutes.

8. Mix the garlic and dried mint. Remove the weighted plate and spoon the garlic mixture into the sauce, shaking the pot to ensure it is thoroughly incorporated.

9. Replace the lid and simmer for about 15 minutes more, then taste and adjust the seasoning, if necessary.

10. Serve the eggplants hot with the sauce on the side. (Recipe may be prepared the day before and refrigerated.)

STUFFED EGGPLANTS IN TOMATO SAUCE
Karniyarik

SERVES 4
PREPARATION TIME: 35 MINUTES
RESTING TIME: 30 MINUTES
COOKING TIME: 30 MINUTES

Karniyarik is a Turkish word meaning "split belly." It is a pleasing dish that brings together fried eggplants, a meat stuffing, and a thick tomato sauce. It is easy to prepare, since there is no coring: the fried eggplants are slit lengthwise (hence the name). The dish is shared between Turkey, Iran, and Aleppo, where it is pronounced *arniari'*. It is considered one of the finest eggplant dishes. Serve this dish with rice.

1 lb/450 g long baby eggplants
    (about 12)

2 teaspoons salt, or to taste

Peanut or vegetable oil, for
    deep-frying

3 tablespoons pine nuts

3 tablespoons olive oil

1 very small onion (3 oz/85 g),
    finely chopped

8 oz/225 g lean ground lamb or beef

1 teaspoon Aleppo spice mix or
    seven-spice powder

¼ teaspoon cinnamon

¼ teaspoon ground black pepper

½ teaspoon ground allspice

14 oz/400 g can peeled tomatoes
    with their juice, puréed in a food
    processor or blender

¾ cup/180 ml meat stock or water

1. Peel off the eggplant's green caps. Cut off part of the stems, leaving about ½ in/1 cm attached. With a potato peeler or sharp knife, peel off thin strips of the skin lengthwise, at intervals of about ½ in /1 cm. Sprinkle with 1 teaspoon of the salt and set aside in a strainer for 30 minutes.

2. Wipe the eggplants with paper towels and fry in the peanut or vegetable oil until light golden. Transfer to a strainer.

3. Fry the pine nuts in 1 tablespoon of the olive oil until golden.

4. In a skillet, heat the remaining 2 tablespoons olive oil over medium heat and sauté the chopped onion for about 1 minute, or until it starts to color. Add the meat, Aleppo spice mix, cinnamon, black pepper, half of the allspice, and the remaining teaspoon of salt. Sauté until the meat is cooked but not colored or dry. Mix in half of the pine nuts. Taste and adjust the seasoning, if necessary.

5. In a small pot, combine the puréed tomatoes, stock or water, and the rest of the allspice and bring to a boil. Pour into an ovenproof dish wide enough to hold the eggplants.

6. Preheat the oven to 350°F/180°C.

7. Make a lengthwise slit on the side of each eggplant and pry it open gently with your fingers. Arrange the eggplants side by side on top of the tomato sauce, open side up.

8. Fill the eggplant openings with the meat stuffing and sprinkle the rest of the pine nuts on top.

9. Bake for about 20 minutes and serve hot with rice.

VARIATIONS

You can add finely chopped green and red peppers to the tomato sauce. You can also add finely chopped parsley to the stuffing.

BULGAR-STUFFED EGGPLANTS
Banjane bi-Burghol

SERVES 8
PREPARATION TIME: 30–35 MINUTES
COOKING TIME: 1 HOUR AND 10 MINUTES

The Kurds are credited for this delicious dish of eggplants stuffed with bulgar, vegetables, and ground lamb, and cooked in a rich lemony sauce with pomegranate molasses.

22 baby eggplants (3 lb/1.4 kg)
A few lamb or beef bones (optional)
1 lb/450 g lamb or beef steaks,
    thinly sliced (optional)

For the stuffing

1 cup/6 oz/170 g coarse bulgar
¼ cup/60 ml vegetable oil
1 cup/5 oz/150 g finely chopped onion
2 medium sweet red peppers
    (8 oz/225 g), finely chopped
3–4 large tomatoes (1½ lb/700 g),
    seeded and finely chopped
2½ cups/3½ oz/100 g finely
    chopped parsley
8 oz/225 g ground lamb or beef
¼ cup/60 ml lemon juice
2 tablespoons pomegranate molasses
1 tablespoon tomato paste
1½ teaspoons Aleppo spice mix or
    seven-spice powder
2½ teaspoons salt, or to taste

For the cooking liquid

3 tablespoons pomegranate molasses
3 tablespoons tomato paste
½ cup/120 ml lemon juice
2 tablespoons sugar
¼ teaspoon chili powder
1½ teaspoons salt, or to taste
1 tablespoon dried mint
9 garlic cloves (1½ oz/40 g), crushed
¼ cup/60 ml olive oil

1. Prepare the stuffing: Wash and drain the bulgar. In a skillet, heat the oil over medium heat and fry the bulgar with the onions for about 2 minutes, stirring well. Transfer to a bowl and mix with the rest of the stuffing ingredients.

2. Cut the green caps and stems off the eggplants. Cut off a ¼ in/½ cm slice from the narrow end of each eggplant to use as a "lid" (optional). Core the eggplants, leaving a thin shell, and set aside in a bowl of cold water for a few minutes.

3. One-by-one, drain the eggplants and fill each with the stuffing, pressing it into the hollow, leaving ½ in/1 cm empty at the opening. Cork the openings with the cut "lids," if using.

4. Place the bones (if using), in the bottom of a pot, top with the steaks (if using); then tightly arrange the stuffed eggplants on top.

5. Prepare the cooking liquid: mix the pomegranate molasses, tomato paste, lemon juice, sugar, chili, and salt with 3 cups/700 ml water and pour over the eggplants.

6. Cover the eggplants with an upturned plate and place a heavy weight on top.

7. Place the pot over high heat and bring to a boil. Lower the heat to very low, cover the pot, and simmer for 45 minutes.

8. Briefly fry the garlic in olive oil with the dried mint.

9. Remove the weight and plate from the pot and spoon the garlic mixture into the sauce, shaking the pot to mix. Replace the lid and continue to cook for a further 25 minutes.

10. Taste and adjust seasoning. Serve hot with sauce on the side. (Recipe may be prepared 1 day in advance.)

VARIATIONS

Add ¾ cup/4 oz/115 g cooked or canned chickpeas to the stuffing and reduce the quantity of the peppers by half.

STUFFED MIXED VEGETABLES
Mahshi Mshakal

SERVES 4–6
PREPARATION TIME: 30–35 MINUTES
COOKING TIME: 1½–2 HOURS

This excellent dish has the advantage of combining the various flavors of zucchini, eggplants, and red and green peppers.

1 lb/450 g small zucchini (about 4)
1 lb/450 g baby eggplants (about 7)
1 very large or 2 medium sweet red
    peppers (8 oz/225 g)
1 very large or 2 medium sweet
    green peppers (8 oz/225 g)
1 medium tomato (4½ oz/125 g)

For the stuffing

1½ cups/10 oz/300 g short-grain
    rice, preferably Egyptian
11 oz/300 g lean ground lamb
    or beef
1 tablespoon tomato paste
1 medium tomato, grated
¼ cup/60 ml olive oil
1 teaspoon Aleppo spice mix or
    seven-spice powder
1 teaspoon ground allspice
½ teaspoon ground black pepper
1½ teaspoons salt, or to taste

For the cooking liquid

¼ cup/60 ml tomato paste
½ cup/120 ml lemon juice
2½ teaspoons salt, or to taste
6 garlic cloves (⅔ oz/25 g)
2 teaspoons dried mint

1. Using the tines of a fork, make small grooves along the length of the zucchini (optional). Slice off the zucchini stems. Cut off the green caps and stems of the eggplants. Use a vegetable corer to hollow out the insides of the zucchini and eggplants, leaving a thin shell. Slice off and reserve the tops of the sweet peppers, and remove and discard the seeds and membranes. Slice off and reserve the top of the tomato and core the tomato using a small spoon.

2. Prepare the stuffing: Wash and drain the rice. Mix in the rest of the stuffing ingredients and 6 tablespoons/90 ml water.

3. Stuff each vegetable with the stuffing, pushing it in gently and leaving ½ in/1 cm empty at the opening. Place the reserved tops back on the tomato and peppers to cover the openings.

4. Arrange the stuffed eggplants and zucchini in the base of a large pot. Top with the stuffed peppers. (The stuffed tomato will be added later.)

5. Prepare the cooking liquid: In a large bowl, mix the tomato paste, lemon juice, and salt and add 4 cups/1 liter water.

6. Pour the cooking liquid over the stuffed vegetables and bring to a boil over high heat. Cover the pot, lower the heat, and simmer gently for 1 hour. Uncover, place the stuffed tomato on top of the other stuffed vegetables, and continue to simmer, uncovered, for a further 30–40 minutes.

7. Crush the garlic with the mint and spoon over the cooking liquid. Cook for a further 5 minutes, or until the vegetables are tender and the sauce has thickened slightly. Serve hot.

VARIATIONS

In the cooking liquid, you can replace the lemon juice with verjuice (sour grape juice), and omit the tomato paste.

VEGETARIAN STUFFED SWISS CHARD
Yalanji al-Siliq

SERVES 6
PREPARATION TIME: 40 MINUTES
COOKING TIME: 1 HOUR AND 25 MINUTES

Swiss chard is a flavorful and nutritious green, rich in vitamins and minerals, with a slightly bitter and salty flavor that is quite refined. Chard is popular in the Mediterranean basin, and Aleppians in particular are fond of it: stuffed, as in this recipe or Stuffed Swiss Chard (with meat, p. 211), or as a salad like Swiss Chard Stems in Tahini Sauce (p.106). Vegetarian Stuffed Swiss Chard has sweet, sour, and salty characteristics, making the balance of flavors crucial for the success of the dish. Do taste the sauce and adjust the seasoning to your taste.

3¼ lb/1.5 kg large Swiss chard (to make about 1¾ lb/800 g leaves)
Ice-cold water, for soaking

For the stuffing

1½ cups/10 oz/300 g short-grain rice, washed and drained
2 teaspoons salt, or to taste
1½ cups/7 oz/200 g finely chopped onion
1¼ cups/5 oz/150 g coarsely chopped walnuts
¼ cup/60 ml olive oil
2 tablespoons red pepper paste
2 tablespoons tomato paste
6 tablespoons/90 ml pomegranate molasses
2 tablespoons lemon juice
2 teaspoons Aleppo spice mix or seven-spice powder
1 tablespoon sugar
1 teaspoon ground black pepper

To make the stuffing

1. Place the rice in a pot over high heat with 1½ cups/350 ml water and about half of the salt. Stir the mixture and bring to a boil. Cover the pot, lower the heat, and cook for 15 minutes. Remove from the heat and set aside for 10 minutes. Fluff the rice with a fork and spread it on a tray to cool.

2. Mix the rice with the rest of the stuffing ingredients.

To prepare the leaves

3. Cut off and discard the thick stems and central ribs of the large Swiss chard leaves, leaving you with lengthwise halves. (You can use the discarded stems to make Swiss Chard Stems in Tahini Sauce, p.106.) Cut the coarse stems off any smaller leaves, leaving them whole, and gently pound the central ribs to flatten them.

4. Boil a pot of salted water and blanch the leaves. Transfer to ice-cold water, then to a strainer to drain.

To stuff the leaves

5. Place a cut leaf on a work surface shiny-side down and with the wide end closest to you. Place about 1 tablespoon of the stuffing a few centimeters from the end closest to you (*see* Photo). Fold the wide end of the leaf over the stuffing diagonally to form a rough triangle, and then fold again diagonally in the opposite direction. Continue folding along the leaf, keeping the triangular shape.

6. Neatly layer the stuffed leaves in the base of a pot.

For the cooking liquid

½ cup/120 ml olive oil
2 tablespoons pomegranate
    molasses
2 tablespoons lemon juice
1½ teaspoons sugar
1½ teaspoons salt, or to taste

To cook and serve

1. Mix the cooking liquid ingredients with ½ cup/120 ml water and pour over the rolled leaves. Place the pot over high heat. Place an upturned plate on top of the stuffed leaves in the pot, and a weight on top of the plate. When the mixture comes to a boil, lower the heat, cover the pot, and simmer for 1 hour.

2. Remove the pot from the heat and set aside to cool for about 2 hours. Remove the weight and plate, and flip or spoon the stuffed leaves onto a serving platter.

VARIATIONS

- You can replace the walnuts with ¾ cup/4 oz/115 g cooked or canned chickpeas (half a 14 oz/400 g can) rinsed, drained, and coarsely chopped.
- You can stuff and roll Swiss chard leaves in cigar-shapes (as on p. 210), if preferred.

VEGETARIAN STUFFED EGGPLANT
Mtabbaq Banjane

SERVES 4
PREPARATION TIME: 35 MINUTES
COOKING TIME: 30 MINUTES

There is a great controversy about the origin of this dish: the Greeks claim it as their own, while the Kurds and Armenians are sure it belongs to them. In Turkey it is called *Imam Baylidi* and is considered one of the great classics of Turkish cuisine. *Imam Baylidi* means "the fainted Imam." Some say this is because a revered Imam fainted from the pleasure of eating this dish; while others claim that the frugal Imam fainted when he discovered how much olive oil his wife used in preparing the dish.

In Aleppo, Vegetarian Stuffed Eggplant is prepared with fried eggplants filled with a stuffing of fried onion, peppers, and tomatoes and baked in the oven. It can be served warm or cold.

1¾ lb/800 g baby eggplants (about 8)

2 teaspoons salt, plus more for salting the eggplants

½ cup/120 ml olive oil

1 very small onion (3 oz/80 g), thinly sliced into half-moons

½ cup/2½ oz/70 g finely chopped sweet green pepper

4 garlic cloves (½ oz/15 g), minced

2 tablespoons tomato paste

1½ teaspoons ground allspice

¼–½ teaspoon chili powder

¼ teaspoon cinnamon

¼ teaspoon ground black pepper

4 cups/1½ lb/680 g finely chopped tomatoes

1 teaspoon sugar, or to taste

¼ cup finely chopped parsley

Parsley leaves, to garnish

1. Peel the caps off the eggplants, leaving about ¾ in/2 cm of the stem attached. Peel the eggplant lengthwise in ½ in/1 cm strips, alternating peeled and unpeeled. Sprinkle with salt and set aside in a strainer for 30 minutes.

2. Wipe the eggplants with a paper towel and fry in ¼ cup/60 ml of the olive oil until light golden in color, but still slightly firm. Transfer to a strainer.

3. Place the remaining olive oil in a skillet over medium to low heat and sauté the onion for a few minutes, stirring, until it begins to color. Add the pepper and sauté for a further 30 seconds, stirring well. Add the garlic, tomato paste, allspice, chili powder, cinnamon, and black pepper and cook for a further 30 seconds. Stir in the chopped tomatoes, sugar, and salt.

4. Bring the mixture to a boil, lower the heat, and simmer for 5 minutes. Remove the stuffing from the heat. Add chopped parsley, taste, and adjust the seasoning, if necessary.

5. Preheat the oven to 375°F/190°C.

6. Place about ⅓ cup/75 ml of the onion-tomato stuffing in the base of an ovenproof baking dish.

7. Make a lengthwise slit on the side of each eggplant and gently open it with your fingers. Place the eggplants on the baking dish in one layer, open-side up. Spoon the stuffing into the eggplants and cover the dish with aluminum foil.

8. Bake for 15 minutes. Remove the foil and bake for a further 15 minutes, or until only a little sauce is left, adding a few tablespoons of hot water if the bottom of the dish dries.

9. Remove from the oven and serve at warm or cold, decorated with parsley leaves. (The dish may be prepared 3 days before serving; refrigerate until needed.)

VEGETARIAN MIXED STUFFED VEGETABLES
Yalanji Mshakal

SERVES 10–12
PREPARATION TIME: 35–40 MINUTES
COOKING TIME: 1½ HOURS

Yalanji is a Turkish word that means liar (in Turkish, *yalanji dolma* is the name given to meatless stuffed dishes), alluding to the Turkish origins of the many *yalanji* dishes that have been popular in the Middle East for over a thousand years.

Stuffing a variety of vegetables and cooking them together enhances the taste of each. In this recipe, eggplants, zucchini, vine leaves, and peppers are stuffed and cooked in olive oil and a sweet-and-sour sauce. Some people like to include stuffed tomatoes, onions, and potatoes with the rest of the vegetables. You can use Swiss chard in place of the vine leaves. Vegetarian Stuffed Swiss Chard (p. 228) typically has a different stuffing containing fewer vegetables and more rice, but the stuffing can be used interchangeably with the one below. You can use the removed zucchini flesh to make Zucchini and Garlic in Olive Oil (p. 46), or Zucchini Omelets (p. 65).

1¾ lb/750 g baby zucchini
    (about 15)
1¾ lb/750 g baby eggplants
    (about 18)
7 oz/200 g vine leaves (canned,
    frozen, or *see* p. 31 to prepare
    from fresh)
3 small sweet green peppers
    (8 oz/225 g)
1 small sweet red pepper (2½ oz/75 g)

For the stuffing

1 cup/240 ml olive oil
2 medium onions (1 lb/450 g),
    finely chopped
¼ cup/1 oz/30 g coarsely grated
    carrots
1¼ cups/9 oz/250 g short-grain rice,
    preferably Egyptian, washed
    and drained
1 lb/450 g ripe tomatoes, peeled,
    de-seeded, and puréed (or
    14 oz/400 g can tomato purée)
½ cup/2½ oz/70 g finely chopped
    sweet green pepper
2 cups/4 oz/115 g chopped parsley
¼ cup/½ oz/15 g chopped mint

1. Cut the ends off the zucchini and eggplants. Using the tines of a fork, make small lengthwise grooves in the skin of the zucchini (optional). Hollow out the zucchini and eggplants with the help of a corer or peeler, leaving thin shells.

2. Rinse and drain the vine leaves and remove the stalks. Cut any very large leaves in half.

3. Cut off and reserve the tops of the sweet peppers. Hollow out the insides using a small knife.

4. Heat the olive oil in a large pan and fry the onion and grated carrots over low heat until the onion is translucent. Add the rice and fry for 2 minutes more.

5. Add the puréed tomatoes and the rest of the stuffing ingredients. Remove the pan from the heat.

6. Place the stuffing in a strainer over a bowl to cool and drain, reserving the liquid to add it to the cooking liquid later.

7. Loosely fill the zucchini and eggplants with the stuffing, leaving ½ in/1 cm empty at the opening.

8. Next, stuff the vine leaves: Place one leaf (or half) on your work surface, shiny side down, and place about 1 teaspoon of the stuffing in a sausage-shape near the stem end. Fold the sides over the stuffing, and tightly roll like a cigarette toward the top of the leaf, folding in the sides as you go (*see* Photo on p. 212). Continue with the rest of the leaves and stuffing.

continued overleaf

5–6 tablespoons/75–90 ml
  pomegranate molasses

¼ cup/60 ml lemon juice

1 tablespoon sugar

½ teaspoon ground Turkish coffee or
  instant coffee granules (optional)

1¼ cups/5 oz/150 g coarsely
  chopped walnuts

1 teaspoon ground black pepper

2 teaspoons salt, or to taste

For the cooking liquid

2 tablespoons lemon juice

2 tablespoons pomegranate
  molasses

1½ teaspoons salt, or to taste

9. Loosely fill the peppers, covering them with the reserved tops.

10. Arrange the vegetables in a pot, layering the zucchini and eggplants first, and then the vine leaves (or these can be cooked separately; *see* Variations). Arrange the sweet peppers, upright, on top.

11. Pour the cooking liquid ingredients into the pot with ½ cup/ 120 ml water and the drained stuffing liquid, and bring to a boil over high heat. Lower the heat to a gentle simmer, cover the pot, and cook for 1½ hours.

12. Remove the pot from the heat and set aside until cooled. (This dish keeps well for one week in the refrigerator.)

VARIATIONS

You can cook the stuffed vine leaves separately from the zucchini and eggplants using half of the cooking liquid. Place a plate on top of the vine leaves in a small pot, and top with a weight before covering. Once cooked, cool and carefully flip onto a serving platter, maintaining the shape of the pot.

VEGETABLE
MAIN DISHES

GREEN BEANS IN OIL
Fasoliah Khadra bi-Zeit (Fawleh bi-Zeit)

SERVES 4–6
PREPARATION TIME: 20 MINUTES
COOKING TIME: 35–40 MINUTES

Fasoliah Khadra, or *fawleh*, is the variety of wide, flat green bean used in Aleppo. Similar to Romano or runner beans, they are often more expensive and lend themselves better to slow cooking. This is a nutritious, easy-to-prepare dish of green beans and tomatoes cooked in olive oil with garlic, and served with Arabic flatbread to mop up the exquisite juices. If preferred, you can substitute French or string beans in this dish. You can find a similar dish with meat on p. 252.

2 lb/1 kg Romano beans
    (or any wide, flat green beans)
⅓ cup/75 ml olive oil
1 cup/5 oz/150 g thinly sliced onion
5 garlic cloves (¾ oz/20 g), crushed
3 tablespoons tomato paste
    (if using fresh tomatoes)
1 tablespoon red pepper paste
    (optional)
1½ teaspoons ground allspice
2 teaspoons ground coriander
½ teaspoon ground black pepper
1 teaspoon sugar
2 teaspoons salt, or to taste
2 lb/1 kg ripe tomatoes, peeled and
    chopped or 28 oz/800 g can
    chopped tomatoes

1. Wash the beans, then snap off the ends using your fingers, and remove any stringy threads that run along the length of the beans. Cut the beans in half lengthwise.

2. Heat the olive oil in a pot and fry the onions briefly over medium heat. Add crushed garlic, tomato paste (if using), red pepper paste, allspice, coriander, black pepper, sugar, and salt and fry for a few seconds more.

3. Mix in the chopped tomatoes and green beans. If using canned tomatoes, add ¾ cup/180 ml water. Stir the mixture and let it come to a boil.

4. Lower the heat to very low, cover the pot, and simmer gently for 35 minutes, or until the beans are tender. Taste and adjust the seasoning. Serve warm or cold.

OKRA IN OIL
Bamia bi-Zeit

SERVES 4–6
PREPARATION TIME: 10–15 MINUTES
COOKING TIME: 30–35 MINUTES

The traditional way to prepare this recipe requires frying the okra, onion, and garlic, but the method below is healthier and easier to prepare, and the result is as delicious. (*See* p. 343 for more information about okra.) I serve this dish with scallions, radish slices, and Arabic flatbread.

2 lb/1 kg small fresh okra,
    1–2½ in/3–6 cm in length (or use
    frozen, canned, or dried okra)
2 lb/1 kg large ripe tomatoes (5–6),
    peeled and chopped
1 small onion (4 oz/115 g),
    thickly sliced
6 garlic cloves (⅔ oz/25 g), peeled
1 cup/2 oz/60 g finely chopped
    cilantro
6 tablespoons/90 ml olive oil
3 tablespoons pomegranate
    molasses
3 tablespoons lemon juice
2 tablespoons tomato paste
½ teaspoon ground cumin
¼ teaspoon ground allspice
¼ teaspoon ground coriander
    (optional)
¼ teaspoon cinnamon
¼ teaspoon ground black pepper
1½ teaspoons salt, or to taste

1. Wash the okra, peel the caps, and cut off the hard stems with a sharp knife so that the top resembles a pyramid. Be careful not to pierce the vegetable flesh or the sauce will become undesirably slimy.

2. Place the okra in boiling salted water and boil over high heat for two minutes, then drain (this is to guard against the slimy texture. Alternatively, the okra can be fried in vegetable oil).

3. In a medium-size pot, combine the drained okra, chopped tomatoes, onion, garlic, and chopped cilantro.

4. In a bowl, combine the rest of the ingredients, and pour the mixture into the pot with the okra.

5. Place the pot over high heat and bring to a boil. Lower the heat to simmer, cover the pot, and cook over low heat for 30 minutes without stirring.

6. Uncover and let cook for another few minutes until the okra is cooked and the sauce has thickened.

7. Remove from the heat and set aside until cooled. (Recipe may be prepared 2 days before serving.)

8. Turn onto a platter and serve cold.

EGGPLANTS IN OIL
Bajane Makmoor

SERVES 4–6
PREPARATION TIME: 20 MINUTES
RESTING TIME: 30 MINUTES
COOKING TIME: 25–30 MINUTES

Eggplants in Oil is a very refreshing summer dish reminiscent of the French ratatouille and the Lebanese or Palestinian *mousaka'a*.

The Arabic word *makmoor* is derived from *maghmoore*, meaning immersed; here the eggplants are cooked immersed in tomato sauce. Serve this dish with Kibbeh with Walnut Stuffing (p. 172) or Pan-Baked Kibbeh (p. 177), with hot peppers on the side.

1½ lb/700 g long, slim eggplants
Peanut or vegetable oil,
    for shallow frying
4 ripe tomatoes (1½ lb/700 g)
6 tablespoons/90 ml olive oil
1 medium-large onion (10 oz/300 g),
    thickly sliced
2 medium sweet red peppers
    (8 oz/225 g), finely chopped
2 medium sweet green peppers
    (8 oz/225 g), finely chopped
5 garlic cloves (¾ oz/20 g), minced
9 garlic cloves (1½ oz/40 g), peeled,
    halved if large
2 tablespoons tomato paste
1 teaspoon sugar
1½ teaspoons salt, or to taste
¼–½ teaspoon ground black pepper
Parsley leaves, to garnish

1. Prepare the eggplants: Cut off and discard the green caps and stems, then peel off strips of skin at intervals of about ½ in/1 cm.

2. Cut in half lengthwise, sprinkle with salt, and leave to sweat for 30 minutes in a strainer or on absorbent paper towels.

3. Wipe the eggplants with paper towels and fry in hot oil until golden. Remove and set aside.

4. Grate the tomatoes, leaving the skin behind, or peel and purée in a food processor.

5. In a large pot, heat the olive oil over medium heat and sauté the onions and red and green peppers until tender, stirring a few times. Add the crushed garlic and fry briefly.

6. Mix in the peeled garlic cloves, tomato paste, ¼ cup/60 ml water, sugar, salt, and black pepper and bring to a boil.

7. Place the fried eggplants in the pot on top of the peppers and onions. Cover the pot and cook over very low heat for about 25 minutes. Uncover and continue cooking to reduce the sauce, if necessary. Set aside to cool.

8. Arrange the eggplants and some of the sauce on a platter, top with the rest of the vegetables, garnish with parsley leaves, and serve cold.

VARIATIONS

You can substitute regular eggplants for the long, slim variety: Prepare as in step 1 and cut into 1½ in/4 cm cubes. Proceed as above.

ISTANBUL ARTICHOKES
Shawki Stambooli

SERVES 5 AS A MAIN DISH OR 10 AS AN APPETIZER
PREPARATION TIME: 15 MINUTES
COOKING TIME: 15–20 MINUTES

This recipe originated in Istanbul, the largest city in Turkey, where it is cooked with the addition of dill. It is a delightful and colorful dish ideal for light eaters.

1 lb/450 g pearl onions
    (or 2 medium sweet onions, chopped)
2 tablespoons all-purpose flour
2–3 teaspoons sugar
1½ teaspoons salt, or to taste
14 large artichoke bottoms
    (2 lb/1 kg; *see* p. 14 to prepare from fresh)
1 lb/450 g carrots, peeled, cut into ¼ in/½ cm rounds
¼ cup/60 ml olive oil
¼–½ teaspoon ground white pepper
¼–⅓ cup/60–90 ml lemon juice
Parsley leaves, to garnish

1. Boil the pearl onions in a large pot of water over medium heat for 1–2 minutes. Drain and immediately plunge in cold water for a few seconds. Drain and peel the onions, leaving the root base intact (or cut off the untidy ends).

2. In a large pot, combine 6 cups/1.5 liters of water, the flour, sugar, and salt and bring to a boil, stirring, over medium heat.

3. Add the artichoke bottoms, carrots, onions, olive oil, and white pepper. When the mixture comes to a boil again, lower the heat and simmer, uncovered, for 15 minutes, shaking the pot from time to time.

4. Add the lemon juice in the last 5 minutes of cooking, and simmer until the sauce is reduced to about ¾ cup/180 ml (if the onions or artichokes become tender before the sauce thickens, remove and set them aside while you reduce the sauce). Taste and add more salt or lemon juice if needed (return the vegetables to the pot at this time and heat through) before removing from the heat.

5. Place the artichoke bottoms on a serving platter and spoon in the rest of the ingredients. Garnish with parsley and serve warm or cold.

VARIATIONS

Green peas may be added, if desired. Add about ½ cup/2½ oz/ 70 g frozen peas 5 minutes before the end of cooking time.

PURSLANE WITH YOGURT
Baqleh bi-Laban (Fattet Baqleh)

SERVES 4–6
PREPARATION TIME: 30–35 MINUTES
COOKING TIME: 10–15 MINUTES

This dish has ancient origins and was originally only made with purslane and yogurt. With time, it gradually evolved to include bread and eggplants. It became a hearty main dish, no doubt influenced by the many *fatteh* dishes from Damascus, in which bread and yogurt are the main ingredients, along with a variety of cooked meats, vegetables, and grains. This dish is often called *Fattet Baqleh*. In it, fried bread is layered with fried eggplant and topped with yogurt and purslane leaves.

Purslane grows wild in many regions and can be found at some farmers' markets or grocery stores. Alternatively, you can use baby spinach or arugula in this recipe.

2 lb/1 kg eggplant (1–2)

1½ teaspoons salt, plus more for
salting the eggplants

1 large loaf Arabic flatbread
(4½ oz/125 g), cut into
1½ in/3 cm squares

Peanut or vegetable oil,
for deep-frying

2 cups/1 lb/450 g plain yogurt,
at room temperature

3 garlic cloves (½ oz/15 g), crushed

1 teaspoon Aleppo spice mix or
seven-spice powder

½ teaspoon dried mint

1 bunch purslane to make
2 oz/60 g cleaned leaves

Pinch Aleppo pepper, to garnish

1. Peel the eggplant and cut into 1½ in/4 cm cubes (these shrink when fried). Place in a strainer and sprinkle with salt. Set aside for 30 minutes.

2. Deep-fry the bread in hot oil until golden and crisp. Remove with a slotted spoon into a deep serving platter with 1½ in/3 cm sides (I used a rectangular dish 11 x 8 in/27 x 19 cm).

3. Wipe the eggplants with a paper towel and deep-fry in the same hot oil. Remove with a slotted spoon and set aside to drain.

4. Mix the yogurt with the crushed garlic and the salt. (Recipe may be prepared to this stage a few hours in advance. Keep the ingredients covered at room temperature, but refrigerate the yogurt until about 15 minutes before serving.)

5. Just before serving: Cover the bread with the fried eggplants and sprinkle with Aleppo spice mix or seven-spice powder and dried mint. Pour the room-temperature yogurt over the eggplants and distribute the purslane leaves on top. Sprinkle with Aleppo pepper. Serve warm or cold.

VARIATIONS

To serve this dish warm, heat the yogurt before adding the garlic. Assemble the dish before the eggplant cools.

FRIED SWISS CHARD
Siliq Mqalla

SERVES 4
PREPARATION TIME: 15 MINUTES
COOKING TIME: 8 MINUTES

This is a simple dish of Swiss chard fried in olive oil with onion, garlic, and herbs. It is typically served cold with Arabic flatbread.

1¾ lb/750 g Swiss chard
⅓ cup/75 ml olive oil
1½ cups/8 oz/225 g finely
    chopped onions
4 garlic cloves (½ oz/15 g), crushed
1 tablespoon red pepper paste
    (or tomato paste with a pinch
    of cayenne pepper)
1 tablespoon dried mint
Dash ground black pepper
1 teaspoon salt, or to taste
½ cup/1 oz/30 g finely
    chopped parsley
Lemon slices

1. Wash and dry the Swiss chard, and separate the leaves from the stems. Remove the threads that cling to the stems: with a small knife, cut away a slice of the stem and pull the threads along the length of the stem. Repeat from other side as necessary.

2. Chop the stems crosswise into thin slices.

3. Cut the leaves in half lengthwise, if large, and chop into ¾ in/2 cm pieces.

4. Place the olive oil in a medium-size pot and fry the onions over medium to low heat until tender. Add the garlic and sauté for a few more seconds.

5. Raise the heat, add the Swiss chard stems, and sauté for 4 minutes, stirring. Add the leaves and continue to stir until most of the liquid has evaporated.

6. Stir in the red pepper paste, dried mint, and black pepper and sauté for a further minute. Taste and add the salt.

7. Remove the pot from the heat and mix in the chopped parsley.

8. Spoon onto a serving platter and serve cold with lemon slices and Arabic flatbread.

LENTILS WITH BULGAR AND CARAMELIZED ONION
Mjaddaret Burghol

SERVES 6 AS A MAIN DISH OR 12 AS PART OF A MEZZE
PREPARATION TIME: 15 MINUTES
COOKING TIME: 30 MINUTES
RESTING TIME: 20 MINUTES

This healthy vegetarian dish is prepared with three main ingredients—lentils, bulgar, and onions—and a good amount of olive oil. It is best served with salad, pickles, radish slices, and yogurt. In Aleppo, Christians customarily serve this dish the first day of Lent, along with Red Lentil and Lemon Soup (p. 82).

Like all legumes, lentils are rich in protein and starch and a good source of B vitamins. However, they do contain phytic acid, which interferes with the absorption of iron, zinc, calcium, and magnesium, which is a particular problem for gout sufferers. This can be remedied when lentils are eaten with foods containing vitamin C, so I serve this dish with Garden Tomato Salad (p. 95). You can find white lentils in Middle Eastern or South Asian grocery stores. You can also replace the bulgar with short-grain rice.

1 medium onion (8 oz/225 g),
    cut into thin wedges
1 tablespoon salt, or to taste
2¼ cups/15 oz/425 g broad white
    lentils (or use brown lentils),
    washed and drained
¾ cup/180 ml olive oil
1 cup/6 oz/170 g coarse bulgar,
    washed and squeezed dry
¼ teaspoon ground black pepper
Mint leaves and tomato slices,
    to garnish (optional)

1. Sprinkle the onions with 1 teaspoon of the salt, place them on paper towels, and set aside for 15 minutes. Squeeze the onions to remove any remaining moisture.

2. In a large pot, combine the lentils with 6 cups/1.5 liters water and bring to a boil over high heat, skimming off the foam that forms on the surface. Lower the heat and cook the lentils uncovered for 15 minutes, or until they are tender but still slightly firm.

3. Drain the cooking liquid from the lentils into a wide-mouthed pot. Reduce by boiling the liquid until it measures 1½ cups/350 ml (or add water if it is not enough). Set aside.

4. Fry the onions in olive oil over medium heat, stirring constantly, until crisp, brown, and caramelized. Drain immediately, reserving the oil.

5. Add the bulgar to the lentils, along with the reduced cooking liquid. Season with the remaining salt and the black pepper.

6. Bring to a boil over medium heat, cover the pot, and lower the heat to simmer for 15 minutes, or until all the liquid is absorbed.

7. Remove the pot from the heat and set aside for 20 minutes, allowing the bulgar to absorb any remaining moisture.

8. Taste the lentils and adjust the seasoning, if necessary. Mix in half the onions and the reserved oil.

9. Garnish with the rest of the onions and the mint leaves and tomato, if using. Serve hot or warm as a main dish, or at room temperature as part of a mezze.

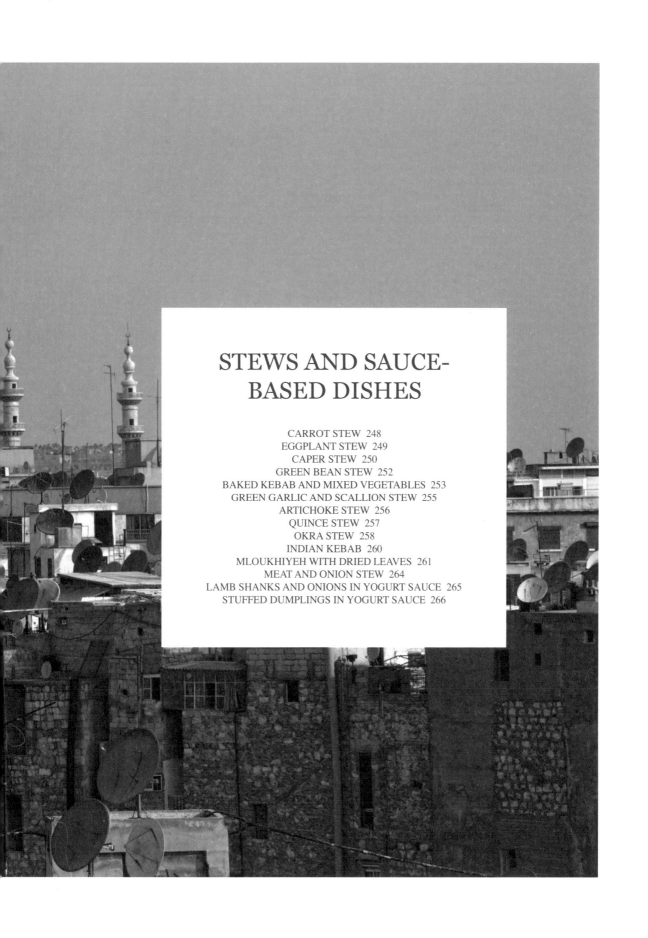

STEWS AND SAUCE-
BASED DISHES

CARROT STEW
Msaqa'et Jazar

SERVES 4–6
PREPARATION TIME: 15 MINUTES
COOKING TIME: 30 MINUTES–1 HOUR

This dish is also known by the name *jazariyeh*. Black carrots are slightly sweeter and tougher to cook than regular carrots. They are not common worldwide but are plentiful in Aleppo. This dish can also be made with orange or purple carrots; it will change the vivid color of the dish but not the flavor. Serve it with rice.

¼ cup/60 ml olive oil

1 small onion (4 oz/115 g),
    finely chopped

2 lb/1 kg black carrots (or use
    orange or purple carrots),
    peeled and sliced

2½ cups/600ml Basic Meat Stock,
    including meat (p. 20),
    or any lamb or beef stock

1 tablespoon tomato paste

¼–⅓ cup/60–75 ml pomegranate
    molasses

2 teaspoons sugar

1½ teaspoons Aleppo spice mix or
    seven-spice powder

½ teaspoon ground black pepper

1½ teaspoons salt, or to taste

1. Heat the oil in a medium pot over low heat. Fry the onion until translucent.

2. Raise the heat to high, add the carrots, and sauté for 1 minute. Pour in the stock and the rest of the ingredients (except for the reserved meat) and mix well.

3. Bring the mixture to a boil, lower the heat, and simmer until the carrots are tender (about 20 minutes, uncovered, for orange or purple carrots; 45 minutes, covered, for black carrots).

4. Add the reserved meat (if using) and bring to a boil again until just heated through. Taste and adjust the seasoning. Serve hot.

VARIATIONS

If using ready-made stock, you can add 8 oz/225 g ground lamb or beef in step 1.

EGGPLANT STEW
Msaqa'et Banjane

SERVES 4
PREPARATION TIME: 10 MINUTES
RESTING TIME: 30 MINUTES
COOKING TIME: 20 MINUTES

This is an easy-to-prepare dish of eggplant, ground meat, onion, and chickpeas. It is served hot with rice or eaten with Arabic flatbread.

1¾ lb/800 g eggplants (1–2)

½ teaspoon salt, plus more for
    salting the eggplants

Peanut or vegetable oil, for
    deep-frying

2 tablespoons olive oil

1 small onion (4 oz/115 g),
    finely chopped

7 oz/200 g lean ground lamb or beef

½ teaspoon Aleppo spice mix or
    seven-spice powder

¼ teaspoon ground black pepper

1 cup/5½ oz/160 g cooked or canned
    chickpeas

1. Peel the eggplant in lengthwise stripes, leaving alternate strips of ½ in/1 cm. Cut into 1½ in/4 cm cubes and sprinkle with salt. Place in a strainer for 30 minutes.

2. Dry the cubes with a paper towel. Deep-fry in the oil and transfer to a strainer. Alternatively, coat the cubes in 2 tablespoons of the oil and grill or broil until tender, turning them once. Set aside.

3. In a large pan, heat the olive oil over medium heat and sauté the onion, stirring until tender. Raise the heat; add the meat, spice mix, black pepper, and salt. Continue stirring until meat browns but does not dry out.

4. Add 1 cup/240 ml water, stir the mixture, and bring to a boil. Lower the heat and simmer, uncovered, for 7 minutes. Mix in the eggplant cubes and chickpeas. Taste and adjust seasoning, if necessary. Serve hot.

VARIATIONS: ZUCCHINI STEW (*MSAQA'ET KOOSA*)

Replace the eggplants with the same measure of zucchini, sliced into rounds. Omit the chickpeas and add 3 tablespoons chopped parsley in step 4, reserving some to garnish, if desired. Serve with rice or Arabic flatbread and Garlic Yogurt (p. 98)

CAPER STEW

Qabbar wa Roz

SERVES 6–8
PREPARATION TIME: 10–15 MINUTES
RESTING TIME: 10–24 HOURS
COOKING TIME: 30 MINUTES

Capers, cultivated in Western Europe, are the unripe flower buds that grow on the new branches of caper shrubs. Before flowering, they range in size from that of a pea to that of an olive. They contain a high amount of rutin: a well-known antioxidant, the medicinal value of which was recognized by the early Greeks and Romans. They have a sharp flavor and a distinctive aroma.

Capers are easy to find in supermarkets pickled in vinegar, oil, or less frequently in brine or sea salt. The latter is by far the best way to preserve capers and a must for the recipe below, as they retain their firmness and flavor better than vinegar- or oil-preserved capers. Look for these in Armenian or Middle Eastern grocery stores, if they are unavailable in your local grocery store.

This dish is very much Aleppian. It is traditionally prepared with lamb shanks, but you can omit the meat and use ready-made stock to reduce the cooking time. The capers impart a unique flavor to the dish, which is best served with Rice Pilaf with Vermicelli (p. 110) and lemon slices. They will need to soak overnight.

2 lb/1 kg capers preserved in salt
½ cup/120 ml oil
1 small onion (4 oz/115 g),
    finely chopped
3 tablespoons flour
3½ cups/830 ml Basic Meat Stock,
    including meat (p. 20), or any
    lamb or beef stock
2 teaspoons Dijon mustard
½ teaspoon ground black pepper
5–6 tablespoons/75–90 ml lemon
    juice, or to taste
1 teaspoon salt, if needed
Lemon slices, to garnish

To prepare the capers

1. Wash capers in a bowl to rinse away the salt. Soak for 10–24 hours in several changes of water. Drain.

2. Bring a large pot of water to a rolling boil over high heat. Add the capers; when the water comes to a boil again, the capers will start rising to the top. Count to 10 and remove the pot from the heat. Drain the capers and rinse under cold running water.

To make the stew

3. Heat the oil over low heat and sauté the onions until tender (8–10 minutes). Add the flour and continue to fry, stirring well until it starts to color.

4. Raise the heat to medium and pour the stock gradually over the onion and flour mixture, stirring until the mixture comes to a boil.

5. Add the capers and reserved meat (if using) and cook for 10 minutes. Add the mustard and black pepper and cook for a further minute. Add the lemon juice and the salt, if necessary. Serve hot, with lemon slices alongside.

GREEN BEAN STEW
Fawleh bi-Lahem (Fasoliah Khadra)

SERVES 4–6
PREPARATION TIME: 15 MINUTES
COOKING TIME: 30 MINUTES

In Arab cooking, *fawleh* or *fasoliah khadra*, a wide, flat variety of green bean, is favored over the thin French variety. They are similar to Romano or runner beans and lend themselves better to slow cooking. Here, they are paired with meat and tomatoes to make an excellent, substantial family meal. The recipe can be prepared with coarsely ground meat to cut down the cooking time (*see* Variations). You can find a similar vegetarian dish on p. 236.

2 lb/1 kg Romano beans (if not available, French green beans will do)

¼ cup/60 ml olive or vegetable oil

1 small onion (4 oz/115 g), finely chopped

5 garlic cloves (¾ oz/20 g), crushed

1 teaspoon ground allspice

1 tablespoon ground coriander

¼ teaspoon ground black pepper

1¼ cups/300 ml Basic Meat Stock, including meat (p. 20), or any meat or vegetable stock (*see* Variations)

14 oz/400 g can crushed tomatoes with their juice

1 teaspoon sugar

2 teaspoons salt, or to taste

1. Wash the green beans and snap off the ends with your fingers, removing the stringy threads that run along the length of the beans. Cut in half.

2. In a large pot, heat the oil over medium heat and briefly sauté the onion, stirring. Stir in crushed garlic, allspice, coriander, and black pepper.

3. Add the stock (with the meat, if using), tomatoes, green beans, sugar, and salt. Bring the mixture to a boil.

4. Lower heat to very low, cover the pot, and gently simmer for about 20 minutes, or until the beans are tender. Taste and adjust the seasoning, if necessary.

5. Serve hot. This dish can be prepared up to 2 days in advance.

VARIATIONS

If using ready-made stock, you can add 8 oz/225 g ground lamb or beef in step 2.

BAKED KEBAB AND MIXED VEGETABLES
Lahmeh bi-Furon

SERVES 6
PREPARATION TIME: 10 MINUTES
COOKING TIME: 50 MINUTES

In this dish, an assortment of vegetables are baked with sour apple and green plums in a tomato sauce and topped with spiced meat patties. It is an easy-to-prepare family meal, which is as delicious with or without the meat. I serve this dish with rice or bulgar, Arabic flatbread, and sliced radishes and scallions. You can half or double this recipe if needed—it freezes well and makes great leftovers.

For the vegetables

1 lb/450 g small zucchini

12 oz/350 g small eggplants

5 oz/150 g green beans

½ medium potato (3½ oz/100 g),
    peeled, chopped, and soaked in
    water until use

1 medium sweet red pepper
    (4 oz/115 g), seeded, chopped

1 medium sweet green pepper
    (4 oz/115 g), seeded, chopped

1¾ lb/800 g tomatoes, peeled,
    seeded, and quartered

1 medium onion (8 oz/225 g),
    thinly sliced

1 teaspoons ground allspice

½ teaspoon ground white pepper

2 tablespoons tomato paste

½ tart apple such as Granny Smith,
    peeled and chopped (optional)

4 oz/115 g green plums (*janarik*; if in
    season, or use greengage plums;
    optional)

1½ teaspoons salt, or to taste

For the kebab

8 oz/225 g lean finely ground lamb
    or beef (pulse in a food processor
    to achieve a fine texture)

1 teaspoons Aleppo spice mix or
    seven-spice powder

½ teaspoon salt, or to taste

1. Cut the tops off the zucchini. Using the tines of a fork, make lengthwise grooves in the skin (optional) and slice.

2. Cut off the tops of the eggplants. With a potato peeler or sharp knife, peel off thin strips of the skin lengthwise, at intervals of about ½ in/1 cm. Chop into bite-size pieces.

3. Trim the ends of the green beans, removing the string, if necessary, and chop.

4. In a large pot, combine the zucchini and eggplants with all of the remaining ingredients for the vegetables. Bring to a boil over medium heat, stirring occasionally with a wooden spoon. Lower the heat and simmer for 10 minutes.

5. Spoon into an ovenproof dish and bake for 25 minutes at 400°F/200°C.

6. Meanwhile, make the kebab: mix the ground meat with the spices and salt and form into 16 thin patties.

7. Place the patties on top of the vegetables and bake for a further 15 minutes. Serve hot.

GREEN GARLIC AND SCALLION STEW
Haloob

SERVES 4–6
PREPARATION TIME: 15 MINUTES
COOKING TIME: 20 MINUTES

The name of this dish, *Haloob*, has origins in the Syriac language, once used across the Fertile Crescent. In Arabic, the word is connected to the word *halaba*, meaning "to extract," which refers to the flavor of the dish that is extracted from the green garlic and scallions. This is an ancient recipe originating from the bordering regions of Syria and Turkey.

Whatever the origin of the recipe or meaning of its name, the sweet-and-sour flavor of this dish is highly enjoyable. The dish is seasonal; prepared in spring when the tender green garlic shoots are harvested while the plants are still very young. The result is a fresh, light garlic flavor. Serve this dish with rice or bulgar on the side.

3 tablespoons vegetable oil

1 small onion (4 oz/115 g),
    finely chopped

1 teaspoon Aleppo spice mix or
    seven-spice powder

2¾ cups/650 ml Basic Meat Stock,
    including meat (p. 20), or any
    meat or vegetable stock

8 oz/225 g green garlic (1 bunch),
    cut into 1½ in/4 cm lengths

1 lb/450 g scallions (4 bunches),
    cut into 1½ in/4 cm lengths

⅓ cup/75 ml red wine vinegar

1 tablespoon tomato paste

⅓ cup/75 ml grape molasses
    (in liquid form) or honey

5 garlic cloves (¾ oz/20 g),
    sliced lengthwise

1 teaspoon salt, or to taste

1. In a medium pot, heat the oil over medium heat and sauté the onion, stirring, until translucent. Add the spice mix, stock, and the green garlic. Bring to a boil, lower the heat, and simmer for 8 minutes.

2. Add the scallions, red wine vinegar, tomato paste, grape molasses or honey, and sliced garlic. Taste and add salt to your liking. Add the meat from the stock (if using), stir, cover the pot, and simmer for a further 10 minutes. Serve hot.

ARTICHOKE STEW
Shawki wa-Roz

SERVES 6
PREPARATION TIME: 10 MINUTES
COOKING TIME: 1–2 HOURS

Tender green artichokes come to the market in early spring in Aleppo, and the season lasts for a few months. In the US, they are mainly grown in California and you can find them year-round, but the peak seasons are spring and fall. They contain 16 essential nutrients and are low in calories.

    Artichoke stew requires little preparation if you buy frozen artichoke bottoms. These are quite good, but fresh artichokes are superior in flavor. If you have the time and patience, get fresh artichokes and prepare them yourself (*see* p. 14). Serve this dish with rice on the side.

⅓ cup/75 ml olive oil

1 small onion (4 oz/115 g),
    finely chopped, or sliced
    into half-moons

2 tablespoons all-purpose flour

½ teaspoon ground allspice

½ teaspoon ground white pepper

¼ teaspoon cinnamon

1 teaspoon salt, or to taste

4 cups/1 liter Basic Meat Stock,
    including meat (p. 20),
    or any lamb or beef stock

12 large artichoke bottoms
    (1½ lb/700 g), quartered

3 tablespoons lemon juice,
    or to taste

1. In a large pot, heat the oil over medium heat and fry the onions until they soften but do not color. Add the flour, allspice, white pepper, cinnamon, and salt and continue to fry, stirring to prevent the flour from browning.

2. Raise the heat and gradually pour the meat stock over the onion-flour mixture. Stir continuously until the mixture comes to a boil.

3. Add the artichoke bottoms. Cover the pot, lower the heat, and simmer for 20 minutes, or until they are tender.

4. Add the lemon juice and the cooked meat from the stock (if using), bring back to a boil, lower the heat, and cook for a few more minutes. Taste and adjust the seasoning, if necessary, then remove from the heat. Serve hot.

VARIATIONS

To give the stew a more vibrant color, you can add a handful of chopped Romaine lettuce with the artichoke bottoms.

QUINCE STEW
Safarjaliyeh

SERVES 4–6
PREPARATION TIME: 10–15 MINUTES
COOKING TIME: 35 MINUTES–1½ HOURS

Quince looks like a rugged yellow apple (*see* Photo on p. 197). It has hard flesh and many seeds in the center. It is too sour and astringent to eat raw, but when cooked, it turns pink and develops an exquisite fragrance.

Quince is mainly used in preserves and jams, but is popular in Aleppo, as well as in Turkey, Iran, and Morocco, as the basis of a stew. In the recipe below, the quince blends with the juices of sour pomegranate, crushed garlic, meat, and a sprinkling of mint, leading to an exceptional culinary experience. Serve this dish with rice.

1 lb 10 oz/750 g quince with skin on

1½ cups/350 ml Basic Meat Stock, including meat (p. 20)

1½ cups/350 ml sour pomegranate juice (*see* p. 24)

1 tablespoon sugar, or to taste

5 garlic cloves (¾ oz/20 g), crushed

1 tablespoon pomegranate molasses

2 teaspoons tomato paste

½ teaspoon ground allspice

¼ teaspoon ground black pepper

1½ teaspoons dried mint

1 teaspoon salt, or to taste

1. Clean the quince and chop into 1–1½ in/2½–3 cm chunks, discarding seeds and the hard core (*see* p. 27 for more).

2. In a large pot, combine the stock with the rest of the ingredients except the reserved meat and quince. Bring to a boil over high heat; then lower the heat and simmer, uncovered, for 2 minutes. Taste and adjust seasoning.

3. Add the quince and reserved meat to the pot and cook for a few minutes, or until the quince is almost tender. (To thicken the broth, you can crush a few pieces of cooked quince with a spoon and mix them back into the pot. Simmer for a few minutes to heat through.)

4. Spoon into a serving dish and serve hot.

NOTES

To cut down on preparation time, you can use 1½ cups/350 ml ready-made meat stock, without stewing meat, but this makes for a less hearty stew.

OKRA STEW
Bamia bi-Lahem

SERVES 6–8
PREPARATION TIME: 20–25 MINUTES
COOKING TIME: 1 HOUR AND 15 MINUTES

Here is another excellent main dish, prepared with baby okra and tomato sauce. It is differentiated from the Lebanese version by the use of red pepper paste, which adds color and depth of flavor. You can use frozen okra if fresh is unavailable (do not defrost before cooking). Use the traditional lamb or beef stock on p. 20 to enhance the dish with meat.

2 lb/1 kg small okra
    (each about 1–2 in/3–6 cm long)
¾ cup/180 ml vegetable oil
4 cups/1 liter Basic Meat Stock,
    including meat (p. 20), or any
    meat or vegetable stock
6 tablespoons/90 ml olive oil
1 very small onion (3 oz/85 g),
    finely chopped
2–3 tablespoons tomato paste
1 tablespoon red pepper paste
½ teaspoon ground allspice
1 teaspoon ground coriander
¼ teaspoon ground black pepper
6 garlic cloves (⅔ oz/25 g), crushed
1 cup/1½ oz/40 g finely chopped
    cilantro
1 lb/450 g ripe tomatoes, peeled and
    puréed in a food processor
2 tablespoons lemon juice
1½ teaspoons salt, or to taste

1. Wash and drain the okra. Using a sharp knife, carefully cut the cap in a pyramid shape without puncturing the cap or cutting the pod itself (cutting into the cap or pod will impart an undesirable slimy texture to the stew).

2. In a medium-size pot, heat the vegetable oil over high heat. Fry the okra in 2 batches, about 3 minutes each batch. With a slotted spoon, transfer to a strainer or a plate lined with paper towels to drain.

3. In a large pot, heat the olive oil over low heat and sauté the onion until tender. Add the tomato and red pepper pastes, allspice, coriander, black pepper, garlic, and cilantro and fry for 1 minute more, stirring well.

4. Add the okra, crushed tomatoes, stock (with the meat, if using), lemon juice, and salt. Raise the heat and bring to a boil. Cover the pot, lower the heat, and simmer for 1 hour, or until the okra is tender. Serve hot.

VARIATIONS

You can broil the okra instead of deep-frying it: lightly brush with oil and cook until just tender, turning once.

INDIAN KEBAB
Kabab Hindi

SERVES 4
PREPARATION TIME: 10–15 MINUTES
COOKING TIME: 25 MINUTES

This dish is an ancient recipe of Persian origin. It is popular in Aleppo, where it is known as *Kabab Hindi*, but it is quite prevalent throughout the Arab world, where it is also known by the name *Dawood Basha*.

In the Turkish version of this dish, *Izmir Koftesi*, the meat is mixed with garlic, onion, and egg and formed into finger-shaped kebabs. It is delicious served with rice.

For the kebab

8 oz/225 g finely ground lamb or
    beef (pulse in a food processor
    to achieve a fine texture)
¾ teaspoon Aleppo spice mix or
    seven-spice powder
1 tablespoon breadcrumbs
    (optional but helps the kebab
    hold their shape)
½ teaspoon salt

For the sauce

¼ cup/60 ml vegetable oil
1½ cups/6 oz/170 g thinly sliced
    onion
4 garlic cloves (½ oz/15 g),
    thinly sliced
2¼ cups/20 oz/600 g tomato purée
1 tablespoon pomegranate molasses
½ teaspoon ground allspice
¼ teaspoon ground black pepper
2 teaspoons lemon juice
2 teaspoons sugar
¾ teaspoons salt, or to taste

1. Make the kebab: Mix the ground meat with the rest of the ingredients and knead briefly. With moistened hands, form into about 15 pieces and roll into balls.

2. In a small pot, heat the oil over medium to low heat and sauté the onions, stirring frequently, until they begin to color. Add the garlic and sauté for a further 30 seconds.

3. Pour in ½ cup/120 ml water and the rest of the sauce ingredients and bring to a boil. Lower the heat and simmer, covered, for 15 minutes, or until the onions are tender.

4. Add the kebab balls, replace the lid, and simmer for a further 10 minutes. Taste and adjust the seasoning.

5. Serve hot.

MLOUKHIYEH WITH DRIED LEAVES
Mloukhiyeh Yabseh

SERVES 4–6
PREPARATION TIME: 15 MINUTES
COOKING TIME: 30 MINUTES

This version of the popular dish is more convenient than Mloukhiyeh with Chicken (p. 133), since it is made with dried leaves. The flavor is slightly different, but lovers of this royal dish will readily accept this slight change when fresh leaves are not available. Dried, crumbled *mloukhiyeh* (Jew's mallow) leaves can be found in Middle Eastern specialty stores.

4 tablespoons/2 oz/60 g butter,
    or more if needed
¼ cup/60 ml olive oil
2 cups/3 oz/90 g dried, crumbled
    mloukhiyeh (Jew's mallow) leaves
5–6 pine nuts
¼ cup ground coriander
9 garlic cloves (1¼ oz/40 g), crushed
5 cups/1.2 liters Basic Meat Stock,
    including meat (p. 20), or any
    meat or vegetable stock
⅓ cup/75 ml lemon juice
1 teaspoon salt, or to taste

To serve

2 teaspoons fried pine nuts
    (optional; *see* p. 23)
2 cups/14 oz/400 g short-grain
    rice, cooked according to your
    preferred method (or *see* p. 30)
½ cup/120 ml lemon juice

1. Heat a medium pot over low heat, and add the butter and oil. Add the dried leaves and pine nuts and sauté for 3–4 minutes, or until the pine nuts start to change color (this step is important as it will prevent a slimy texture).

2. Add the ground coriander and stir for a further minute. Add the crushed garlic and continue to fry for 1 minute more, adding a little more oil if the mixture dries.

3. Pour in the hot meat stock and lemon juice. Raise the heat to medium and simmer, covered, for 20 minutes. Taste and add the salt, adding a little more stock or water if needed (the consistency should be that of a thick soup). Add the meat (if using) and simmer until it is heated through.

4. Ladle into soup bowls and serve hot, garnished with fried pine nuts, if using. Serve the rice and lemon juice on the side.

MEAT AND ONION STEW
Baransa bi-Lahem

SERVES 6
PREPARATION TIME: 1½ HOURS–2 HOURS
COOKING TIME: 1½ HOURS–2½ HOURS

Leeks are called *barasia*, *baransa*, or *kurrat* in Arabic. They are known to have been used for food in the Middle East as far back as the ancient Egyptians. Aleppo and Turkey share this stew of leeks, meat, and small whole onions, which makes an excellent family meal. Serve this dish with lemon wedges and plain rice, Bulgar Pilaf with Vermicelli, p. 110, or Arabic flatbread.

9 oz/250 g fresh pearl onions, unpeeled

2½ lb/1.2 kg leeks (white and tender green parts)

⅓ cup/75 ml olive oil

1–2 tablespoons red wine vinegar

½–1 teaspoon ground white pepper

1½ teaspoons salt, or to taste

For the stock

2 lb/1 kg lamb shanks or stewing beef with bones

2–3 cinnamon sticks

1 bay leaf

1 medium onion (8 oz/225 g), quartered

1 small carrot, chopped (optional)

1. Place the meat in a large cooking pot with cold water to cover by about 2 in/5 cm. Bring to a boil over high heat, skimming the foam that forms on the surface. Add the stock ingredients, cover the pot, and simmer very gently (the surface of the liquid should barely tremble) for 35 minutes–1½ hours, or until the meat is very tender. Remove the meat and set aside, discarding the bones.

2. Strain and measure the stock and return it to the pot. Boil, uncovered, until it is reduced to about 4 cups/1 liter.

3. Blanch the onions for 1–2 minutes in boiling water, drain, and transfer to cold water for a few seconds. Drain and peel the onions, leaving part of the root end intact to keep them whole.

4. Chop the leeks into 2 in/5 cm lengths. Wash and drain well. Sauté the leeks briefly in the oil until they soften.

5. Place the leeks, stock, vinegar, white pepper, and salt in a pot and bring to a boil. Lower the heat, partially cover, and simmer for 25 minutes.

6. Add the pearl onions and continue to simmer for a further 20 minutes, or until tender. Add the meat to the pot and cook just until heated through. Serve hot.

NOTES

To cut down the preparation time, you can use frozen peeled pearl onions. Add them, still frozen, in step 6, and simmer for 10 minutes.

LAMB SHANKS AND ONIONS IN YOGURT SAUCE
Arman

SERVES 6
PREPARATION TIME: 10–15 MINUTES
COOKING TIME: 35 MINUTES–1½ HOURS

The name of this dish, *Arman*, originates from a Turkish word meaning forest, and possibly also from a Persian word meaning desire or pleasure. In this very old dish, lamb shanks are cooked with small, whole onions in a yogurt sauce. It is also known by the name *shakriyeh* in Damascus, and in Lebanon it is called *Laban Immo* ("mother's milk"). It is a soothing and nourishing dish loved by many. Serve it with cooked rice or Bulgar Pilaf with Vermicelli, p. 110.

1¾ lb/800 g lamb shanks with bones

1 lb/450 g baby onions
    (such as cipollini or large pearl
    onions), unpeeled

4 cups/2 lb/1 kg sheep's, goat's,
    or cow's milk yogurt

¼ cup/1 oz/30 g cornstarch mixed
    with ¼ cup/60 ml water
    (if using cow's milk yogurt)

1 egg white (you can use the whole
    egg but this will tint the yogurt)

1½ teaspoons salt, or to taste

Aromatics

2–3 cinnamon sticks

1 bay leaf

1 medium onion (8 oz/225 g),
    quartered

1 small carrot, chopped (optional)

½ teaspoon salt, or to taste

To garnish

1 tablespoon fried pine nuts (*see* p. 23)

1. Place the meat in a large cooking pot with cold water to cover by about 2 in/5 cm. Bring to a boil over high heat, skimming the foam that forms on the surface. Add the aromatics, cover the pot, and simmer very gently (the surface of the liquid should barely tremble) for 35 minutes–1½ hours, or until the meat is very tender. Remove the meat and set aside, discarding the bones.

2. Strain and measure the stock and return it to the pot. Boil, uncovered, until it is reduced to about 1 cup/240 ml.

3. Blanch the onions for 1–2 minutes in boiling water, drain, and transfer to cold water for a few seconds. Drain and peel the onions, leaving part of the root end intact to keep them whole.

4. Place the onions in a small pot with water to cover and bring to a boil. Lower the heat and cook for about 10 minutes, or until almost tender. Drain.

5. Place the yogurt in a large bowl and whisk well. If using cow's milk yogurt, stir in the cornstarch-water mixture. Add the meat stock, egg white, and salt. Pass through a fine mesh strainer into a medium-size pot.

6. Place the pot over medium heat and stir continuously with a wooden spoon, always in one direction, until the mixture comes to a boil. Taste and adjust seasoning.

7. Add the meat and onions. Return to a boil, lower the heat, and simmer briefly until the meat is heated through. Garnish with the pine nuts, if using, and serve hot.

NOTES

To cut down the preparation time, you can use 1 small onion (4 oz/115 g), finely chopped. Sauté the onion in 3 tablespoons olive oil or melted butter until tender.

STUFFED DUMPLINGS IN YOGURT SAUCE
Shish Barak

SERVES 4–6
PREPARATION TIME: 1 HOUR–1½ HOURS (SEE VARIATIONS FOR SHORTCUT)
COOKING TIME: 10–15 MINUTES

This traditional Arabic recipe is prepared in Syria, Lebanon, Palestine, and other Arab countries (varying a little from country to country). The name *Shish Barak* has multiple meanings: thin pastry (in Turkish), thin pastry on a skewer (in Farsi), or six sides (in Kurdish).

It is a well-flavored dish of meat-filled dumplings in a rich, creamy yogurt sauce, garnished with fried garlic and coriander (some countries use fresh cilantro, and some like to use dried mint, but I prefer dried coriander for this dish). You can serve it with rice, but it is good without.

Greek-style yogurt suits this recipe best, since it is a little sourer than regular plain yogurt, but sheep's milk yogurt is best if you can find it. Preparing the dough and shaping it into small hat-shaped dumplings is time-consuming and requires dexterity. Shaping the dumplings into half-moons is slightly easier. In the Middle East, you can find these dumplings ready-made, but you can also substitute tortellini with meat stuffing to save time (*see* Variations).

For the dough

Generous 1 cup/5 oz/135 g
    all-purpose flour, plus more
    for dusting
½ cup/120 ml cup milk or water
½ teaspoons salt

For the stuffing

3 tablespoons olive oil or butter
2 tablespoons pine nuts
½ small onion (2 oz/60 g),
    finely chopped
12 oz/350 g lean finely ground lamb
    or beef (pulse in a food processor
    to achieve a fine texture)
1 teaspoon ground allspice
1 teaspoon cinnamon
¼ teaspoon ground black pepper
1 teapoon salt, or to taste
2 tablespoons finely chopped parsley

To make the dough

1. In a large bowl, combine the flour and salt. Gradually pour in the milk, mixing with a wooden spoon until a soft dough has formed. Transfer the dough to a work surface dusted with flour and knead for 3 minutes, adding a little flour if it is too sticky. Form into a ball, cover with plastic wrap, and let it rest in the refrigerator for 30 minutes.

To make the stuffing

2. In a large pan, heat the butter or oil over medium heat and fry the pine nuts until golden. Remove with a slotted spoon and set aside.

3. Lower the heat and fry the onions until tender but not colored (about 8 minutes).

4. Raise the heat and add the meat and the rest of the ingredients except the parsley and pine nuts. Fry, breaking up the meat with a wooden spoon, until it loses its color. Remove from the heat. Mix in the parsley and nuts and allow to cool.

5. Knead the mixture with a little water to make a thick paste. Divide into 55 small balls.

To form the dumplings

6. Divide the dough into 3 parts, keeping them covered with plastic wrap or a damp cloth until use.

continued overleaf

For the sauce

1 egg

1 tablespoon salt, or to taste

6 cups/3 lb 3 oz/1.5 kg sheep's or
    cow's milk yogurt

1 tablespoon cornstarch mixed with
    2 tablespoons water (if using
    cow's milk yogurt)

To garnish

5 garlic cloves (¾ oz/20 g)

¼ teaspoon salt

⅓ cup/75 ml olive oil or butter

1½ tablespoons ground coriander
    (or 1½ cups finely chopped
    cilantro, if preferred)

7. On a floured surface, roll the first part until paper-thin. Cut into 2½ in/6 cm rounds using a glass or cookie cutter. Repeat with the rest of the dough (you should have about 55).

8. Place one ball of stuffing in the center of each round. Fold the dough over it, forming a semicircle, and press the edges together to seal. Wrap the semicircle around your finger and press the 2 points together to seal, forming a hat shape (*see* Photo on page 268).

To cook

9. Preheat the oven to 350°F/180°C. Arrange the dumplings on an oiled baking sheet and bake for 10 minutes, or until lightly colored.

10. In a small bowl, mix the sauce ingredients. Using a wire whisk, beat the mixture until smooth. Pass through a strainer into a medium-size pot.

11. Place the pot over medium heat and bring to a boil, stirring continuously with a wooden spoon in one direction. Simmer for a few seconds.

12. Add the dumplings to the yogurt and continue simmering on low heat, stirring gently a few times with a wooden spoon. Cook for 10–15 minutes, or until the dumplings are puffy. The sauce may thicken as it cools; add a little hot water if needed.

To serve

13. With a mortar and pestle, pound the garlic to a paste with the salt.

14. Heat the oil or butter in a small pan and add the garlic, fry for a few seconds then add the coriander and fry for a few seconds more.

15. Stir a few teaspoons of the garlic mixture into the pot, and serve the rest as a garnish or on the side.

VARIATIONS

- You can simmer the baked dumplings in the cooked yogurt, as above, or add them to the sauce just before serving, keeping them crisp.
- You can skip step 9 and cook the raw dumplings in the yogurt sauce, if preferred.
- Alternatively, the dumplings (either baked or from raw) can be cooked in hot water then drained and added to the yogurt sauce just before serving.
- To save time, you can substitute the dumplings with 10 oz/300 g tortellini, cooked according to the package instructions and added to the finished yogurt sauce. If using tortellini, add 1 additional tablespoon cornstarch to the yogurt mixture.

BREAD

ARABIC FLATBREAD
Khobez Arabeh

MAKES 6 LOAVES, EACH ABOUT 6 IN/15 CM IN DIAMETER, ¼ IN/½ CM THICK
PREPARATION TIME: 15–20 MINUTES
RESTING TIME: 2–3 HOURS
COOKING TIME: 3–4 MINUTES

Khobez is the Arabic word for bread. Arabic flatbread is available throughout the Middle East. It is considered an essential part of every meal; torn pieces are used to scoop up food. The bread is also toasted and broken into pieces to be used like croutons. In Aleppo, it is sliced and placed under many dishes to soak up the juices (*see* Meatballs in Sour Cherry Sauce, p. 158).

The rounds of flatbread are typically 13 in/34 cm in diameter and ½ in/¼ cm thick (though smaller sizes exist) with a hollow interior. An air pocket forms in the process of baking, lifting the upper flap, forming a large ball that deflates as it cools.

In the old days, Aleppian families would send their dough to a communal oven, where it was baked and sent back via a young employee. Today, people usually buy their bread from local bakeries or from shops and supermarkets where it is available fresh every day.

Arabic flatbread can be made with white or whole wheat flour and, like pizza, it is best baked in a very hot oven and placed directly on a pizza stone (an inexpensive alternative is to use unglazed quarry tiles or fire bricks or an upturned baking sheet).

3 cups/13 oz/360 g all-purpose or
    bread flour
2 teaspoons instant or
    active dry yeast
1½ teaspoons salt
1½ teaspoons sugar
1¼ cups/300 ml room-
    temperature water

1. If using active dry yeast, warm ¼ cup/60 ml of the water to about 110°F/40°C and add ½ teaspoon of the sugar. Stir to dissolve, then sprinkle the yeast on top. Set aside until it is dissolved and frothy.

To mix the dough in a stand mixer

2. Place flour, instant dry yeast or yeast-water mixture, salt, and sugar in the bowl of an electric mixer with the dough hook attached. Process on low to mix the ingredients.

3. Add the rest of the water and work the machine on medium speed for about 7 minutes, or until the dough pulls away from the sides of the bowl and is slightly sticky. Add a little water if the dough is too stiff or a little flour if it is too sticky.

4. Transfer the dough to a work surface and knead for a few minutes by pressing down on the dough with the palm of the hand, away from you, then folding it toward you, repeating this step a few times until smooth and elastic.

To mix the dough by hand

5. In a large mixing bowl combine the flour, instant dry yeast or yeast-water mixture, salt, and sugar.

6. Make a well in the center and gradually add the water, mixing with a wooden spoon.

7. Turn dough on to a lightly floured working surface and knead for 12 minutes, or until the dough is smooth and elastic.

To shape and bake

8. Shape the dough into a ball and transfer to a large bowl brushed with vegetable oil. Roll the dough in the oil so it is coated all over. Cover with plastic wrap and place in a warm, draft-free place for about 2 hours (less in warm weather), or until the dough doubles in volume.

9. Punch down dough and knead lightly. Roll it into a log shape and divide it into 6 pieces (more if you want to make smaller loaves). Shape the pieces into balls, cover, and let them rest for 20 minutes.

10. Preheat the oven to 475°F/240°C (or the maximum setting on your oven), and place the pizza stone (or baking sheet) on the lowest shelf.

11. On a lightly floured surface, roll the balls of dough to rounds 6 in/15 cm in diameter and ¼ in/½ cm thick. Place rounds on a lightly floured tray.

12. Transfer the rounds in batches to the hot pizza stone or baking sheet using a paddle if you have one and bake for about 3 minutes, or until they puff up and are slightly colored (the precise time depends on how thick and moist the bread is and how hot the oven gets so watch carefully).

13. Remove the loaves from the oven and transfer to wire racks. They are best eaten fresh and warm out of the oven. (Store in airtight containers in the freezer; they are ideal to freeze since they defrost quickly at room temperature, in a toaster oven, or over a gas flame.)

ALEPPO MEAT PIES
Lahem bi-Ajine Halabi

MAKES 12
PREPARATION TIME: 10 MINUTES (USING PREMADE DOUGH)
RESTING TIME: 30 MINUTES
COOKING TIME: 10–15 MINUTES

These are pizza-like pies prepared with simple bread dough, thinly rolled, and covered with a mutton or lamb topping, which is patted into the dough before baking. They are so good to have on hand in the freezer, to be taken out and reheated when needed (you can quickly reheat them—open or folded—in a nonstick skillet, which will crisp the bottom). I have prepared them with very thinly rolled dough, but the thickness and size depends on personal choice. For a nice texture, sprinkle the baking sheet with fine semolina instead of flour.

In Syria, one can prepare the topping at home and take it to a local bakery to be spread on thinly rolled bread dough and baked in the bakery oven.

½ recipe Arabic Flatbread
    dough (p. 272), or 14 oz/400 g
    premade pizza dough
1 very small onion (3 oz/85 g),
    finely chopped
2 teaspoons salt, or to taste
1½ lb/700 g lean ground lamb
    or beef (pulse in a food processor
    to achieve a fine texture)
1¼ teaspoon Aleppo spice mix or
    seven-spice powder
½ teaspoon ground black pepper
¼–⅓ cup/60–75 ml pomegranate
    molasses
Sliced cucumbers, radishes, and
    scallions, to garnish (optional)

1. If using store-bought pizza dough, follow the instructions on the package. Preheat the oven to 475°F/240°C.

2. Sprinkle the chopped onion with 1 teaspoon of the salt and set aside for 30 minutes. Squeeze to remove all the moisture from the onions and mix in a bowl with the rest of the ingredients, except the garnishes. (The dough and stuffing can be prepared ahead and refrigerated; bring the meat to room temperature before rolling and baking.)

3. Divide the dough into three parts. On a lightly floured surface, roll one part paper-thin, flouring the rolling pin if it sticks to the dough. Cut into 7 in/18 cm rounds.

4. Continue with the rest of the dough and place the rounds on a lightly floured baking sheet.

5. Divide the meat mixture between the rounds and pat to spread evenly over the surface of the dough, leaving only a narrow crust around the edge (the meat will shrink during cooking).

6. Bake the pies on the lowest shelf of the oven for 10–15 minutes. (You may need to bake them one sheet after another in the oven. Do not put raw rolled dough on hot baking sheets.)

7. Serve hot or warm with the cucumber, radish, and scallion slices, if desired.

BIWAZ BREAD
Khobez Biwaz

MAKES ONE LARGE FLATBREAD
PREPARATION TIME: 10 MINUTES
COOKING TIME: 2–3 MINUTES

Biwaz is a word of Persian origin meaning onion. In this recipe, Arabic flatbread is topped with sliced onion and other ingredients (which vary by country) and grilled. It is known as *pide* in Turkey, where it is flavored with sumac.

In Aleppo the bread is smeared with a thin layer of red pepper paste and topped with thinly sliced onion and chopped parsley. The bread is often used to cover kebab dishes, like Aleppo Kebab (p. 146), to keep them hot and to be eaten alongside the dish. Sometimes Biwaz Bread is sprinkled with sliced red peppers or crushed grilled tomatoes, or used to make a kebab sandwich.

¼ cup/60 ml red pepper paste

2 tablespoons olive oil

1 Arabic flatbread, about 13 in/
    34 cm in diameter (*see* p. 272
    to make your own)

1 very small onion (3 oz/85 g), sliced
    paper-thin into half-moons

¼ cup/½ oz/15 g coarsely chopped
    parsley

1. Mix the red pepper paste with olive oil and spread on top of the bread.

2. Scatter the sliced onion on top. Sprinkle with the chopped parsley.

3. Using the palm of your hand, press lightly on top to smooth the surface as much as possible.

4. Grill briefly over a charcoal flame or under a broiler until warm.

5. Cut into 8 triangles and serve as a snack, sandwich, or on top of grilled kebab.

RED PEPPER BREAD
Khobez Fleifleh

MAKES 5
PREPARATION TIME: 10–20 MINUTES
RESTING TIME (IF USING HOMEMADE DOUGH): 2–3 HOURS
COOKING TIME: 15 MINUTES

In this recipe, flatbread dough is thinly rolled and baked with a thin covering of red pepper paste, onion, sesame seeds, spices, and olive oil. The bread can be of any size, but it is easier to make 5–7 in/15–18 cm rounds and cut them up as desired. Red Pepper Bread can be served as is, or with white cheese, mint, and scallions. Armenians make a version called Chili Bread, or *Khobez al-Harr*, and the Lebanese cover their version, *Man'ousheh*, with a dried herb mixture called *za'atar*.

Ingredients for 1 recipe Arabic
    Flatbread dough (p. 272),
    or 28 oz/800 g premade
    pizza dough
1 very small onion (3 oz/85 g),
    finely chopped
Scant ½ cup/100 ml olive oil
2½ tablespoons red pepper paste
2 teaspoons pomegranate molasses
3 tablespoons sesame seeds
2 teaspoons poppy seeds
1 tablespoon ground coriander
1 teaspoon ground cumin
¼ teaspoon cayenne pepper,
    or more to taste
1 teaspoon salt, or to taste

1. If making your own dough, follow the method on p. 272 until step 6. If using store-bought dough, follow the package ingredients.

2. Divide the dough into 5 pieces and roll each to ¼ in-/ 6 mm-thick rounds. Place them on an oiled baking sheet and lightly prick the surface all over with a fork, being careful not to puncture the dough all the way through.

3. Preheat the oven to 475°F/240°C and place a pizza stone or upturned baking tray on the bottom shelf.

4. Combine the rest of the ingredients in a bowl and mix well.

5. Cover each round of bread with about 1¼ tablespoons of the mixture, leaving a very narrow crust around the edges.

6. Place the rounds on the pizza stone or baking sheet in the oven and bake for 15 minutes.

7. Serve hot or warm, whole or cut into quarters. The bread keeps well for 8 days in the refrigerator and can be frozen for up to 6 months (to reheat: heat in a nonstick skillet, topping-side up).

VARIATIONS

1 teaspoon dried thyme or ¼ cup/1 oz/30 g finely chopped walnuts can be added to the topping mixture, if desired.

PICKLES AND PRESERVES

GREEN ALMOND PICKLES
Mukhallal Aqqabiyeh

MAKES 4 CUPS/1 QUART/1 LITER
PREPARATION TIME: 15 MINUTES
RESTING TIME: 4 DAYS–1 MONTH

Fresh green almonds can be eaten as a snack with a little salt or sliced and mixed into salads. They are sometimes also cooked with meat and served with rice. They complement many dishes and stand out on the mezze table.

Green Almond Pickles are not common, but are a delightful way to preserve fresh almonds for year-round use. The almonds have to be bought in early spring, when they are fresh and tender (in Aleppo, the best variety is called *Imm Omar*, mother of Omar). This recipe is simple, but the end result is pickles with a delightful bite. You will need a quart-size canning jar with a nonreactive lid.

1 lb/450 g green almonds
¼ cup/1¾ oz/50 g coarse pickling
   or other noniodized salt
½ cup/120 ml red wine vinegar

1. Wash the green almonds and dry with paper towels.

2. Remove the stalks, make a small incision along the length of each almond with the tip of a knife, and place them in a sterilized jar.

3. In a nonreactive pot, combine the salt with 2 cups/480 ml water and bring to a boil, stirring until the salt dissolves. Once the brine has come to a full boil, skim off any foam that may have formed. Mix in the vinegar.

4. Pour the hot liquid over the green almonds in the jar. They will float to the top, and settle after about 30 minutes (you can add more almonds if needed to fill the jar). Make sure that the almonds are completely covered by the liquid. Allow to cool, and cover with the lid.

5. Store in the refrigerator. Pickled green almonds will be ready after 4 days.

PICKLED GREEN TOMATOES
Mukhallal Banadoora

MAKES 3 CUPS/1½ PINTS/700 ML
PREPARATION TIME: 7 MINUTES
RESTING TIME: 4 DAYS–1 MONTH

Green tomatoes are simply unripe tomatoes. They have a tart flavor and apple-like texture that is ideal for pickling. The pickling solution below is a mild one, less sour and less salty, and flavored with garlic and hot peppers (if desired). You will need a large glass canning jar with a nonreactive lid.

1¼ lb/550 g small green tomatoes, quartered

Peeled garlic cloves (2–4; optional)

Hot red chili peppers (2–4; optional)

2 tablespoons coarse pickling or other noniodized salt

6 tablespoons/90 ml white wine vinegar

1. Arrange the tomato quarters, garlic cloves, and peppers (if using) in a sterilized canning jar.

2. Bring 2 cups/480 ml water and the salt to a boil in a nonre-active pot, stirring until the salt dissolves. Once the brine has come to a full boil, skim off any foam that may have formed. Mix in the vinegar.

3. Pour the hot liquid over the ingredients in the jar, making sure they are completely covered by the liquid. Allow to cool, and cover with the lid.

4. Store in the refrigerator: the pickles will be ready in 4 days but are at their best after a few weeks.

PICKLED TURNIPS
Mukhallal Lifit or *Shalgham*

MAKES 3 CUPS/1½ PINTS/700 ML
PREPARATION TIME: 7 MINUTES
RESTING TIME: 6 DAYS–1 MONTH

Pickled vegetables with vibrant colors are a must in Aleppo. They are served as snacks, with mezze, and with certain dishes.

Pickled turnips are available in Aleppo's markets year-round, but many households make their own in fall and winter, priding themselves on their vibrantly colored pickles.

Choose young, fresh half-white, half-purple turnips: avoid the older and larger ones, as they tend to be thick-skinned and somewhat bitter. Raw, sliced beets are added to enhance the color of the pickles; the more beet, the more vibrant the color. You will need a large glass canning jar with a nonreactive lid.

1¼ lb/550 g baby purple-topped turnips of similar size

Up to 1 large red beet, peeled and thickly sliced

½–1 hot red chili pepper (optional)

3 tablespoons coarse pickling or other noniodized salt

½ cup/120 ml red wine vinegar

1. Wash the turnips, cut off the ends, and peel if the turnips are large or not in season. Keep turnips whole if small and tender, or slice thickly or quarter if large, or you can cut deep slits into them, keeping them intact at the base. Sliced turnips mature quickly, while whole turnips take longer.

2. Evenly layer the turnips, beet slices, and peppers (if using) into a sterilized glass jar.

3. Bring 2 cups/480 ml water and the salt to a boil in a nonreactive pot, stirring until the salt dissolves. Once the brine has come to a full boil, skim off any foam that may have formed. Mix in the vinegar.

4. Pour the hot liquid over the turnips in the jar, making sure that they are completely covered by the liquid. Allow to cool, and cover with the lid.

5. Store in the refrigerator: the pickles will be ready in 6 days but are at their best after a few weeks.

ROSE PETAL JAM
Mrabba al-Ward

MAKES ABOUT 3 CUPS/1½ PINTS/700 ML
PREPARATION TIME: 10–15 MINUTES
COOKING TIME: 18 MINUTES

If you walk through Aleppo during the month of May, you will notice that the air is filled with the sweet fragrance of the roses sold in the markets. This is the season for making rose petal jam (also known by the Turkish name *gulba shaker*) from the famous Damask rose, or *ward al-joury*. The colorful pink blossoms are grown throughout Syria and are prized for their strong fragrance. The jam is a typical part of the Aleppian breakfast and is usually eaten with white cheese. But I have discovered many other uses: it is a tasty topping for vanilla ice cream or filling for tarts or cake. Make sure to use young fragrant roses that haven't been treated with pesticides or chemical fertilizers. *See* Variations for a less sweet option.

8 oz/225 g rose petals

½ cup/120 ml lemon juice

3 cups/1 lb 5 oz/600 g sugar

¼ teaspoon citric acid

1. Carefully wash and dry the rose petals. Remove the white base and sepal (the green part connecting the petal to the stem) and discard any blemished petals. In batches, place the petals in a strainer with large holes and shake to remove any pollen (pollen is bitter and will spoil the flavor).

2. Transfer the petals to a bowl. Using both hands, rub them with the lemon juice, squeezing and pressing on the petals. They should disintegrate and reduce considerably in size.

3. Pulse half of the petals in a food processor until they are coarsely chopped.

4. In a large pot, combine all the rose petals with ¾ cup/ 180 ml water and bring to a boil. Cover the pot and simmer for about 15 minutes.

5. Uncover the pot and add the sugar in three batches, stirring with a wooden spoon between each addition.

6. When the mixture returns to a boil, simmer uncovered for a few seconds, or until the sugar has dissolved. Remove from the heat and stir in the citric acid.

7. Pour the jam into sterilized jars and allow to cool. Cover and store in the refrigerator until use. (Use within 3 weeks, or freeze the jam for longer-term storage.)

VARIATIONS

For a less sweet jam, you can reduce the sugar to 1¾ cups/ 12 oz/350 g.

SOUR CHERRY JAM
Mrabba Karaz al-Washneh

MAKES 4 CUPS/1 QUART/1 LITER
PREPARATION TIME: 10–15 MINUTES
COOKING TIME: 35 MINUTES

Sour cherries (*washneh*) are available for a short season during the months of June and July. At this time, Aleppians busy themselves preparing Sour Cherry Jam and Sour Cherry Liqueur (p. 330) to last throughout the year. The tartness of the cherries combined with the sweetness of the sugar makes a superb jam, usually served with cheese and bread to balance the sweetness.

The jam can be prepared any time with frozen pitted sour cherries (available in Middle Eastern and Armenian shops) or from dried sour cherries that have been soaked in water. Morello cherries are not a bad substitute. Traditionally, the jam is made in the sun, and I have included this variation below (though this requires patience and a hot, dry climate).

2 lb/1 kg fresh sour cherries
3½–5 cups/1½–2 lb/700 g–1 kg
    sugar
Dash citric acid or 2 tablespoons
    lemon juice (bottled is best)

1. Wash and drain the cherries. Remove the pits, placing them in a small bowl with 1 cup/240 ml water.

2. Using your fingers, rub the pits in the water to remove all the filaments and juice. Discard the pits, reserving the water.

3. Place the cherry water, pitted cherries, and the sugar in a pot over low heat. Cover and cook for about 5 minutes, stirring a few times until the sugar dissolves.

4. Remove the cover, raise the heat to medium, and continue to simmer the mixture for 30 minutes, or until it thickens to a syrup and large air bubbles are seen on the surface of the jam (at this point the temperature should have reached 233°F/112°C, or what is called the soft ball stage: when a little bit of the syrup dropped into cold water will form a soft ball when pressed with the fingers). Add the citric acid or lemon juice in the last few minutes of cooking.

5. While still hot, pour the jam into sterilized jars, filling them to within ¼ in/50 mm of the top. Allow them to cool, cover, and store in the refrigerator until use. (Use within 3 weeks, or you can process or freeze the jam for longer-term storage.)

VARIATIONS: TO MAKE JAM IN THE SUN

Remove the cherry stalks and pits. Mix the cherries with sugar and leave overnight. The next day, spread the cherries across a large, shallow, nonreactive tray and place under a hot sun, stirring three times a day until the sauce thickens, about 3–4 days if you live in a warm, dry climate (bring them inside overnight if you live in a more humid climate). Other jams, such as apricot jam, are prepared in Aleppo using the same method.

MELON JAM
Mrabba al-Battikh

MAKES 1½ CUPS/12 OZ/350 ML
PREPARATION TIME: 10–15 MINUTES
COOKING TIME: 35–40 MINUTES

Melon comes in so many varieties and colors; the flesh can be white, yellow, or green. But whether you prefer cantaloupe (which has the best flavor in my opinion), muskmelon, or winter melon, you can use the rind to prepare this tasty, fruity jam (*see* Watermelon Jam, p. 288). In Aleppo, it is served for breakfast with salty white cheese and bread.

Seeds from 1 melon with filaments attached (optional)

1 lb/450 g peeled melon rind (with outer skin and inner flesh removed)

1 yellow apple

15 whole cloves

1 cinnamon stick

1 tablespoon lemon juice (bottled is best)

1 cup/7 oz/200 g sugar

1. Place the seeds with any attached filaments in a strainer set over a bowl. Press the seeds with a spoon to squeeze out as much juice as possible.

2. Cut the melon rind into ½ in/1 cm cubes.

3. Peel and core the apple and cut into ½ in/1 cm cubes.

4. Tie the cloves and cinnamon stick in a small muslin bag.

5. In a medium pot, combine the melon rind, melon juice (from seeds, if using), apple pieces, sugar, and the spice bag.

6. Cover the pot and place over low heat for about 10 minutes, or until the sugar dissolves, stirring once after 5 minutes.

7. Remove the cover and continue to simmer for 20 minutes. Add the lemon juice, raise the heat, and simmer a further 5 minutes, or until the liquid becomes syrupy and large air bubbles are seen on the surface of the jam (at this point the temperature should have reached 233°F/112°C, or what is called the soft ball stage: when a little bit of the syrup dropped into cold water will form a soft ball when pressed with the fingers). Mix in the seeds, if using.

8. Pour the jam, while still hot, into sterilized glass jars, filling them to within ¼ in/50 mm of the top.

9. Allow the jam to cool, then cover and store in the refrigerator until use. (Use within 3 weeks, or you can freeze the jam for longer-term storage.)

WATERMELON JAM
Mrabba al-Jabass

MAKES ABOUT 2½ CUPS/20 OZ/600 ML
PREPARATION TIME: 10 MINUTES
COOKING TIME: 40–45 MINUTES

Why discard the watermelon rind when it can be turned into a delicious jam? Try it and you will never throw away the rind again. Like many other jams in Aleppo, Watermelon Jam is served with salty white cheese and bread. You will need canning jars with a nonreactive lids.

2 lb/1 kg peeled watermelon rind (with outer green skin and all the pink flesh removed)
3½ cups/1½ lb/700 g sugar
3 tablespoons lemon juice
1 tablespoon lemon zest

1. Cut the rind into strips about ¼ x 2 in/1 x 5 cm.

2. Place the rind in a pot, cover with water, and bring to a boil over high heat. Lower the heat and simmer for 7 minutes. Drain.

3. Mix the rind with the sugar and place in a pot over low heat. Cover and cook for 10 minutes, stirring the mixture once, until the sugar dissolves.

4. Remove the lid, raise heat to medium, and simmer for about 15 minutes, until the rind is just tender (but still has a little bite to it). Using a slotted spoon, transfer the rind to a bowl and set aside.

5. Add the lemon juice to the pot and continue simmering the ingredients for a further 8 minutes, or until the liquid becomes syrupy and large air bubbles are seen on the surface of the jam (at this point the temperature has reached 233°F/112°C, or what is called the soft ball stage: when a little bit of the syrup is dropped into cold water it will form a soft ball when pressed with the fingers).

6. Add the reserved rind and lemon zest, return to a boil, then remove from heat.

7. Pour the jam, while still hot, into clean jars, filling them to within ¼ in/50 mm of the top. Allow the jam to cool, then cover and store in the refrigerator until use. (Use within 3 weeks, or you can freeze the jam for longer-term storage.)

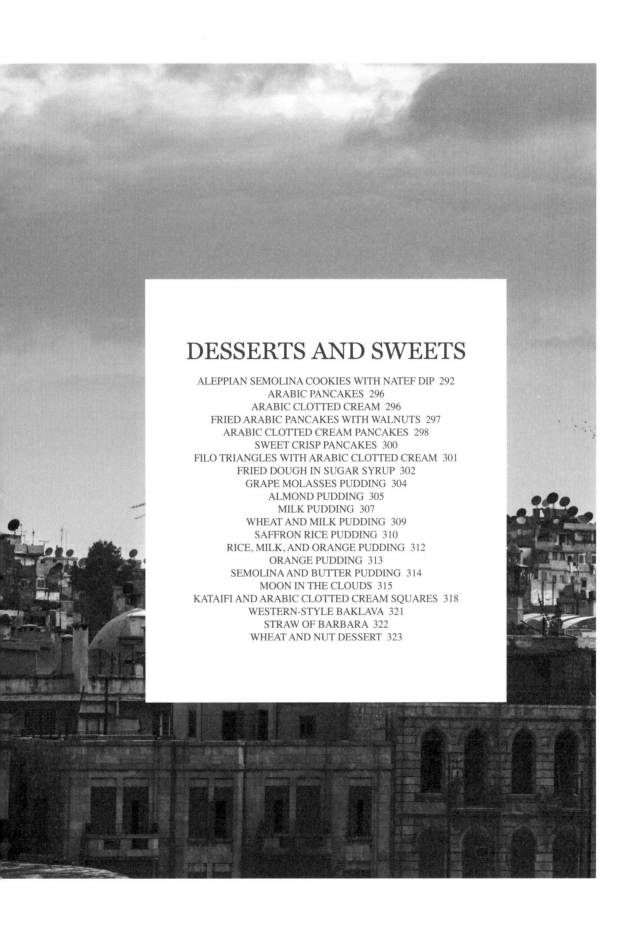

DESSERTS AND SWEETS

ALEPPIAN SEMOLINA COOKIES WITH NATEF DIP
Karabeej Halab wa Natef

MAKES 42 COOKIES AND 2¼ CUPS/550 ML DIP
FOR COOKIES: PREPARATION TIME: 40–45 MINUTES; COOKING TIME: 10–15 MINUTES
FOR NATEF DIP: PREPARATION TIME: 15 MINUTES; RESTING TIME: 12 HOURS; COOKING TIME: 25 MINUTES

These divine morsels of buttery pastry filled with nuts are a treat for sweet lovers and a pleasure to look at, served with the shiny white Natef Dip. They originated in Aleppo, but are made throughout the Middle East.

The cookies are not difficult to prepare but disappear quickly from the plate. This Natef Dip requires accuracy, and a good candy thermometer to achieve good results. *Natef* is made from *shirsh el-halaweh* (*see* soapwort or Panama bark, p. 346) and sugar syrup. It looks like whipped cream but is shinier and denser. You may be able to find it in Arab sweet shops. A good substitute to Natef Dip is marshmallow cream mixed with a little rose water. Aleppian Semolina Cookies are pictured on p. 294.

For the cookies

2⅓ cups/1 lb/450 g very fine
    semolina (*see* Notes)
¼ teaspoon mahlepi (*mahlab*;
    optional)
½ teaspoon instant dry yeast
¼ teaspoon salt
2 sticks butter (1 cup/8 oz/225 g)
¼ cup/60 ml rose water
2 tablespoons orange blossom water

For the stuffing

1¾ cups/8 oz/225 g unsalted
    pistachios or walnuts
⅓ cup/1½ oz/40 g confectioner's
    sugar
¼ cup/60 ml orange blossom water

For Natef Dip

1¾ oz/50 g dried Panama bark or
    soapwort root (*see* p. 346)
2 teaspoons rose water

For the sugar syrup

1 cup/7 oz/200 g sugar
¼ teaspoon lemon juice

To make the cookie dough

1. In a bowl, mix the semolina, mahlepi (if using), yeast, and salt.

2. Place the butter, rose water, and orange blossom water in a small pot with ¼ cup/60 ml water and bring to a boil.

3. Pour the hot butter mixture over the semolina in the bowl. Mix with a fork until cool enough to handle. Knead briefly, cover the bowl, and refrigerate for 8–10 hours (the recipe can be prepared a few days in advance to this stage). Bring the dough to room temperature before filling.

4. When ready, knead the dough, adding a little water or rose water if needed, to result in a supple dough. Divide into 42 balls (each about ¾ oz/20 g).

To make the stuffing

5. Pulse the nuts in a food processor until they resemble breadcrumbs. Mix in the confectioner's sugar and blossom water.

To mold the cookies

6. Preheat the oven to 475°F/250°C. Grease two baking sheets.

7. Hollow each ball like you would a kibbeh ball (p. 163) and fill with the stuffing (about ¼ oz/8 g per cookie). Seal the opening. Form into an egg-shape or place it in a mold (*see* Photo on p. 294) sealed-side up, flattening with the palm of your hand; flip the mold and tap it so the cookies fall out. Arrange on baking sheets.

8. Bake for 10–15 minutes, or until lightly colored (no more than 20 minutes). Cool on wire racks.

9. Serve with Natef Dip on the side. These will keep for a several weeks in airtight containers.

To make Natef Dip

10. Wash the Panama bark or soapwort, place in a bowl, and cover with water (no need to peel or pound the bark). Soak for a minimum of 12 hours.

11. Place the bark with the soaking water in a large pot over high heat and bring to a boil (be careful: the mixture will foam and may overflow). Simmer over low heat, uncovered, until only about ⅓ cup/75 ml remains.

12. Strain through cheesecloth placed over a strainer and cool. Refrigerate to very cold before use.

13. Make the sugar syrup: place the sugar in a small pot with ½ cup/120 ml water. Bring to a boil over medium heat. Stir gently only if needed to melt the sugar. Continue cooking the mixture for about 5 minutes, or until large bubbles appear at the surface, then add the lemon juice. The syrup should reach the firm ball stage and 244–249°F (118–121°C) on a candy thermometer.

14. While the sugar is cooking, start whisking the Panama bark or soapwort liquid on medium speed in a large bowl with an electric mixer, until it becomes foamy, shiny, white, and almost quadrupled in volume.

15. When the sugar syrup reaches the required stage, remove from the heat and start pouring the syrup in a steady stream into the foam between the beater and the side of the bowl. The mixture will whiten more and thicken, and almost double in volume. Mix in the rose water.

16. Natef Dip will keep at room temperature for one month if properly prepared. Serve warm or cold.

NOTES

- You can grind the nuts in different textures, ranging from very finely ground to whole nuts.
- If you don't like the flavor of rose or orange blossom water, you can use plain water.
- The grains of fine semolina differ from country to country. Fine semolina in Aleppo is finer than fine semolina in Lebanon, for example. Look for the finest grain semolina for these cookies. If you can, use firkha flour (*see* p. 341) or mix Lebanese fine semolina with firka in the ratio of 4:1.

VARIATIONS: DATE COOKIES (*AKRASS BI-AJWEH*)

These beautiful cookies are shaped with a special wooden mold and dusted with confectioner's sugar. They are usually prepared during holidays.

- Prepare and divide the dough as per the recipe above.
- Place 1½ lb/700 g pitted dates, 1 stick (½ cup/4 oz/115 g) butter, and a dash of cinnamon and cloves in a small pot over medium to low heat, stirring until the butter melts. Transfer to a food processor and pulse until a paste has formed. Divide the stuffing into 42 parts, each weighing about ¾ oz/20 g, and roll each into a ball.
- Preheat the oven to 475°F/240°C and grease your cookie sheets.
- Stuff, mold, and bake as above. When cool, dust with confectioner's sugar.

ARABIC PANCAKES
Ajinet al-Qatayef

MAKES ABOUT 25 PANCAKES, 3 IN/8 CM IN DIAMETER
PREPARATION TIME: 5 MINUTES
RESTING TIME: 1 HOUR
COOKING TIME: 15 MINUTES

Qatayef are small Arabic pancakes, which are usually filled with nuts or cream to make a dessert popular throughout the Arab world (*see* pp. 297-299), especially for holidays like Holy Ramadan and Saint Barbara night. The pancakes are spongy and fried only on one side.

1¼ cups/5½ oz/160 g all-purpose
   flour
½ teaspoon instant dry yeast
1 teaspoon baking powder
1½ teaspoons sugar
Pinch salt
1 cup/240 ml milk

1. Mix the dry ingredients in a bowl. Mix the milk with ½ cup/120 ml water and gradually pour over the dry ingredients, whisking until smooth. Set aside for 1 hour to rest.

2. Heat a nonstick skillet over medium to low heat. Using a ladle, pour in about ¼ cup/60 ml batter (less for smaller pancakes; refer to your recipe) and cook until bubbles appear and the surface loses its shine. The bottom should be slightly golden. Transfer to your work surface to cool.

3. Check the result: You may need to adjust the heat. Add water if the pancake is too thick or flour if it is too thin. Continue making pancakes with the rest of the batter.

ARABIC CLOTTED CREAM
Qashta

MAKES 1½ CUPS/13 OZ/360 G
PREPARATION AND COOKING TIME: 5 MINUTES
RESTING TIME: 30 MINUTES

Some Middle Eastern specialty stores in the US carry traditional *qashta*, flavored clotted cream, a popular dessert ingredient in the Middle East. English clotted cream (sometimes Cornish or Devonshire clotted cream) is similar and can be used in its place. But if you can't find either, the recipe below is a quick substitute. It is used in other desserts, but makes an excellent treat in itself with honey and pine nuts.

⅓ cup/1¾ oz/50 g powdered milk
⅓ cup/150 ml cream or whole milk
1 tablespoon cornstarch
1½ tablespoons sugar
1–2 slices white bread, crusts removed
   (1 oz/30 g), broken into pieces
½ cup/120 ml warm water
1 tablespoon orange blossom water
1½ teaspoons rose water

1. In a small pot, combine all the ingredients except the orange blossom water and rose water.

2. Place the pot over medium heat and stir continuously with a wooden spoon until the mixture comes to a boil and thickens, about 2 minutes. Turn down the heat and simmer for a few more seconds, stirring well.

3. Mix in the orange blossom and rose waters, and remove from heat. Set aside to cool. Chill for at least 30 minutes before use.

FRIED ARABIC PANCAKES WITH WALNUTS
Qatayef bi-Joze

MAKES 12
PREPARATION TIME: 15 MINUTES
COOKING TIME: 20 MINUTES

In Aleppo, these fried stuffed pancakes are sold in various sizes, though they are most commonly made with 4–5 in/10–12 cm pancakes and stuffed with walnuts, Arabic clotted cream (*qashta*), sweetened Akkawi cheese, or colostrum (*lebeh, see* p. 339), and served with sugar syrup.

The syrup is often spiced with cinnamon and cloves, which adds to the aroma and enjoyment of the dish, but this is optional (add 1 cinnamon stick and 3 cloves when you make the syrup). You can also bake these pastries, if desired, or fill with a clotted cream, colostrum, ricotta, or cheese filling (*see* Variations).

1 recipe spiced sugar syrup (p. 322), warm

1 recipe Arabic Pancake batter (p. 296), made into 12 pancakes, 4–5 in/10–12 cm in diameter

1¾ cups/6 oz/170 g walnuts, lightly dry-toasted, finely chopped

¼ cup/1¾ oz/50 g sugar

2 teaspoons ground cinnamon, plus more to garnish

2 tablespoons orange blossom water

¾ cup/180 ml peanut or vegetable oil

Cinnamon sticks, to garnish (optional)

1. Mix the walnuts with the sugar, ground cinnamon, and orange blossom water (the mixture should be sticky and not crumbly, add more orange blossom water if needed).

2. Place about one tablespoon of the stuffing in the center of each pancake, fold the pancake in half over the stuffing, and firmly pinch the edges closed (at this point you can freeze the pancakes).

3. Heat the oil in a large pot and fry the stuffed pancakes in batches for 3 minutes, or until golden, turning them once. Dip in the warm sugar syrup while still hot.

4. Sprinkle with ground cinnamon, garnish with the cinnamon sticks, and serve hot or warm.

VARIATIONS

- To bake: Preheat the oven to 400°F/200°C. Brush the filled pancakes with melted butter and arrange on a greased baking tray. Bake in the oven for about 5 minutes, or until the outer shell is crisp and golden (over-baking will burn the walnuts). Dip in the warm sugar syrup while still hot.
- For colostrum, ricotta, or cream stuffing: Mix 1½ cups/ 13 oz/360 g Arabic Clotted Cream (p. 296), colostrum, ricotta, or English clotted cream with cinnamon according to taste and use this to fill the pancakes as above.
- For Akkawi cheese filling: Slice 1 lb/450 g Akkawi cheese and soak in several changes of water to remove the salt. Process to fine crumbles before using to fill the pancakes.

ARABIC CLOTTED CREAM PANCAKES
Qatayef bi-Qashta (Asafiri)

MAKES 25
PREPARATION TIME: 10 MINUTES
COOKING TIME: 5 MINUTES

This dish is fresher-tasting than Fried Arabic Pancakes with Walnuts (p. 297). The sweets are not fried but rather served cold, stuffed with Arabic clotted cream, with sugar syrup on the side. They make a beautiful dessert; they look like horns filled with white cream and covered with green pistachios.

Arabic Pancakes (*qatayef*) and Arabic Clotted Cream (*qashta*) can be found in some Middle Eastern specialty stores, but you can also make your own (*see* p. 296). You can prepare the cream up to two days ahead and refrigerate until needed; prepare the pancakes the same day they are to be filled (or they can be frozen for later use).

1½ cups/13 oz/350 g Arabic Clotted
    Cream (p. 296)
1 recipe Arabic Pancakes (p. 296)

To garnish

¼ cup/1 oz/30 g unsalted pistachios,
    finely chopped
1 tablespoon orange blossom jam
    (optional)

For the sugar syrup

2 cups/14 oz/400 g sugar
¼ teaspoon lemon juice
2 tablespoons orange blossom water

1. Place one tablespoon of the cream in the center of a pancake. Fold the pancake in half over the filling, and pinch the edges together on one side, leaving one end open to expose some of the cream (*see* Photo).

2. Holding the closed end of the pancake, dip the cream end in the chopped pistachios. Garnish with about ¼ teaspoon of the orange blossom jam, if desired, and place on a serving platter. Repeat with the rest of the pancakes.

3. Prepare the sugar syrup: In a small pot, combine the sugar with ¾ cup/180 ml water. Bring to a boil over medium heat; then lower heat and simmer, uncovered, for about 4 minutes, or until the syrup thickens, skimming off the foam that forms on the top. Add the lemon juice and simmer for 1 more minute. Add the orange blossom water. Remove from the heat and set aside to cool.

4. Serve the stuffed pancakes cold with the sugar syrup on the side.

NOTES

You can use honey instead of the sugar syrup, and English clotted cream instead of Arabic clotted cream.

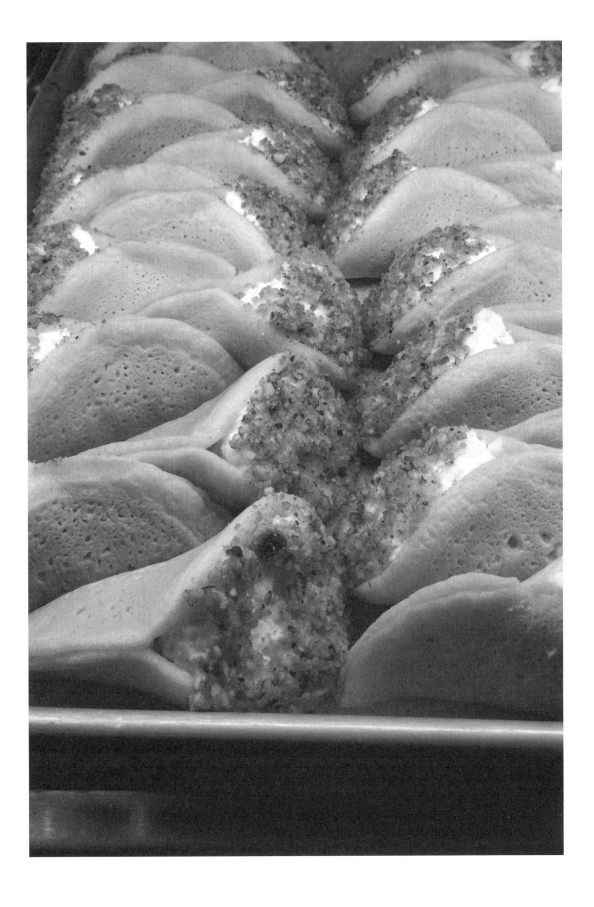

SWEET CRISP PANCAKES
Zalabia

SERVES 6
PREPARATION TIME: 10 MINUTES
COOKING TIME: 10–15 MINUTES
RESTING TIME: 1 HOUR

Zalabia is a very old Arabic word referring to a variety of sweets made by frying dough, such as this popular dessert. Aleppo is known for the best kind of *zalabia*—the dough is stretched very thinly by hand then fried and quickly rolled with Arabic clotted cream and sprinkled with cinnamon and sugar. These are made in only one shop in Aleppo, and the chefs who make them have learned the method from their grandfathers.

The famous poet Ibn al-Rumi (born in Baghdad 836) wrote this beautiful Arabic poem about the making of this dessert, comparing the frying oil to silver and the thin pancakes to gilded lace.

روحي الفداء له من منصب صعب   ومستقر على كرسيه تـعب

في رقة القشر والتجويف كالقصب   رأيتـه سحرا يقلي زلابيـة

كالكيمياء التي قالوا ولـم تصب   كأنما زيته الفضـي حين بدا

فيستحيل شبابيكا مـن الذهب   يلقي العجين لجينـا مـن أناملـه

Settled in his chair, tired
I'd give my soul to ransom him, high seated, yet exhausted
I saw him at dawn, frying zalabia, thin crusted and hollow, like reeds or golden emroidery
His silver oil, is like that alchemy they keep talking about, but never find
The paste drops as silver from his finger tips, and turns into nets of gold

It is impossible to prepare the sweet exactly as it is found in Aleppo, but this recipe will allow you to make a homemade version: fried dough dusted with confectioner's sugar and cinnamon. You can serve it with Arabic Clotted Cream (p. 296) on the side, if desired.

1 cup/4½ oz/125 g all-purpose flour

1 cup/4½ oz/125 g cornstarch

½ teaspoon instant dry yeast

Vegetable oil

⅓ cup/1½ oz/40 g confectioner's
   sugar

1 tablespoon cinnamon

1. Sift the flour and cornstarch into a bowl. Add 1 cup/240 ml water and the yeast, and mix well until a soft dough has formed. Cover the bowl and refrigerate for 1 hour.

2. Heat about ¼ in/½ cm oil in a wide skillet over medium heat.

3. Cut a small piece of dough (about 1 tablespoon) and roll gently on an oiled surface. Lift with oiled hands, letting the dough hang to stretch it further. Place it in the hot oil. Repeat with more dough, as much as the skillet can hold in one layer. Flip the pancakes when the bottom is golden and fry the other side until golden. Transfer to a plate lined with paper towels to drain.

4. Sprinkle with the confectioner's sugar and cinnamon while still hot and serve immediately or within a few hours.

FILO TRIANGLES WITH ARABIC CLOTTED CREAM
Sh'aibiyat

MAKES 12 TRIANGLES, EACH 3 IN/8 CM
PREPARATION TIME: 10–15 MINUTES
COOKING TIME: 25 MINUTES

This sweet is popular throughout the Arab world. It is, however, of Turkish origin, dating back 500 years. It was made in Aleppo and Idlib due to their proximity to Turkey and usually served at weddings and large ceremonies. Layers of pastry are stuffed with Arabic clotted cream, baked, and soaked in sugar syrup. There are variations with walnut or pistachio stuffing, and a lighter option using less butter.

5 sheets filo pastry, each 9½ x 12½ in/ 24 x 32 cm

1½ sticks butter (¾ cup/6 oz/170 g), melted

1½ cups/13 oz/350 g Arabic Clotted Cream (*see* p. 296)

2 tablespoons finely chopped pistachios, to garnish

For the sugar syrup

1¼ cups/9 oz/250 g sugar
Few drops lemon juice
1½ tablespoons orange blossom water

1. Brush 4 filo sheets with melted butter and stack them on your work surface. Place the unbuttered filo sheet on top. Using a sharp knife, cut the pastry into 3 in/8 cm squares (you will have 12; alternatively you can make larger or smaller squares).

2. Preheat the oven to 400°F/200°C and grease a baking pan.

3. Place 1 tablespoon of the cream into the center of each square and fold the pastry over it to form a triangle.

4. Arrange the triangles on the baking tray. Using a small spoon, pour the rest of the butter on top of the triangles.

5. Bake for 20 minutes, or until golden. Remove the pan from the oven and place the pastries on a platter.

6. Prepare the sugar syrup: In a small pot, combine the sugar with ½ cup/120 ml water. Bring to a boil over medium heat; then lower the heat and simmer, uncovered, for 1 minute, or until the syrup thickens, skimming off the foam. Add the lemon juice and simmer for 1 more minute. Remove from heat, mix in the orange blossom water, and set aside to cool.

7. Hold a large slotted spoon over the hot pastries and pour the syrup through the spoon, moving it around to make sure all the pastries are covered. Set aside for 5–10 minutes.

8. Transfer the pastries to a serving platter and sprinkle with chopped pistachios. The pastries stay crisp until the next day. They will keep refrigerated for 4 days if using home-prepared cream, or 2 days with store-bought cream.

VARIATIONS

- You can make these pastries with thinly rolled puff pastry instead of filo pastry.
- You can also sprinkle the filo layers with confectioner's sugar instead of sugar syrup.
- For walnut or pistachio stuffing: Combine 1½ cups/6 oz/170 g whole pistachios or chopped walnuts with 1 tablespoon/½ oz/15 g room-temperature butter, ¼ cup/1¾ oz/50 g sugar, and 1 teaspoon cinnamon.

FRIED DOUGH IN SUGAR SYRUP
Louqam or A'awwamat

SERVES 6
PREPARATION TIME: 10 MINUTES
RESTING TIME: 4–5 HOURS
COOKING TIME: 25–30 MINUTES

In this very old recipe, deep-fried balls of yeast dough are dipped in a thick sugar syrup. It is of Turkish origin and is prepared in many surrounding countries. In Greece, it is called *loukoumades* and served with honey.

For the thick sugar syrup

2 cups/14 oz/400 g sugar
¼ teaspoon lemon juice
2 teaspoons orange blossom water
1 teaspoon rose water
⅔ cup/145 ml liquid glucose
    (optional; *see* Notes)

For the dough

1 cup/4½ oz/125 g all-purpose flour
1½ tablespoons cornstarch
1 tablespoon powdered milk
1 tablespoon/½ oz/15 g butter,
    at room temperature
½ teaspoon instant dry yeast
Dash of salt
Peanut or vegetable oil,
    for deep-frying

To prepare the syrup

1. In a small pot, combine the sugar and ¾ cup/180 ml water and place over medium heat. Stir gently until the sugar melts, making sure the grains don't stick to the sides of the pot.

2. Raise the heat, add the lemon juice, and bring the mixture to a boil. Simmer for a few seconds and remove from the heat. Stir in the flower waters and the liquid glucose, if using.

To make the fried dough

3. Sift the flour, cornstarch, and powdered milk into a bowl. Add the butter, yeast, about ¾ cup/180 ml water, and the salt. Mix by hand or in an electric mixer to obtain a soft dough.

4. Cover the bowl and set aside in a warm place free of drafts for 4–5 hours, or until the dough doubles in volume and bubbles appear on top (do not punch down).

5. In a wide pot, heat the oil to 340°F/170°C over medium heat.

6. Place a piece of dough in your left hand and close your hand, pushing a small ball of dough out between your thumb and index finger. Cut the piece with a spoon and let it drop into the hot oil. Repeat with the rest of the dough, deep-frying the balls in batches, stirring from time to time and removing them before they color. Transfer cooked dough to a strainer.

7. Raise the heat to 375°F/190°C and fry the balls a second time, stirring them until they color. Remove the cooked dough with a slotted spoon and tranfer immediately to the warm sugar syrup. Leave the balls in the syrup for 8 minutes, stirring them a few times to make sure they are evenly coated. Using a slotted spoon, transfer them to a serving platter. Serve warm or cold.

NOTES

Liquid glucose is thick and transparent. It reduces the sweetness of sugar syrup and gives shine to the fried dough. It can be found in the baking section of some grocery stores.

GRAPE MOLASSES PUDDING
Khabisa

SERVES 10
PREPARATION TIME: 5 MINUTES
COOKING TIME: 10–15 MINUTES
RESTING TIME: 1 HOUR

Khabisa (meaning scrambled or muddled) is a very old Aleppian dessert. It is easy to prepare, with ingredients high in nutritional value: grape molasses (*see* p. 341), walnuts, and ground ginger.

In the old days, wheat was used to thicken the dessert instead of cornstarch, and incense granules were flamed to infuse the dish, enriching it with a very special smoky aroma.

1 cup/14 oz/400 g thick Turkish grape molasses (*see* p. 341)

⅔ cup/3 oz/85 g cornstarch

1½ teaspoons ground ginger

1 cup/3½ oz/100 g walnut halves, toasted, half chopped and half kept whole, to garnish

For incense infusion (optional)

1 small piece charcoal

4 to 5 incense granules (*see* p. 342)

Small heatsafe bowl

A sturdy strip of cardboard or aluminum (just longer than the diameter of the serving platter but not as wide)

Aluminum foil or a pot and lid large enough for the serving platter

1. In a small pot, combine the grape molasses with 2 cups/480 ml water and bring to a boil, stirring. Remove from heat.

2. Mix the cornstarch with ½ cup/120 ml water, then gradually pour it into the pot, stirring.

3. Return the pot to medium heat and bring to a boil, stirring continuously. Simmer for a count of ten seconds and remove from the heat.

4. Sprinkle the ginger on a 9½ in/24 cm round serving dish that is at least ¾ in/2 cm deep. Scatter the chopped walnuts on the base. Pour the hot pudding on top of the walnuts.

5. Garnish with the toasted whole walnuts. Cool to room temperature and refrigerate. Serve cold.

To infuse with incense

6. Place the piece of charcoal over an open flame until it ignites.

7. Place the ignited charcoal in a very small heatsafe bowl. Place the incense granules on top; the smoke will start coming out, filling the room with its scent.

8. Suspend a narrow strip of sturdy cardboard or aluminum across the dish of pudding, making sure most of the pudding is still exposed. Place the bowl of incense granules on top of the strip. Cover the whole thing tightly with a tent of aluminum foil or place it in a large pot with a lid. Set aside for 15 minutes, allowing the smoke to infuse the pudding, then remove the cover, incense bowl, and aluminum or cardboard and serve.

ALMOND PUDDING
Pudding al-Loze

SERVES 8–10
PREPARATION TIME: 20–25 MINUTES
COOKING TIME: 15–20 MINUTES

In this easy-to-prepare dessert, a creamy pudding is layered with nuts and served with apricot sauce. Though it is traditionally called almond pudding, it is often prepared with mixed nuts, as below (you can adjust the relative quantities to your liking). You will need a 7 cup/1.75 liters charlotte mold, or similar deep dish, such as a soufflé dish.

To prepare the pan

2 tablespoons/1 oz/30 g butter, room temperature
2 tablespoons sugar

To garnish (optional)

A few dried prunes or other dried fruits
Whole walnuts, almonds, and pistachios

For the pudding

4 cups/1 liter milk or almond milk
⅔ cup/3 oz/85 g cornstarch
⅔ cup/160 ml whipping cream
⅔ cup/5 oz/150 g sugar

For the nut layer

¾ cup/4 oz/115 g almonds, soaked in water, peeled, and coarsely chopped
¼ cup/1 oz/30 g shelled pistachios, soaked in water, peeled, and coarsely chopped
¾ cup/2½ oz/75 g walnuts, coarsely chopped

For the apricot sauce

5 oz/150 g dried apricots
⅓ cup/2½ oz/70 g sugar

1. Butter the sides of a 7 cup/1.75 liter charlotte mold or soufflé dish and sprinkle with sugar. Fit the base with a sheet of parchment paper.

2. Arrange the dried fruits and nuts for the garnish in a decorative design on the parchment paper, if desired.

3. Mix 1 cup/240 ml of the milk with the cornstarch.

4. In a medium-size pot, combine the rest of the milk with the cream and sugar. Bring to a boil over medium heat, stirring. Remove from the heat.

5. Stir the milk-cornstarch mixture and gradually pour it into the pot, stirring.

6. Place the pot on low heat and stir until the mixture comes to a boil and thickens. Simmer for a few seconds and remove from the heat.

7. Mix the coarsely chopped almonds, pistachios, and walnuts for the nut layer.

8. Spoon a third of the hot pudding into the bottom of the charlotte mold, smoothing the top with the back of a spoon. Top with half of the nut mixture and gently press.

9. Spoon half of the remaining pudding on top. Top with the rest of the nuts, followed by the rest of the pudding.

10. Refrigerate for a few hours until chilled. (The pudding can be made up to 2 days before serving.)

11. Make the apricot sauce: In a small pot, combine the apricots, sugar, and 2½ cups/360 g water and bring to a boil. Stir, lower the heat, cover, and simmer for 8 minutes, or until tender. Using an immersion blender or food processor, purée the sauce and set aside to cool. Refrigerate until cold.

12. To serve, turn out the pudding onto a serving platter and serve cold, with the chilled apricot sauce on the side.

MILK PUDDING
Haytaliyeh or *Hilatiyeh*

SERVES 8–10
PREPARATION TIME: 15–20 MINUTES
COOKING TIME: 15 MINUTES
RESTING TIME: 4–5 HOURS OR OVERNIGHT

Milk pudding is a delicate, refreshing dessert ideal for hot summer days. It is easy to prepare, largely with ingredients most people have at home: milk, sugar, crushed ice (and sometimes ice cream). The dish is very similar to the milk pudding *mhalabiyeh*, in which the sugar is typically added to the pudding rather than serving it with syrup on the side. This version has Chinese origins, and it is still served in Chinese cups and with Chinese spoons in Aleppo.

The name *Hilatiyeh* comes from the Arabic word *halata*, meaning to eat in one gulp. The pudding is typically served without any toppings, symbolizing purity. Christians traditionally serve it on the first day of the New Year to represent purity and luck in the year to come. There is an Arabic saying, *Al-dayem dayem*, meaning that what takes place on the first day of the year, whether good or bad, will determine the rest of the year. Thus, this spotless pudding will keep the rest of the year free of blemishes.

The dish is sometimes prepared with a burned flavor that is much loved by Aleppians—some even claim that it is not the real thing without burning the milk. I feel the dessert is excellent without it, but I have given instructions on how to give the dessert this distinctive flavor, if desired (*see* Variations). The dessert is usually served with pure milk ice cream, which does not contain eggs or vanilla. It is called *zahret al-haleeb* (flower of milk); though some serve the dessert with only crushed ice and sugar syrup.

Prepare this dish a few hours in advance, refrigerate until firm, and serve cold.

For the pudding

Vegetable oil, for greasing
6 cups/1.5 liters milk
1 cup/4½ oz/125 g cornstarch
¼ teaspoon mastic (Arabic gum;
    see p. 343), pounded with
    1 tablespoon sugar
1 package/¼ oz/7 g unflavored
    gelatin powder (*see* Notes to
    use leaf gelatin)
2 cups/480 ml ice-cold water

For the sugar syrup

¾ cup/5 oz/150 g sugar
Few drops lemon juice
3 tablespoons rose water
2 tablespoons orange blossom water

To serve (optional)

Milk or Sweet cream ice cream
Crushed ice

1. Lightly grease a 9 x 13 in/33 x 22 cm rectangular pan that is at least 1½ in/4 cm deep (or any similar pan, bearing in mind that the pudding should be about 1 in/2 cm thick).

2. In a large bowl, combine 1 cup/240 ml milk and the cornstarch and stir to mix. Set aside.

3. In a medium pot, heat the rest of the milk over medium heat, stirring with a wooden spoon until it comes to a boil. Remove the milk from the heat.

4. Stir the milk-cornstarch mixture well, and gradually pour it into the warm milk, stirring continuously.

5. Return the pot to medium heat and continue stirring until the mixture comes to a boil again and thickens. Sprinkle the mastic-sugar mixture on top, simmer for a few seconds, stirring well, and remove from the heat.

6. Place ¼ cup/60 ml of cold water in a small pan and sprinkle gelatin all over the surface. Set the pan aside for 5 minutes. Place the pan over very low heat and stir until the granules have dissolved. Stir into the hot milk and mix well.

continued overleaf

7. Pour the pudding into the prepared pan. Make shallow indentations on the surface with your fingers and sprinkle the ice-cold water on top of the hot pudding. The surface should wrinkle in nice ripples and the water should completely cover the pudding, preventing the formation of a crust. Cover the pudding with plastic wrap and refrigerate for 4 to 5 hours, or until very cold. (I prefer to prepare it the day before.)

8. Prepare the sugar syrup: In a small pot, combine 2 cups/480 ml water and the sugar and heat over medium heat, stirring until the sugar dissolves. Bring the mixture to a boil, add the lemon juice, cover, and simmer for 2 minutes. Add the rose water or orange blossom water and remove from the heat. Cool.

9. To serve: Cut the pudding into 1 in/3 cm squares. Using a slotted spoon, transfer the squares to a serving bowl or individual Chinese bowls, leaving the water behind.

10. Serve the pudding with the sugar syrup, ice cream, and crushed ice, if using.

NOTES: TO USE LEAF GELATIN

Soak 1½ gelatin leaves in cold water for a few minutes, or until tender, remove and squeeze out any excess water. (If you leave them for too long, they will disintegrate in the water.) Add gelatin leaves to the milk in step 5, after the pot has been removed from the heat, stirring until they dissolve completely.

VARIATIONS: BURNED MILK PUDDING

The flavor is better achieved by using a copper pot to heat the milk. One method is to heat the pot until it is very hot, then pour in the milk and leave it to simmer for a few seconds without stirring until it burns slightly. For another, easier method: Heat the pot over a high heat until it is very hot. Pour ¼ cup/60 ml of the milk into the pot and wait until the milk has evaporated, leaving a coating of medium-dark brown burned milk. Pour in the rest of the milk and bring it to a boil, stirring gently. The burned coating will separate into pieces. Strain the milk, discarding the burned pieces, and place the milk in a clean pot to continue with the recipe.

WHEAT AND MILK PUDDING
Qameh bi-Haleeb

SERVES 6
PREPARATION TIME: 10 MINUTES
SOAKING TIME: 8 HOURS OR OVERNIGHT
COOKING TIME: 1 HOUR AND 20 MINUTES

Also known by the name *Mhalabiyet al-Qameh*, this is a very old recipe. It used to be called *Hboub* when prepared with wheat and water, or *Qameh bi-Haleeb* when prepared with wheat and milk.

In this distinctive pudding, crushed wheat berries are simmered with milk to a creamy consistency, making a welcome and soothing breakfast, afternoon snack, or dessert.

I usually soak and cook two cups of wheat berries, crush them (step 2), and freeze half so I can make this dessert at short notice.

1 cup/3½ oz/100 g hulled
    wheat berries
6 cups/1.5 liters whole milk
1 cup/7 oz/200 g sugar
⅓ cup/1½ oz/40 g cornstarch
¼ cup/60 ml orange blossom water
7 small pieces of mastic (Arabic
    gum; *see* p. 343), pounded with 1
    tablespoon sugar

To garnish

½ cup/2 oz/60 g pistachios, soaked
    in hot water, drained, and peeled
½ cup/1½ oz/40 g sliced almonds

1. Wash and drain the wheat berries and place them in a bowl with water to cover. Set aside for 8 hours or overnight.

2. The next day, drain the wheat and place it in a pot with 4 cups/1 liter water. Bring to a boil over high heat, then lower the heat and cook for 45 minutes, stirring from time to time, and adding about 1 cup/240 ml hot water if needed to prevent it drying out (about ¼ cup/60 ml liquid should be left at the end of cooking). The wheat must be very tender.

3. While still hot, transfer the wheat and cooking liquid to the bowl of a food processor and pulse until the kernels are the texture of very fine bulgar.

4. Place the processed kernels back into the pot and add the milk. Place the pot over high heat and stir with a wooden spoon until the mixture comes to a boil. Lower the heat and simmer for 30 minutes, stirring occasionally, scraping the bottom.

5. Add the sugar and continue to cook the mixture for a further 5 minutes, stirring frequently.

6. Mix the cornstarch to a paste with ⅓ cup/75 ml water, and stir this into the simmering mixture. Stir until the mixture returns to a boil and thickens further.

7. Add the orange blossom water. Stir briefly, then sprinkle on the mastic-sugar mixture and stir for a few seconds to mix. Remove from the heat.

8. Pour the pudding into a 5 cup/1¼ liter serving dish, or individual serving dishes. Cool to room temperature, then refrigerate until chilled. Serve cold, garnished with pistachios and almonds.

SAFFRON RICE PUDDING
Zarda

SERVES 9
PREPARATION TIME: 5 MINUTES
COOKING TIME: 1 HOUR
RESTING TIME: 3 HOURS

This is an old, festive dessert that was common in the Ottoman Topkapi palace in the sixteenth century. It was served at weddings, birth celebrations, and during the first ten days of Muharram (the first month of the Islamic calendar and one of the four sacred months of the year in which any fighting is prohibited). The dessert is currently considered an Aleppian heritage dish, and it is still served during Muslim marriage celebrations and appears on the menus of several restaurants.

There is a well-known saying in Aleppo, "*Baad al-ours mafi zarda*," or "After the wedding, there is no saffron rice pudding," meaning, enjoy it while you can! (Because of the high cost of saffron, it was a dish reserved for special occasions.)

The ingredients are simple: rice, sugar, saffron, and orange blossom water, but the result is a delicious dessert with a wonderful fragrance, due to the presence of the most expensive spice in the world—saffron.

The word *zarda* stems from a Persian word meaning egg yolk (*zard* means yellow), referring to the rich golden-yellow color of the dessert. It is known as *Sholeh Zard* in Iran, where it is made with the addition of butter and cardamom, and is associated with the giving of alms during religious ceremonies. I discovered that a version is also made in Pakistan, with basmati rice, cardamom, and cloves. In parts of India, yet another version is prepared with carrots.

1 cup/7 oz/200 g short-grain rice
½ teaspoon ground saffron or
    1 teaspoon saffron threads, ground
2 tablespoons hot water
2 cups/14 oz/400 g sugar
6 tablespoons/90 ml orange
    blossom water
Peeled almonds, soaked in water,
    or pine nuts, to garnish

1. Wash the rice in a bowl in several changes of water and drain.

2. Pound the saffron in a mortar and pestle, leaving a few threads whole. Steep the ground saffron in 2 tablespoons hot water.

3. In a large pot, combine the rice with 9 cups/2.12 liters water and bring to a boil, skimming off any foam that rises to the surface. Lower the heat to medium, cover, and simmer for 35 minutes, stirring occasionally until the rice is very soft.

4. Add the sugar and saffron water, cover the pot, and simmer for 25 minutes more, stirring the ingredients a few times. Mix in the orange blossom water and remove from the heat.

5. Spoon the pudding into individual serving bowls and set aside to cool. Refrigerate until chilled, and decorate with almonds or pine nuts before serving

VARIATIONS

The less expensive safflower is sometimes used to replace saffron, but it does not impart a color and is inferior in smell and flavor.

RICE, MILK, AND ORANGE PUDDING
Roz bi-Haleeb Mbattan

SERVES 4–6
PREPARATION TIME: 5 MINUTES
COOKING TIME: 25–30 MINUTES
RESTING TIME: 3–4 HOURS

A beautiful two-layered cold dessert of thickened milk pudding topped with a layer of thick orange pudding.

For the rice and milk layer

⅓ cup/2½ oz/70 g short-grain rice,
    preferably Egyptian
3¾ cups/890 ml milk
¼ cup/1¾ oz/50 g sugar
¼ cup/1 oz/30 g cornstarch

For the orange layer

2½ cups/600 ml orange juice
Zest of 1 orange
½ cup/3½ oz/100 g sugar,
    or to taste
¼ cup/1 oz/30 g cornstarch

Peeled pistachios or almonds,
    to garnish

To prepare the rice and milk layer

1. Wash and drain the rice. Place it in a small pot with 1 cup/240 ml water and bring to a boil over medium heat. Cover the pot, lower the heat, and cook over low heat for 15 minutes. Remove from the heat.

2. Mix the milk with the sugar and pour into a medium pot. Add the rice.

3. Place the pot over high heat, stirring continuously until the mixture comes to a boil. Lower the heat and continue to cook, stirring, for a further 8 minutes.

4. Stir the cornstarch into ¼ cup/60 ml cold water and pour gradually into the simmering milk. Stir continuously until it returns to a boil and thickens. Simmer for a few seconds, then pour into small glass serving dishes or into one large glass bowl. Cool and refrigerate for a few hours.

To prepare orange layer and serve

5. Place the orange juice, zest, and sugar in a pot over medium heat and bring to a boil. Simmer for a few seconds then pour through a fine mesh strainer to remove the zest. Return the juice to the pot.

6. Stir the cornstarch into ¼ cup/60 ml water, then stir the mixture into the orange juice in the pot.

7. Place the pot over medium heat and stir continuously until mixture comes to a boil and thickens. Simmer for a few seconds. Remove from the heat and cool slightly. Pour slowly over the milk layer. Cool then refrigerate.

8. Serve cold, decorated with pistachios or almonds.

ORANGE PUDDING
Balooza bi-Burtoqal

SERVES 4–6
PREPARATION TIME: 10 MINUTES
RESTING TIME: 3–4 HOURS
COOKING TIME: 5–10 MINUTES

This is an easy-to-prepare, very refreshing pudding best served on hot summer days. It can be made up to two days before serving. The main ingredients are orange juice (or any fruit juice of your choosing) and fruit syrup diluted with water. The juice is thickened with cornstarch and served very cold.

It looks like opaque white glass with an orange tint. It moves jello-like when served, which is why it is compared to the tummy of a belly dancer.

4 cups/1 liter orange juice

⅓ cup/2½ oz/70 g sugar, or to taste

Zest of 3 oranges

⅓ cup/1½ oz/40 g cornstarch

¼ cup/1½ oz/40 g whole almonds,
　to garnish

¼ cup/1 oz/30 g peeled pistachios,
　to garnish

1. Place the orange juice, sugar, and zest in a pot over medium heat and bring to a boil. Lower the heat and simmer for a few seconds. Remove from the heat and strain through a fine mesh strainer to remove the zest. Return juice to the pot.

2. Mix the cornstarch with 6 tablespoons/90 ml water, then gradually pour the mixture into the juice.

3. Place the pot over medium heat and stir continuously until the mixture comes to a boil. Lower the heat and simmer for a few seconds. Pour into a heat-resistant glass container or any other container of choice. Cool.

4. Refrigerate for a few hours, or until very cold. (The recipe can be made up to 2 days in advance to this stage.)

5. Garnish as desired and serve very cold. (I like to serve it with more peeled almonds and pistachios on the side.)

VARIATIONS

- Chopped almonds or pistachios may be added to the pudding in step 3.
- A few teaspoons of orange blossom water or rose water can be added to the juice in the last few seconds of simmering.

SEMOLINA AND BUTTER PUDDING
Mamouniyeh

SERVES 6
PREPARATION TIME: 5 MINUTES
COOKING TIME: 10–15 MINUTES

Semolina and Butter Pudding is a specialty of Aleppo. It is a delicious dessert and a very popular breakfast treat that no gourmet should miss. It is often served on special occasions and sometimes to nursing mothers right after childbirth, since it is thought to be a good source of energy. The ingredients are simple and easily sourced for such a delicate treat.

This dessert was most likely named after the Caliph al-Ma'moun, who reigned in the tenth century. It is said that he ordered his chef to mix something in a hurry from items he had on hand. The enterprising chef combined semolina, honey, and ghee (clarified butter), and ended up with this mouthwatering treat. Sugar was later substituted for honey. If serving for breakfast, you may wish to serve it with Arabic flatbread.

3½ oz/100 g mild white cheese such as *msannara*, *shilal*, Akkawi, halloumi, or firm mozzarella (optional), briefly soaked in water if very salty

2 cups/14 oz/400 g sugar (1½ cups/10 oz/300 g if not using cheese)

¼ cup/60 ml ghee (clarified butter) or a mixture of vegetable oil and butter

1 cup/6 oz/170 g fine semolina

2 tablespoons orange blossom water (optional)

¼ cup/1 oz/30 g unsalted pistachios or walnuts, chopped

½ teaspoon cinnamon

1. If using, drain the cheese and cut it into thin slices or string into threads (the cheese should still be slightly salty).

2. In a small pot, combine the sugar with 4 cups/1 liter water and bring to a boil. Reduce heat to low and simmer, covered, for 6 minutes.

3. In a medium-size pot, melt the ghee or oil and butter over low heat. Add the semolina and cook, stirring continuously with a wooden spoon, for 5 minutes or until light golden.

4. Pour the simmering syrup over the semolina, stirring continuously until the mixture comes to a boil. Lower the heat and simmer, stirring, for a further minute. (Fresh semolina opens and swells quickly, while older semolina takes a few minutes longer.)

5. Cover the pot and set aside for a few minutes until the semolina grains swell. Add the orange blossom water, if using. (You should be able to pour the pudding rather than having to spoon it.)

6. Pour the pudding into a bowl or individual serving dishes. Top with the chopped nuts and some of the cheese, if using, and a sprinkling of cinnamon.

NOTES

Cheese is a new addition to Semolina and Butter Pudding. It is used as decoration or accompaniment, and sometimes stirred into the dessert until it melts (do this in step 5). Personally, I love a small portion of the slightly salty cheese with every mouthful.

MOON IN THE CLOUDS
Qamar bi-'Ib al-Gheim

SERVES 6
PREPARATION TIME: 15 MINUTES
COOKING TIME: 15 MINUTES

A beautiful title for a beautiful dessert. Kataifi (shredded pastry) is one of the main ingredients of this new sweet in the Aleppian repertoire. The other main ingredient is Arabic clotted cream, along with confectioner's sugar, cinnamon, and an array of colorful nuts. It is an opulent dessert to serve for guests after a meal.

5 oz/150 g fresh or frozen kataifi (shredded pastry dough or *uthmaliyeh, see* p. 342)

4 tablespoons/2 oz/60 g butter

1½ teaspoons cinnamon

½ cup/2 oz/60 g confectioner's sugar, sifted

½ cup/2 oz/60 g coarsely chopped walnuts, lightly toasted

¼ cup/¾ oz/20 g peeled and sliced almonds

2 tablespoons vegetable oil or melted butter

¼ cup/¾ oz/20 g whole shelled pistachios

1½ cups/13 oz/350 g English or Arabic Clotted Cream (*see* p. 296 to make your own)

2 tablespoons chopped pistachios, to garnish

1. Using a pair of scissors, cut the kataifi pastry into ¾ in/2 cm lengths (it may be easier to cut it into longer pieces and pulse it in a food processor to the desired length).

2. Melt the butter in a large skillet over low heat. Add the shredded kataifi and fry, stirring gently, until the strands are crisp and slightly colored (this step can take up to 15 minutes; taste to make sure the shreds are crunchy). Cool.

3. Mix the kataifi with the cinnamon and half of the confectioner's sugar. Mix in the walnuts.

4. Fry the almonds in butter or vegetable oil until light golden in color. Add the pistachios and stir briefly. Drain.

5. Using a fork, mix the clotted cream with the rest of the confectioner's sugar. (The recipe may be prepared to this step a day in advance: refrigerate the cream and store the rest of the ingredients in airtight containers at room temperature.)

6. A few hours before serving, place a third of the kataifi in a 11 in/28 cm serving platter and spoon half of the cream over the top in scattered dollops. Sprinkle half of the remaining kataifi and then another layer of cream. Spread the remaining kataifi over the cream, leaving gaps (it will look like the moon peeking out among the clouds).

7. Top with the fried nuts and garnish with the finely chopped pistachios. Serve at room temperature.

VARIATIONS: SPILLED KATAIFI (*KNAFEH MADLOUAH*)

This is an old recipe and a simpler version of Moon in the Clouds: Follow steps 1–3 as above, without mixing in the walnuts. Omit the almonds, and fry the walnuts and pistachios separately. Arrange the kataifi on a serving platter, top with the nuts, and serve with clotted cream on the side (if desired).

KATAIFI AND ARABIC CLOTTED CREAM SQUARES
Knafeh

MAKES 30
PREPARATION TIME: 20–30 MINUTES
COOKING TIME: 40 MINUTES
RESTING TIME: 10 MINUTES

Bein Narain, meaning "between two fires," refers to the process of baking the dessert with the flame coming from above and below the dish. It is a signature Aleppian dessert with Turkish origins, made with 2 layers of kataifi (shredded pastry) and a stuffing of a thick Arabic clotted cream (*qashta*). During spring when the sheep give birth, a colostrum filling is used in place of the cream (*see* p. 339). This dessert is pictured on p. 319.

1¼ lb/600 g fresh or frozen kataifi
    (shredded pastry dough,
    see p. 342)
2½ sticks butter (1¼ cups/
    10 oz/300 g), plus more
    for greasing

For the filling

1¼ cups/5½ oz/160 g powdered
    milk
1¾ cups/415 ml whipping cream
    or milk
3½ tablespoons cornstarch
⅓ cup/2½ oz/70 g sugar
8–9 slices soft white bread
    (5 oz/135 g after removing crust)
¼ cup/60 ml orange blossom water
2 tablespoons rose water

For the sugar syrup

2 cups/14 oz/400 g sugar
1 teaspoon lemon juice

To garnish

3 tablespoons finely chopped
    pistachios

To make the filling

1. In a small pot, combine all the ingredients except the orange blossom and rose waters. Add 1½ cups/350 ml water.

2. Place the pot over medium heat and stir continuously with a wooden spoon until the mixture comes to a boil and thickens. Simmer for a few seconds, stirring.

3. Mix in the orange blossom and rose waters, and remove from heat. Set aside to cool.

To make the sugar syrup

4. In a small pot, combine the sugar with 1½ cups/350 ml water. Bring to a boil over medium heat; then lower heat and simmer, uncovered, for about 4 minutes, or until the syrup thickens, skimming off the foam that forms on the top. Add the lemon juice and simmer for 1 more minute. Remove from the heat and set aside to cool.

To make the dessert

5. Cut the kataifi with scissors into ½ in/1 cm lengths (it may be easier to cut it into longer pieces and pulse it in a food processor to the desired length). Place the pieces into a large pan or pot.

6. Melt the butter and pour it over the kataifi in the pot. Mix with a fork until cooled slightly then rub gently with your hands to ensure the strands are well coated. Divide into 2 parts, one slightly larger than the other. The larger part will be the bottom layer (which will later become the top layer after baking and flipping).

7. Preheat the oven to 475°F/250°C.

8. Generously butter an 11 in/29 cm baking pan that is at least 2 in/5 cm deep. Spread the larger quantity of kataifi over the bottom of the pan and push it up the sides by ½ in/1½ cm. Press on the bottom and sides with the palm of your hand, then with a spatula. Cover with plastic wrap, place a slightly smaller pan on top, and press on it firmly to make sure the pastry is well compacted (some use weights).

9. Remove the top pan and the plastic. Spread the filling on top and level with a spatula.

10. Sprinkle the second half of the kataifi on top, distributing it evenly. Press with the palm of your hand to compact the pastry. Cover with plastic, then press down using the smaller pan, as before.

11. Remove the top pan and the plastic covering. Return the top pan and place a weight on top (I use a piece of marble; any heavy stone will do).

12. Bake in the middle of the oven for 10 minutes. Remove the weight and the top pan and bake for 30 minutes more, or until the top is golden.

13. Remove the pan from the oven and set aside for 10 minutes. Flip the dessert onto a cutting board or work surface and pour the cooled syrup over it, a tablespoon at a time. Set aside to cool. Then cut it into squares and garnish with the chopped pistachios. Serve warm or cold.

WESTERN-STYLE BAKLAVA
Baqlawa Franjiyeh

MAKES 24 PIECES
PREPARATION TIME: 5–10 MINUTES
COOKING TIME: 20–25 MINUTES
RESTING TIME: 1–2 HOURS

Western-Style Baklava is a soft and easy-to-prepare diamond-shaped pastry of milk, semolina, and sugar. The shape in which this dessert is cut is similar to the well-known Middle Eastern baklava (prepared with thin filo pastry, nuts, and sugar syrup).

2 tablespoons/1 oz/30 g butter,
    room temperature
4 cups/1 liter whole milk
1 cup plus 2 tablespoons/7 oz/200 g
    fine semolina
¾ cup/5 oz/150 g sugar
2 cinnamon sticks
1 teaspoon vanilla extract

For the top and garnish

2 tablespoons/1 oz/30 g chilled
    butter (optional)
1 teaspoon cinnamon
1 tablespoon confectioner's sugar

1. Generously grease an ovenproof 8 x 11 in/20 x 28 cm dish (or a slightly smaller one will do) with the butter and preheat the oven to 350°F/180°C.

2. Place the milk, semolina, sugar, and cinnamon sticks, and vanilla in a medium-size pot over high heat. Bring to a boil, stirring with a wooden spoon. Lower the heat and simmer, stirring, for 30 seconds and remove from the heat.

3. Discard the cinnamon sticks and pour the semolina into the prepared dish.

4. Once cool enough to handle, level the top with moistened hands. Set aside to cool.

5. Cut through the dessert diagonally into 24 diamonds. Bake for 20 minutes.

6. Remove from the oven and place under the broiler for a few minutes, or until the top turns golden (this is not obligatory but gives the final dish a nice color).

7. Pass the chilled piece of butter gently over the hot semolina (this allows the cinnamon to stick) and sprinkle immediately with cinnamon. Cool.

8. Cut again along the previous cuts. Using a spatula, remove the diamonds and sprinkle with confectioner's sugar before serving.

STRAW OF BARBARA
Qash al-Barbara

SERVES 8–10
PREPARATION TIME: 10–15 MINUTES
RESTING TIME: 30 MINUTES
COOKING TIME: 8–10 MINUTES

Saint Barbara's Day is celebrated in honor of a martyred saint said to have lived somewhere in Syria in the third century AD. She converted to Christianity in secret at an early age in defiance of her father, who is said to have punished her and then beheaded her. Her life story is the subject of various myths, as is her exact place of birth. Catholics celebrate the holiday on December 4th, while the Greek Orthodox Church celebrates it on December 17th. The celebrations are similar to Halloween, when children dress up and knock on neighbors' doors. Middle Eastern Christians celebrate the holiday by preparing special delicacies.

In Aleppo, it is traditional to prepare this dessert; the threads of pastry symbolize the straw (*qash*) bedding of baby Jesus. These are baked in ghee (clarified butter) and sold in sweet shops, and the crunchy threads are mixed with sugar syrup, cinnamon, and nuts for the whole family to enjoy. It is so tempting to the palate that it can be addictive! Use the traditional Straw of Aleppo (*knafe qash*) if you can find it, but below is a method using more widely available shredded pastry.

9 oz/250 g kataifi (shredded pastry), cut into 8 in/20 cm lengths

Vegetable oil, if frying or

5 tablespoons/2½ oz/75 g butter, melted, if baking

Scant ½ cup/1¾ oz/50 g pistachios, fried in vegetable oil (*see* p. 23)

½ cup/1 oz/35 g slivered almonds, fried in vegetable oil (*see* p. 23)

½ cup/1¾ oz/50 g walnuts, chopped and lightly dry-toasted

2 teaspoons ground cinnamon

Whole cinnamon sticks, to garnish

For the sugar syrup

1½ cups/10 oz/300 g sugar

1 cinnamon stick

6 cloves

¼ teaspoon lemon juice or a dash citric acid

2 tablespoons orange blossom water

2 tablespoons rose water

1. Separate the kataifi into threads, tossing them to make sure they don't stick together (*see* Photo on p. 316). Scrunch them into mounds so they wrinkle (they will crumble if cooked flat).

2. If frying: In 4 batches, deep-fry the threads in hot oil until golden; transfer to a strainer. To oven-bake: Preheat the oven to 300°F/150°C. Rub the melted butter into the kataifi and place the kataifi on a large baking sheet. Bake until golden, about 15 minutes.

3. Using two forks, toss the fried or baked threads to make sure they don't stick together. (These can be made up to 3 days ahead; store in an airtight container.)

To prepare the sugar syrup

4. In a small pot, combine the sugar, cinnamon, and cloves with ¾ cup/180 ml water and bring to a boil over medium heat. Lower the heat and simmer, uncovered, for 3 minutes, or until the syrup thickens, skimming off any foam that forms.

5. Add the lemon juice or citric acid and simmer for 1 minute. Add the flower waters and remove from the heat. Cool. Remove and discard cinnamon stick and cloves.

To serve

6. Gently crush the pastry "straw" and layer it with the nuts and ground cinnamon, drizzling a spoonful of syrup on top of each straw layer. Decorate with ground cinnamon and cinnamon sticks, and serve with extra syrup on the side.

WHEAT AND NUT DESSERT
Sliqa

SERVES 6–8
PREPARATION TIME: 10 MINUTES
SOAKING TIME: 8 HOURS OR OVERNIGHT
COOKING TIME: 35 MINUTES

This nutritious dessert is prepared with wheat and a variety of nuts and flavored with anise, fennel, cinnamon, and pomegranate seeds, when available. Traditionally, mothers and grandmothers rush to buy the many ingredients needed to make this dessert during the first appearance of a child's tooth, calling it *snouniyeh,* meaning "pertaining to teeth." It is also served on December 4th, along with Straw of Barbara (previous page) and other sweets made to celebrate Saint Barbara's Day.

1½ cups/8 oz/225 g hulled wheat berries, picked through, rinsed, and drained
4 cinnamon sticks
1 cup/7 oz/200 g sugar, or to taste
3 tablespoons anise seeds
½ cup/2½ oz/75 g pine nuts
½ cup/2½ oz/75 g raisins
1 tablespoon fennel seeds
1 cup/4 oz/115 g chopped walnuts
½ cup/2 oz/60 g peeled unsalted pistachios
½ cup/2½ oz/75 g peeled unsalted almonds
3 tablespoons rose water

To garnish

3–4 tablespoons/¾–1 oz/ 25–30 g sugarcoated anise seeds (*aghizmiskeh*, *see* Notes)
Seeds of half a sweet pomegranate, if in season
A few whole walnuts
¼ cup/¾ oz/20 g shredded or grated coconut (optional)
A few blue sugared almonds

1. Soak the wheat berries overnight in ample water to cover.

2. Drain wheat berries and place in a pot over high heat with 5 cups/1.25 liters water and the cinnamon sticks. Bring to a boil, lower the heat to simmer, and cook, covered, for 20 minutes, or until the berries open. Remove from the heat and set aside, covered, for 15 minutes.

3. Drain the wheat, reserving the cooking liquid. Discard the cinnamon sticks and place 1 cup/240 ml of the cooking liquid (¼ cup/60 ml more if you like the dessert with little sauce) in a medium-size pot.

4. Add the sugar, drained wheat, anise seeds, pine nuts, raisins, and fennel. Bring to a boil and simmer for a few seconds, stirring until the sugar dissolves. Cover the pot and set aside for a few minutes. Add the chopped walnuts, pistachios, almonds, and rose water. Mix well, adding a little extra sugar if desired.

5. Spoon the dessert into a deep serving bowl and decorate with the garnishes. Serve hot or warm, but it is also delicious cold and keeps for a few days in the refrigerator.

NOTES

Sugar-coated anise seeds, or *aghizmiskeh*, are widely available in Aleppo and Turkey, and in Turkish, Armenian, and South Asian specialty shops around the world. Sprinkles or sugared seeds or nuts can be used if these are not available.

DRINKS

ALMOND MILK
Sharab al-Loze

MAKES 4 CUPS/1 LITER
SOAKING TIME: 10 HOURS OR OVERNIGHT
PREPARATION TIME: 15–20 MINUTES

This non-alcoholic drink is prepared as a special treat to be served during engagement parties and weddings. It is often made with a few bitter apricot seeds, but the drink is still excellent without this extra addition. Commercial versions include Panama bark (*see* soapwort, p. 346), which gives the drink a brighter color and a lighter texture.

1 cup/5 oz/150 g whole peeled almonds, soaked in cold water overnight
¾ cup/5 oz/150 g sugar
2 cups/480 ml hot milk

1. Place the almonds and sugar in the bowl of a food processor or blender and pulse until a paste has formed.

2. Add the hot milk and blend for 30 seconds. Set aside for 30 minutes to infuse.

3. Line a strainer with clean cheesecloth or muslin and place it over a bowl. Pour the almond mixture in the strainer and stir to allow the liquid to seep into the bowl.

4. Squeeze the cloth to force all the almond milk into the bowl.

5. Transfer the almond residue in the cloth to a bowl and mix in 1½ cups/350 ml water. Strain as above, adding it to the infused milk.

6. Refrigerate the almond beverage until cold and serve with crushed ice, adding a little water to dilute to taste.

NOTES

- A few teaspoons of orange blossom water or rose water can be added, if desired.
- Froth can be created on the top by processing some of the almond milk in a blender or shaking vigorously before serving.
- To make this recipe lactose free, you can substitute water for the milk.

ORANGE BEVERAGE
Sharab al-Burtuqal

MAKES 2¾ CUPS/650 ML CONCENTRATED SYRUP (ABOUT 11 SERVINGS)
PREPARATION TIME: 5–8 MINUTES
COOKING TIME: 2–3 MINUTES

This is a very easy way to make concentrated orange juice. Keep it in the refrigerator to serve as needed.

2 cups/480 ml orange juice
(from about 8 oranges)
Zest of about 8 oranges
2 cups/14 oz/400 g sugar
Crushed ice cubes, to serve

1. Place the orange juice, zest, and sugar in a small pot over medium heat and stir until the sugar melts and the juice is heated through (do not let the mixture come to a boil). Remove from the heat and set aside until cooled.

2. Line a strainer with cheesecloth or a coffee filter and strain the mixture into a clean glass bottle. Refrigerate until serving.

3. To serve: Pour ¼ cup/60 g of the syrup (or more or less to taste) into a tall drinking glass. Add crushed ice and fill with cold water.

VARIATIONS

Tangerines and other citrus fruits may be used in this recipe.

LEMONADE
Limonada

MAKES 3½ CUPS/830 ML CONCENTRATED SYRUP (ABOUT 14 SERVINGS)
PREPARATION TIME: 5–8 MINUTES
COOKING TIME: 2–3 MINUTES

This is an easy-to-prepare concentrated lemonade that you can keep on hand in the refrigerator.

2 cups/480 ml lemon juice
(from about 10 lemons)
Zest of about 10 lemons
4 cups/1¾ lb/800 g sugar
Orange blossom water, crushed ice
cubes, and mint sprigs, to serve
(optional)

1. Place the lemon juice, zest, and sugar in a small pot over medium heat and stir until the sugar melts and the juice is heated through (do not let the mixture come to a boil). Remove from the heat and set aside until cooled.

2. Line a strainer with cheesecloth or a coffee filter and strain the mixture into a clean glass bottle. Refrigerate until serving.

3. To serve: Pour ¼ cup/60 g of the syrup (or more or less to taste) into a tall drinking glass. Mix in 2 teaspoons of orange blossom water (if desired). Add crushed ice, fill with cold water, and garnish with mint sprigs.

ORANGEADE
Sharab al-Hamod wal-Burtuqal

MAKES 2½ CUPS/600 ML
PREPARATION TIME: 10 MINUTES

This easy-to-prepare drink is refreshing on hot summer days.

1 lb/450 g oranges (about 3)
8 oz/225 g lemons (2–3)
½ cup/3½ oz/100 g sugar,
or to taste
3 thin slices lemon peel,
without the pith
Crushed ice cubes, to serve
Mint sprigs, to garnish

1. Peel the oranges and lemons, making sure you remove all the pith. Slice them, discarding any seeds.

2. Place the sliced oranges and lemons in a blender with the sugar and lemon peel, and purée.

3. Strain into a jug, and taste the juice, adding more sugar if desired.

4. Refrigerate until chilled.

5. Serve very cold, with crushed ice and a mint garnish.

SOUR CHERRY LIQUEUR
Anbariyeh

MAKES 8 CUPS/2 LITERS
PREPARATION TIME: 5 MINUTES
RESTING TIME: 1 MONTH

Anbariyeh is a Turkish word meaning liqueur. Sour cherries make excellent liqueur appreciated by Aleppians and visitors to the city. The liqueur can only be prepared from fresh sour cherries, which are available for a short period during the month of June and the beginning of July. Both cherries and the liqueur are sold in shops throughout Syria.

The liqueur is ready to be served after two months, but it gets better as it ages. It is usually made in summer to be served during the holiday season. It is often served in small glasses with a few cherries placed at the bottom and a small spoon or toothpick.

2 lb/1 kg fresh sour cherries
(*see* p. 346)
25 fl oz/750 ml bottle eau de vie
(about 3 cups)
1 cup/240 ml vodka or whisky
(or more eau de vie)
2–3 cups/14 oz–1 lb 5 oz/
400–600 g sugar, to taste
1½ tablespoons whole cloves
3 cinnamon sticks (optional)

1. Remove the cherry stalks (these can be boiled with water to make a healthy drink). Wash and drain the cherries.

2. Pour the alcohol into a wide-mouth half-gallon/2 liter glass jar with a tight-fitting lid. Add the sugar and stir until it partially dissolves.

3. Add the sour cherries. If using, tie the cloves and cinnamon sticks in a muslin bag sealed with string, and place it in the jar. Cover tightly and keep at room temperature, preferably in a cool dark place, shaking the sealed jar once or twice a day until the sugar dissolves completely.

4. The liqueur may be served after a month, but it improves as it ages.

TAMARIND BEVERAGE
Tamer Hindi

MAKES ABOUT 10½ CUPS/2½ LITERS
PREPARATION TIME: 20–30 MINUTES
RESTING TIME: 3 HOURS

Tamarind is a contraction of the Arabic term *tamer hindi* which means "Indian date." It is actually the name given to the syrup, paste, and the beverage prepared from the fruit of the tamarind tree. These are long, hard, shiny pods with brown seeds surrounded by a sour pulp. The trees grow in the wild but are cultivated for food in certain countries. Tamarind is a good source of vitamin B and calcium and is used as a mild laxative in some countries. It is used in some parts of the world as a souring agent to replace lemon. In the Arab world, it is only used in a few dishes and to make this beverage.

Tamarind is available in semi-dried, packed blocks of sticky, dark, fibrous pulp and seeds. These are typically produced in India and have a shelf life of about 3 years. With the addition of water and sugar, it becomes a pleasant and refreshing drink with a sweet-and-sour flavor.

12 oz/350 g block of semi-dried
   tamarind paste
3 cups/700 ml boiling water
3 cups/1 lb 5 oz/600 g sugar

1. Separate the tamarind mass into chunks and place in a bowl. Cover with the boiling water and set aside for a few hours until the pulp dissolves in the water.

2. Rub the tamarind pulp and seeds with your fingers, and add 3 cups/700 ml cold water.

3. Place the mixture in a fine mesh strainer set over a large bowl and press on the tamarind to extract all the juice.

4. Transfer the pulp residue to a small bowl and add 2 cups/480 ml cold water, rubbing the mixture with your fingers. Strain into the large bowl as above.

5. Repeat the procedure a third time with 1 cup/240 ml water.

6. Add the sugar to the tamarind juice in the large bowl and stir to dissolve.

7. Refrigerate and serve very cold with ice and water to dilute as desired (about ¼ cup/60 ml water per cup/240 ml juice).

NOTES

After step 3, the sour juice can be used as a substitute for lemon juice in some recipes.

DRINKING YOGURT
Ayran

SERVES 2–3
PREPARATION TIME: 3 MINUTES
RESTING TIME: 1 HOUR

Ayran is an ancient summer thirst-quencher. Healthy and savory, it is popular in many parts of the Arab world, especially in hot regions like the Gulf, particularly during the Muslim holy month of Ramadan. It is also popular in Turkey, particularly in kebab shops, where heavy cream is added for richness.

   Ayran is simply yogurt diluted with water with the addition of salt. It is sold in bottles in Middle Eastern grocery stores but can be prepared at home in a matter of minutes. You can use any good quality yogurt (it used to be made with camel's milk yogurt), but in my opinion, it is best with full-fat sheep's milk yogurt.

1 cup/8 oz/225 g sheep's or cow's milk yogurt
2 cups/480 ml cold water, or more depending on the consistency desired
1 teaspoon salt, or to taste
Ice cubes, to serve (optional)
Mint sprigs, to garnish

1. Place the yogurt in a bowl and beat with a wire whisk.

2. Mix in the cold water and salt.

3. Refrigerate until chilled, if necessary.

4. Serve cold with ice (if desired), garnished with mint sprigs.

VARIATIONS

You can add ½ teaspoon dried mint in step 2.

SALEP
Sahlab

MAKES 3 CUPS/700 ML
PREPARATION TIME: 5 MINUTES
COOKING TIME: 5–8 MINUTES

This is a hot, sweet drink prepared with milk and thickened with the white powdered salep, which is made from the roots of wild orchids. You can find it in Middle Eastern or Greek grocery stores. This drink is best served alongside cookies or sweets.

2 teaspoons salep powder

2 teaspoons cornstarch

¼ cup/1¾ oz/50 g sugar, or to taste

2½ cups/600 ml milk

1 tablespoon rose water

¼ teaspoon cinnamon

1. Mix the salep powder, cornstarch, and sugar in a small bowl. Gradually pour in ½ cup/120 ml of the milk, stirring well.

2. Place the rest of the milk in a small pot over medium heat and bring to a boil, stirring a few times. Remove from the heat. Gradually stir the milk-salep mixture into the hot milk.

3. Return the pot to medium heat and stir continuously until the mixture comes to a boil. Lower the heat and simmer for a few seconds. Mix in the rose water and remove from the heat.

4. Pour into teacups, sprinkle with cinnamon, and serve hot.

CUMIN TEA
Sharab al-Kammoon

SERVES 2–3
PREPARATION TIME: 5 MINUTES
RESTING TIME: 30 MINUTES

Here is a very easy-to-prepare savory beverage with lots of health benefits. It is especially good after a heavy meal. It is believed that it helps the process of digestion, eliminates gas, fights inflammation, pain, and swelling, and aids in the absorption of iron to the body. Serve it hot or warm after a heavy meal, or cold on summer days.

1 tablespoon freshly ground cumin

1½ teaspoons salt, or to taste

2 cups/480 ml very hot water

⅓ cup/75 ml lemon juice

1. Place the ground cumin and salt in a small bowl.

2. Add hot water and stir for a few seconds. Set aside for 30 minutes.

3. Pour the cumin-water mixture through a strainer lined with cheesecloth or a coffee filter into a bowl, discarding the cumin residue left in the cloth.

4. Mix in the lemon juice.

TURKISH COFFEE AND ARABIC COFFEE
Qahweh Turkiyeh wa Qahweh Arabiyeh

PER SERVING
PREPARATION TIME: 3 MINUTES
COOKING TIME: 3–5 MINUTES

Turkish Coffee (*Qahweh Turkiyeh*) is a general term that refers to the way coffee is prepared throughout the Arab world and beyond (in Greece, it is called "Greek Coffee"). The coffee is made of high-quality 100% Arabica coffee beans, which are dark-roasted and ground to a fine powder. It is sometimes mixed with a little ground cardamom for flavor. Nowadays, the coffee is usually brewed, with or without sugar, in a narrow, long-handled copper pot shaped like an urn and called a *rackweh* or *ibriq*. The handle helps to keep the hands away from the strong heat required (you can use a small pot with good results). When I was young, I remember my grandmother brewing coffee slowly in the hot coals placed in the brazier that heated the room. The coffee took longer to brew, but all agree that it had a superior flavor.

Turkish coffee is typically served in demitasse cups with small handles. It is a ritual among Arabs to serve this coffee to guests as a sign of hospitality. In some regions, your fortune is told by analyzing the patterns of the coffee grounds left behind in the cup: The emptied cup is flipped upside down onto a saucer, left to sit for a few minutes, and then turned upright to reveal the pattern made by the grounds. Large gaps indicate happiness and rest, the form of a bird indicates travel, and the form of a snake indicates an enemy.

Arabic Coffee (*Qahweh Arabiyeh*) is an unsweetened version prepared from chopped coffee beans boiled in water and allowed to rest for 24 hours. It is then simmered to produce a more concentrated brew with no residue. It is prepared in a special metal (usually copper) pot called a *dalleh*, which has two compartments: the top one for the coffee, and a perforated lower compartment for hot coals. The coffee is served in bowl-shaped demitasse cups with no handles. The portions are very small, covering only about a third of the cup. In restaurants, it is served by specially clad waiters called *qahwaji*, and usually offered with the compliments of the house, though it is customary to tip the *qahwaji*.

½ cup/120 ml cold water

1 teaspoon sugar (for medium-sweet coffee), or to taste

1 tablespoon very finely ground Turkish coffee

Dash of ground cardamom (optional)

1. In an *ibriq*, *rackweh*, or small pot, bring the water and sugar, if using, to a boil over medium heat, stirring a few times.

2. Remove the pot from the heat. Lower the heat and add the coffee and cardamom, if using. Return to the heat until it comes to a boil, watching carefully so it doesn't boil over.

3. If you like foam on top of your coffee, remove the pot from the heat and spoon some foam into your demitasse cup. For those who do not like foam, simmer the coffee for a few seconds, stirring until no foam appears.

4. Set the pot aside without stirring, and let the coffee rest in the pot for a few seconds until the grounds sink to the bottom.

5. Pour the coffee into the cup, leaving the grounds behind.

NOTES

You can find a *rackweh* or *ibriq* (the narrow, long-handled pot used to brew Turkish coffee) in most shops selling Middle Eastern food or home decor. They are usually made from copper, brass, enamel, or stainless steel, and range in size from very small (1 to 2 cups) to very large (10 to 12 cups).

GLOSSARY

ALEPPIAN SOUJOK *Qadid* Pronounced 'adid, the literal translation is "dried meat." *Qadid* is a distinctly Aleppian cured sausage made from lamb, garlic, and spices. The mixture is molded into a thin rectangle, placed in a muslin cloth under a weight and hung to air-dry. It is sliced and usually fried with eggs or used as a topping for flatbread.

ALEPPO PEPPER *Fleifleh Hamra Halabiyeh* or *Fleifleh Na'meh* Aleppo pepper, also called Halabi pepper or *Pul Biber*, is a ground red pepper coarser than paprika with a vibrant color and a deep, sweet, fruity, smoky flavor (somewhat like ancho chili). It is prepared from a variety of *Capsicum annum* called Aleppo red peppers or *baladi* (and sometimes a few hot peppers). The peppers are sun-dried, ground, then rubbed with olive oil and sometimes salt. You can find it in Middle Eastern or Turkish stores. The flavor can't be replicated but combining ¼ cup paprika with ¼ teaspoon cayenne pepper is an acceptable substitute.

ALEPPO SPICE MIX *Daqqa* Similar to the Lebanese seven spice mix, Aleppo spice mix is a famous mixture of six or seven ground ground spices. It is used in many dishes, in particular kibbeh and meat. The main ingredients are allspice, black pepper, cinnamon, nutmeg, and cloves, sometimes with additions like red chili, mahlab, and cardamom. Every household in Aleppo swears by its own blend. The old souqs, in particular Souq al-Attarine, will prepare a blend chosen by the client, to be ground on the spot. *See* p. 14 to make your own.

ALLSPICE *Bhar Helou* This spice consists only of the green berries of the *Pimenta dioica plant*, which are sun-dried and ground. The dried berries are larger than peppercorns and have a mild, sweet aroma. Allspice is widely used in the cuisine of the Arab world. The literal translation of *bhar helou* is "sweet spice."

ARABIC FLATBREAD *Khobez* Known simply as *khobez* ("bread"), Arabic flatbread is the most common bread in the Arab world (*see* recipe, p. 272). The loaves are round and flat, prepared with flour and yeast, and most commonly about 12 in/33 cm in diameter, ¼ in/½ cm thick, with a hollow pocket inside. The bread puffs up in the oven and deflates when cool. The bread is usually ripped into bite-size pieces and used to scoop food. It is also placed under some dishes to soak up the sauce. *Saj* bread (named for the utensil it is cooked on, a domed metal griddle) is a similar flatbread, but one-layered. Tannour bread is similar only it is baked in a *tannour* (a brick, ceramic, or stoneware oven). The pita bread that is commonly available in the US and Europe is thicker and smaller than the typical Syrian loaf.

ARAK *Arak*, meaning "to sweat," is a colorless, sweetened alcoholic drink flavored with aniseed. It is traditional in much of Syria and Lebanon. It is typically 100-proof, so it is usually served mixed with water in the proportion of one measure arak to 2–3 measures water, turning the drink a milky color.

BASTURMA *Basturma* is a cured meat, prepared in Aleppo with lamb or beef. The meat is salted and then covered with a paste called *shemen* (fenugreek mixed with garlic, red food coloring, and ground spices such as cumin, paprika, and chili). It is then hung to air-dry.

There is a lively debate as to the origin of basturma. Both the Turks and the Armenians claim its origins. Folklore has it that basturma was discovered by horsemen, who dried the meat on their saddles, pressing it between their legs and the saddle. Basturma is a noun derived from the verb *bastırmak*, meaning "to press." It probably has a kinship to pastrami, which originated in Eastern Europe. In Aleppo it is served with butter and eaten with bread as part of a mezze, fried with eggs, or prepared in pastries such as Basturma Beurak (p. 62). Basturma is available in Arabic and Turkish specialty stores.

BAY LEAVES *Waraq Ghaar* These leaves are widely used to flavor soups, stews, and many other dishes. They are picked from the evergreen bay tree, which has been known since ancient times. A crown of bay leaves used to be placed on the heads of warriors, poets, and athletes as a symbol of victory. The tree produces fruits resembling green olives that contain the much sought after bay laurel oil, which is the main ingredient and distinguishing characteristic of Aleppo soap.

Freshness is important; look for green, unbroken leaves. Store sealed in a cool, dry place.

BULGAR *Burghol* Also known as burghul or bulghur, bulgar is a fiber-rich grain, high in protein and minerals, and a staple in Middle Eastern cuisine. To make it, wheat is parboiled, sun-dried, and milled, removing the outer bran. It is ground in three sizes: fine (#1), medium (#2), and coarse (#3). In Aleppo, there is an even finer grain called *smeismeh*; *sreisirah* elsewhere. Coarse bulgar is used in place of rice as a side dish. Fine bulgar is used to prepare kibbeh paste. The full range of bulgar varieties can be found in Middle Eastern grocery stores, but the coarser grind is often available in supermarkets. There are two varieties: white bulgar (sometimes labeled yellow) is made from white wheat; a dark variety (sometimes labeled black or brown bulgar) is made from durum wheat. The white is slightly softer than the dark, while the dark has a more nutty flavor. Grains sold and labeled as "cracked wheat" are often made from raw wheat berries without parboiling and should not be confused with bulgar.

CARDAMOM *Habb al-Hal* Cardamom is a spice belonging to the ginger family. It is one of the most expensive spices (after saffron and vanilla) and has a strong flavor. Cardamom is used widely in the Arab world to flavor coffee and sweet and savory dishes. Some claim it aids digestion. It is also a breath freshener—chewing pods can mask the pungency of onion or garlic.

Cardamom pods are picked three quarters ripe, washed, then dried. They can be white or green (white pods are dried in the sun while green pods are dried in the shade). The spice is available as whole pods, or the seeds can be purchased whole or ground. Whole pods are most potent and retain their flavor for longer than ground. One needs to crush the seeds of about 10 pods to yield ½ teaspoon of ground cardamom.

CHEESES *Jibneh* "Green" cheese, *jibneh khadra*, is a fresh, salty white cheese used abundantly in Aleppo ("green" refers to the fact that it is unripened, rather than its color). It is usually prepared from sheep's milk, and available during the spring. It is served as an appetizer either raw or grilled, and sometimes used as a stuffing for kibbeh (*see* p. 174) or beurak (*see* p. 61). You can substitute salty fresh cheeses such as halloumi.

Akkawi cheese is a hard, salty, white cow's milk cheese native to Acre, Palestine. It is now produced mostly in Syria, Lebanon, and Cyprus. It melts when cooked. It is used in many Arabic sweets after desalting. Depending on the dish, halloumi or ricotta can be substituted.

Braided cheese, *jibneh majdooleh*, is a sheep's milk cheese formed into threads and typically woven into a tight braid, sometimes with the addition of nigella seeds. It is similar to Armenian string cheese.

Halloumi cheese is a hard and slightly rubbery cheese made of sheep's milk. After slicing, it is ideal for grilling or frying in a nonstick pan as it holds its shape when cooked.

CINNAMON *'Irfeh* There are two types of laurel trees that produce cinnamon sticks: the slightly more expensive real cinnamon, and cassia. Real cinnamon is the dark inner bark of laurel trees found in India and Sri Lanka. Cassia bark comes from the laurel trees in China, Vietnam, and Indonesia. It is darker in color, thicker, and is less expensive. Ready-ground cinnamon is usually a mixture of both.

Cinnamon is one of the spices that constitute Aleppo spice mix, which is used in most meat dishes. It is also used widely in Aleppo and the Arab world in savory and sweet dishes or to garnish rice.

CITRIC ACID *Milih al-Laymoon* Citric acid is a colorless, mild, organic acid in granular form, which dissolves in liquid. It is derived from citrus fruits. It is effective in preserving food from spoilage and prevents discoloration in pickling and preserving.

COLOSTRUM *Lebeh* Colostrum is the name for the "first milk" from the mammary glands of all female mammals immediately after giving birth, and lasting for around 2 to 3 days. It is thick yellowish milk, low in fat and sugar, and very rich in vitamins and minerals. It has vital antibodies that protect from disease. In Arabic the "first milk" is called *lebeh*, *al-louba* or *al-loubeh*, and sometimes *shamandoor* or *arisheh*. The colostrum used in Aleppian cooking is that of sheep, and it can be found from December to February. It thickens and becomes like cottage cheese when cooked. It is most commonly used to stuff Arabic Pancakes (p. 298) and also a dessert similar to baklava called *bein narain*. Unfortunately is not generally available outside of the Middle East, but it is processed similarly to ricotta, which is an acceptable substitute.

CORIANDER/CILANTRO *Kouzbara* When fresh, the herb is known as cilantro in the US and fresh coriander in the UK. The dried seeds of the plant are used as a spice, which is most commonly known as coriander. Coriander seeds are available whole or ground.

CUMIN *Kammoon* Cumin seeds are the dried seeds of an annual herb of the parsley family. It is the second most popular spice in the Middle East, after black pepper. The seeds are native to Syria and traces have been found in many archeological sites there. They are also grown in parts of East Asia. It is believed that cumin aids digestion, eliminates gas, fights inflammation, and aids in the body's absorption of iron.

Cumin seeds are available whole or ground. Ground cumin is used extensively in Aleppian cuisine in kibbeh dishes, salads, and as a tea (p. 335). For the best flavor, dry-toast the seeds, shaking the pan until they pop. Remove and grind to a powder. To preserve their freshness, only grind the quantity needed.

DESERT TRUFFLE *Kamayeh* Known by the name *kamaa* or *fiqa'* in Saudi Arabia, *terfezia* in Morocco, and *terfas* in Egypt, the desert truffle is actually a fungi classified as a distant cousin of the European truffle, and is considered a seasonal delicacy in the Middle East. It is available in rural Syria, stretching from Palmyra to the northeast, as well as in Jordan, North Africa, and Saudi Arabia. The name is a misnomer; it has nothing to do with the desert, since it does not germinate in the sand, but it is found in arid areas.

It develops underground during the fall as a result of rain, thunder, and the clap of lightning that hits the ground. It sprouts in January and February. Gatherers, who are usually farmers in the area, depend on memory and knowledge of the land to collect the truffles, helped by the fact that the growth often causes a small elevation and a slight crack in the earth.

Desert truffles range in size from 1–4 in/3–10 cm in diameter. The flesh is dense, smooth, and creamy in color, similar to mushrooms in texture, with a good fungal smell. The outside looks like a rough potato. The color ranges from creamy white to black; the darker shades are more valued. Their flavor is deep, earthy, and nutty and the texture is firm, but yields to the bite. Desert truffles are not as strongly flavored as their distant relatives, European forest truffles, but they add a lot of flavor, especially to meat dishes.

In Aleppo, desert truffles are very precious and served to honored guests. They are most commonly prepared as a salad in Desert Truffle Salad (p. 95) or in stews; they are also added to meat and grain dishes (they are especially good with freekeh), grilled on a barbecue, stuffed, or cooked with Freekeh with Chicken (p. 130), where they stand out as jewels on a crown.

Desert truffles pass their peak after five days out of the ground. Once they rise to the surface they have two enemies: sunlight and humidity. It is best, therefore, to store them in a cool, drafty, shaded place. When not in season, desert truffles are available frozen or canned in Middle Eastern specialty stores. *See* also p. 17.

EGGPLANT *Banjane* Also known as aubergines in France and the UK, *banjane* in Aleppo, and *batinjan* by most other Arabs, eggplants are actually fruits. They are native to India and come in an assortment of shapes and sizes, and range in color from white to purple to almost black.

Eggplants are the star of many Middle Eastern dishes. They are served grilled and puréed as a cold appetizer in Baba Ghanouj (p. 40), fried as a hot appetizer in Eggplant Beurak (p. 61), stewed with kibbeh as a main dish in Kibbeh in Pomegranate Stock (p. 195), stuffed as in Stuffed Eggplants in Tomato Sauce (p. 224) and Lamb-Stuffed Eggplants (p. 223), and grilled as in Grilled Kebab and Eggplant (p. 150).

Eggplants have a distinctive ability to soak up oil when fried. It has, therefore, been customary to slice and sprinkle them with salt to draw out the water and collapse the cells. Some eggplants may have some lingering bitterness, but with modern eggplants, especially those in season, bitterness is not a problem.

Select eggplants that are firm to the touch and have a glossy skin. Pick those that are lighter in weight when equal in size; the heavier ones have more seeds. Store them uncut (they oxidize quickly when cut) and unwashed in plastic bags in the refrigerator. In this manner they can keep for about a week.

Eggplant can be prepared with or without the skin, but peel when not in season. If you peel the eggplant, cook immediately as it will quickly turn brown when exposed to air.

In Aleppo, the small, striped *tadfi* eggplants are considered the best for their soft skin and sweet flesh.

FAVA BEANS *Fool Akhdar Fool* is the general Arabic name for a variety of fava beans, also called broad beans, that grow in plump, green pods. When dried, they are light to dark brown.

This is the bean of the old world and has served as a good source of protein for thousands of years. It originated in the Middle East, where it is still a staple food, especially in Egypt.

The beans come in various sizes; the small size is preferred in Lebanon and Egypt while the larger size is preferred in Syria. Their main use is in the preparation of a much sought after treat where the beans are boiled until very tender and then mixed with garlic, lemon juice, and olive oil described in the recipe Fava Beans (p. 58). The dish is served for breakfast with bread and vegetables, or as part of a mezze. It is also available pre-cooked in cans.

FENNEL *Shamra* Fennel is a plant of Mediterranean origin. It has feathery leaves and produces yellow flowers. The seeds are used in savory dishes, either whole, as in Wheat and Nut Dessert (p. 323), or ground. A different variety, usually called Florence fennel, is grown for its white bulbs, which are eaten cooked, or raw in salads. The leaves and stems are used as seasoning, or as a garnish, and are excellent with fish.

The plant has a slight aniseed-licorice flavor. Whole seeds should be kept in closed containers in a cool, dark place and they can last about a year. They should be roasted before grinding. Ground fennel seeds lose their aroma quickly so it is best to grind only what you need.

FENUGREEK *Hilbeh* This is the name of a plant that produces elongated pods containing oblong seeds, which are used as a spice. The seeds are very hard and can only be ground commercially or with a heavy mortar and pestle. The spice is one of the ingredients in curry powder and used to make basturma.

FIRKHA FLOUR *Theen Firkha* This wheat flour is slightly coarser than ordinary flour, and much finer than fine semolina. It is used mainly in the preparation of sweets like Aleppian Semolina Cookies. Mixing firkha into fine semolina makes less crumbly dough that is easier to handle.

FREEKEH *Freek* Like bulgar, freekeh is a durum wheat product but it undergoes a different process. The wheat stalks are picked still green, with the soft wheat berries still attached. The wheat is dried for a short period then burned in a process in which the sheaves are set on fire until the shaft turns black and the tips of the grains are charred. This process produces chewy wheat berries with a sweet and appealing smoky flavor. The kernels are used whole, milled to a coarse texture, or ground to a fine texture.

Freekeh may be stored in an airtight container in a cool, dark place for 6 months but loses its green color with time. Refrigeration is the best way to preserve it. It freezes quite well before and after cooking (*see* p. 19). (Note: The name Greenwheat Freekeh is trademarked by an Australian company. The freekeh is produced using modern roasting methods that eliminate the traditional field fires.)

GHEE *Samneh* All butter consists of about 80% fat; the rest is milk or water. Ghee, sometimes labeled clarified butter, dry butter, or pure butter, is where the water, milk, and solids have been removed through a slow heating process, making it safe to use for frying over high heat. For this English-language edition, I have substituted butter, olive oil, or a mixture of both. But if you prefer to use ghee, the flavor will be more authentic. You can find it in Middle Eastern, South Asian, and some healthfood stores.

GRAPE MOLASSES *Dibs al-'Inab* This is a product of cooked white grape juice. It is believed that it retains all the health benefits of the fruit. It comes in two consistencies: one syrup-like, and another somewhere between syrup and paste. The thicker of these is produced in Turkey and used in Grape Molasses Pudding, or served with Fried Vegetable Patties.

GREEN PEPPER *Fleifleh Haskouriyeh* Aleppian green peppers are long, wrinkled, and taper to three or four lobed ends. They are available in in mid-summer in two varieties: mild, which has a light green color (similar to Italian sweet peppers) and hot, which are dark green in color (similar to poblano peppers).

INCENSE *Bakhoor* This is the name given to granules of tree resin from certain trees. They are beige in color and emit a pleasing scent when heated, so they are often burned in homes or sacred places. In the Middle East, they are used to infuse a much-loved fragrance into dishes like Grape Molasses Pudding (p. 304).

JEW'S MALLOW *Mloukhiyeh* (*feuille de corête* in French; bush okra in parts of Africa; *bai po* in Thai; botanical name: *Malvaceae corchorus olitorius*) is the edible leaves of a variety of corchorus.

In the Middle East, the leaves are typically prepared as a stew topped with rice, toasted bread, and an onion and vinegar sauce. In Arabic, *Mloukhiyeh* refers to both the plant and the dish (*see* p. 19, p. 133, and p. 261). The word *mloukhiyeh* is a derivative of *malek* ("king"), implying that the dish is befitting royalty. It is said that a sick Egyptian king was cured when given this dish.

Mloukhiyeh has antioxidant properties, more carotene than carrots, more vitamin A than parsley, more calcium than spinach, and is high in vitamins B1 and B2.

The leaves should be prepared and cooked with care, otherwise they can become slimy and glutinous. Follow the proper techniques and the result will be a superb, nutritious, low-calorie dish. *Mloukhiyeh* is available in Middle Eastern stores in the US frozen, dried, and occasionally fresh. The plant may be grown in one's backyard as all it needs is warmth and plenty of water in summer.

KATAIFI *Uthmaliyeh* This is a flour pastry formed into long, very thin threads. It is made commercially by pouring a thin stream of dough over a hot, rotating iron plate.

Knafeh is the name of the dough when formed into fine grains and also the name of a famous dessert prepared with a cheese stuffing, which originated in Palestine in the city of Nablus. It is not easy to travel to Nablus these days to compare, but it is still claimed that this is where the best knafeh is made, using the famous Nabulsi cheese.

The dough is widely used in the Arab world, Turkey, and Greece to prepare many kinds of sweets. Kataifi is available frozen in most supermarkets and fresh in Middle Eastern grocery stores.

KEBAB MEAT *Kabab* In Syria, "kebab" (often called *kabab halabi*) refers to finely ground meat for grilled dishes. Ground lamb is often used, but if you use beef, make sure it has 15%–20% fat content. Too little fat and the kebab will be dry; too much fat and the kebab will crumble.

If your meat is coarsely ground (as is most common in the US), you must grind or chop it for many of the dishes in this book. If you have a meat grinder, pass the meat through on the fine setting once, then knead and chop as needed. Alternatively, briefly pulse the ground meat in a food processor.

KIBBEH is the national dish of Syria and Lebanon, but it is also popular across the Arab world. It comes in many varieties: raw, layered and baked, or hollowed and stuffed to be fried or grilled. It is usually based on a supple paste of bulgar mixed with pounded lean mutton, lamb, or beef, onions, spices, and salt. Vegetarian versions can be made with pumpkin, rice, potatoes, lentils, or simply flour and semolina.

Before the invention of the food processer, chopped meat was pounded to a paste with a little salt in a stone mortar and pestle. One onion was also pounded with small amounts of salt and spices. This process used to take at least an hour, but the advent of the food processor has shortened the preparation time.

LENTILS *Adess* Lentils are among the earliest legumes known to the Mediterranean and Southeast Asia. They are high in protein, iron, and fiber. In the Middle East three varieties are widely available; red, brown, and white lentils. Red lentils are, in fact, orange in color, and available as split lentils. They are used mainly in soups (*see* p. 79-85). Brown lentils are the most common. White lentils are a lighter brown, larger in size, and slightly flattened. Brown and white lentils yield similar results when cooked.

Lentils do not need to be presoaked but sometimes need to be picked over to remove stones or impurities. The best way to do this is to spread them on a tray in one layer. Always skim off the foam that forms on the surface of the cooking water. Add salt only at the end of cooking.

MAHLEPI *Mahlab* This powdery white spice is made from the dried seeds of the St. Lucie Cherry, a tall shrub with white flowers and dark, edible cherries. The powder has a strong sweet and spicy aroma. It is used sparingly in sweets, breads, and cheese. It has been in use for centuries in the Middle East, Iran, Armenia, Greece, and Turkey. It can be bought ground or whole, but always grind before using.

MASTIC/ARABIC GUM *Miskeh* or *masticha* Mastic is a plant resin collected from the native Greek *Pistacia lentiscus* tree. The resin solidifies to pea-size, translucent, crystal-like shapes. The best mastic is found in the Greek island Chios, where the granules are light yellow. White mastic is inferior in quality.

The name is derived from the Greek word *mastichon*, the root of the English verb masticate, meaning "to chew." Mastic was the first known chewing gum and is still being used as such, sometimes with a small piece of wax to tenderize it. It is used in small amounts as a binding agent in puddings. It is also used to flavor ice cream, and in certain meat and chicken marinades.

Mastic should be used sparingly, as too much of it gives a bitter taste to the dish. Because it is chewy, it should always be pounded in a mortar and pestle with salt or sugar, depending on whether the dish is savory or sweet. It can be found in Arabic, Greek, or Turkish stores (not to be confused with gum Arabic).

MUTTON Definitions of mutton vary from country to country. Generally, lamb is the meat of a sheep slaughtered under the age of one year. Mutton is the meat of a female or castrated male between two and three years old. It should be hung on the bone for two to three weeks to develop flavor and tenderness.

Before World War II, mutton was extremely popular in Europe and more common in the US. The 1918 edition of Fannie Farmer's popular cookbook gave instructions for preparing leg, saddle, chops, and curry of mutton. It is said that a steady diet of very poor quality boiled mutton, given to troops during the war, gave the meat a bad reputation and virtually destroyed the market for it.

More recently, mutton has been making a comeback in the West, with small specialty farms producing excellent quality meat and the rising popularity of the cuisines of India, the Mediterranean, and North Africa.

Mutton has a more complex flavor than lamb and benefits from long, slow cooking. In the Middle East and much of Asia, it has never gone out of fashion, and is very well suited to the spicy flavors of the region. Look for it in Asian, Middle Eastern, and Carribbean neighborhoods. In the Caribbean, "mutton" often describes both adult sheep and goat meat, so you'll need to specify sheep mutton.

NUTMEG *Jozet al-Teeb* This is the seed of the nutmeg tree, native to Indonesia but now cultivated in tropical Asia and America. In Aleppo, is most frequently used to spice sweets, and savory dishes such as Rice Kibbeh (p. 180), Stuffed Black Carrots (p. 207), and Leg of Lamb with Freekeh (p. 138). Though available ground, it is best to buy whole nutmeg; the flavor is far more pronounced when freshly ground.

OKRA *Bamia* Sometimes called ladies' fingers, okra are the green pods of an annual plant in the mallow family (like *mloukhiyeh*). It is a very popular vegetable in the Arab kitchen, most commonly used in stews with meat, or in a cold appetizer with olive oil. Okra pods can be found in two varieties: long (3–5 in/ 6–12 cm), or short (1–1½ in/3–4 cm). Smaller okra is more prized in the Arab world. Okra is available fresh, frozen, dried, or canned, but I prefer to use fresh or frozen.

Care should be taken when trimming the vegetable. Use a sharp knife to peel the cap without cutting into the pod itself, unless otherwise specified in the recipe. Okra contains a glutinous product that acts as a thickening agent to stews and soups, but in other dishes, piercing the pod will result in a slimy texture.

OLIVES *Zeitoon* Olive trees are as old as civilization itself in the Middle East, and olives are Syria's oldest and most important agricultural produce (along with pistachios). The country rates second in the Arab world after Tunisia in the production of olive oil. Olives are found on every Arab table.

Green and black olives are picked and treated to remove bitterness. Then they are cured in a salty solution with a few additions for flavor. Buyers are offered a number of choices, including pitted green olives stuffed with red chilis or walnuts. In Aleppo, the choices include olives that have undergone a different method of curing: they are boiled in a lye solution (*attroune;* a commercial alkaline solution used in soap making and some food preparations, sometimes sold under the name "red devil"). These olives are kept whole. Their color is vivid and they have a pleasant crunch. Green olives are harvested earlier than black, i.e., before they mature. They need more soaking to remove their bitterness.

ORANGE BLOSSOM WATER *Ma' al-Zaher* Orange blossom water, or orange-flower water, originated in the Middle East and is the end product of the distillation of the flowers of the bitter orange tree (known as Seville orange, *Abou Sfeir*, or sour orange). It is a highly fragrant essence used in various Middle Eastern sugar syrups used to flavor desserts. It is also mixed with hot water and sugar to make an after-dinner beverage called "white coffee" in some Arab countries.

PISTACHIOS *Fistoq Halabi* Along with olives, pistachios are one of Syria's major agricultural exports. Plantations of pistachio trees are found mainly in the city of Morek, north of Hama, and in the area near Idlib.

Pistachios are used extensively in Aleppo as a garnish and in sweets and savory dishes. Unsalted pistachios are available whole, ground, or thinly sliced. They can be found in most supermarkets.

POMEGRANATE *Rimman* This fruit originated in Persia, and has been cultivated in the Mediterranean region since antiquity. It was at one time considered a sign of love and fertility. It is slightly larger than an apple, with red or yellow skin that houses lots of seeds and a sweet or sour pulp ranging in color from dark red to white. Pomegranate has many nutrients, including potassium and vitamin C.

There are three main varieties of pomegranate. The sweetest variety has red seeds and is good for eating raw, cooking, and decoration. It is used in the making of grenadine. Another variety of pomegranate is the sweet-and-sour *laffaneh*, which is also good for eating and sometimes used for the making of pomegranate molasses, a thick syrup used in many sweet and savory dishes. The sourest variety of pomegranate is also used to make pomegranate molasses. A less common variety is called *assfooreh*, meaning bird-related. It is available for a shorter season. It has soft seeds and is hence classified as seedless. Its sweet fragrance and taste make it excellent for eating raw. The first of these pomegranates were found in ancient Palestine before spreading to other regions.

Fresh pomegranate juice is used extensively in Aleppo to replace lemon juice in savory dishes. The beautiful red seeds are used in fruit salads and as a garnish.

POMEGRANATE MOLASSES *Dibs al-Rimman* or *Rub al-Rimman* This flavorful sweet-and-sour syrup has been used since ancient times in Syria, Lebanon, Turkey, and Iran. It is made by boiling down the pinkish juice of pomegranates until it forms a shiny, thick, crimson-brown syrup. This syrup is used extensively in Aleppian cuisine. It can be found in specialty Middle Eastern or gourmet food stores or it can be made at home (*see* p. 26). Do not confuse the pomegranate molasses with grenadine syrup, which is much thinner and sweeter, and made from a different variety of pomegranates.

PRESERVES AND PICKLES Jams and pickles are an important part of the Aleppian table. The preserving methods in this book are traditional and still widely used in Aleppo; however they have not been pH tested for safe canning, so I have recommended storing in the refrigerator or freezer. Some of them may be safe for processing; if you are an experienced canner and would like to process the acidic jam and pickle recipes in this book, I advise you to do so according to the USDA guidelines, which can be found at http://nchfp.uga.edu. Otherwise, you can store them in the refrigerator or freezer without processing.

In our grandmothers' time, and even today in the Middle East and Europe, where many people still make their own vinegar, the acidity level of vinegar can be as high as 18%. Most commercially sold vinegar in the US has 5% acidity or higher. The pickle recipes in this book are based on vinegar with at least 5% acidity so check the level of the vinegar you plan to use.

QUINCE *Safarjal* This autumnul fruit is of Caucasian origin (pictured on p. 199). It is more acidic than apples and slightly bitter and astringent when raw, though some eat it raw with a sprinkling of salt. When cooked, its color changes from yellow to pink, or red with the addition of sugar, and with a longer cooking time, the taste sweetens. Like the apple, it produces pectin when cooked, making it ideal for the preparation of jam. The high acidity of the quince makes it an excellent accompaniment to fatty meats.

In the Middle East, quince is considered a modern food. Aleppians prize the fruit and have integrated it in their cuisine: in a stew served with rice (*see* Quince Stew, p. 257); in a soup with kibbeh and meat (*see* Kibbeh with Quince, p. 198), and other dishes.

RED PEPPER PASTE *Dibs Fleifleh* Similar in texture to tomato paste, red pepper paste has a vibrant red color, strong flavor, and is popular in Aleppo and the surrounding region. In late summer, the rooftops of Aleppo offer the beautiful sight of red peppers spread out in the sun to dry for its preparation.

Aleppian cuisine uses the paste fairly extensively. Generally speaking, the paste blends well with dishes that contain tomatoes. The pepper best for the purpose is the native Baladi, but the paste may be prepared from all kinds of sweet red peppers. It can be found in Middle Eastern and Turkish grocery stores.

ROSE WATER *Ma' al-Ward* This fragrant liquid is distilled from the petals of Damask roses (*Ward al-jouri*). Its use is widespread in the Middle East and beyond, to perfume some savory dishes and many sweet dishes. It can be found in Middle Eastern, international, and heathfood stores. Concentrated rose extracts, which are often packaged in small bottles, are not water-based and should not be used here.

SAFFLOWER *Osfor* This spice is the dried petal of the thistle-like flower of the safflower plant. Though mild in flavor, it lends a yellow color to dishes, hence the name *osfor*, which is a derivative of *asfar*, meaning yellow. It is sometimes referred to as false saffron, or poor man's saffron, since it is an inexpensive alternative. A dye is produced from the flowers, and the seeds produce oil, which is used in cooking, paint, and medicine.

SAFFRON *Za'faran* This spice is made of the dried red-orange stigmas of the saffron crocus flower. These are threads about 1 in/2 cm long, commonly available whole and sometimes ground. It is the most expensive spice in the world, as each flower has only three stigmas and these can only be picked by hand. Only a small amount is needed to flavor a dish and give it a beautiful light golden color. The best saffron comes from Iran and Valencia, Spain. In Aleppo, it is the dominant flavor of the sweet Saffron Rice Pudding (p. 310). The spice should be soaked in warm milk or water in order to best bring out its color and aroma.

SEMOLINA *Smeed* The semolina that is used in the Middle East is in the form of granules extracted from hard (durum) wheat. It is available in two textures—coarse or fine. Fine semolina is used to make sweets such as Aleppian Semolina Cookies, Western-Style Baklava, and Semolina and Butter Pudding. It is also excellent for savory dishes such as vegetarian kibbeh. It is available from Middle Eastern and Greek stores and health food stores. Stored in an airtight container, it keeps well in the refrigerator.

SEVEN-SPICE POWDER *Sabe' Bharat* This Lebanese spice mixture is used widely in Middle Eastern cooking. It is made up of equal amounts of allspice, cinnamon, cloves, nutmeg, ginger, *mahlab* (mahlepi; sour cherry seeds), and black pepper. Some slight variations occur between blends; sometimes fenugreek is used instead of *mahlab*. It can be found in some Middle Eastern grocery stores.

SHEEP'S TAIL FAT *Liyyeh* The types of sheep that are most commonly found in the Middle East are the fat-tailed breeds (such as the Awassi). A mature ram's tail can carry up to 25 lb (12 kg) of prized fat, softer and more delicately flavored than fat stored in the body's interior. Cooking with *liyyeh*, the rendered fat, has been around for a very long time. The oldest existing Arabic cookbooks (both called *Kitab al-Tabikh* and written between the tenth and thirteenth centuries) use it. There is even a reference to it in the Bible (Leviticus 3:9). Sheep's tail and Arabic *samneh* (fat from sheep or cow's milk), though still used, is in steady decline. Nowadays vegetable oils are preferred in daily cooking, yet when folks crave that old-time flavor, it is still *liyyeh*. In rural areas of Syria, you can still find rendered sheep's tail fat in grocery stores.

SOAPWORT OR PANAMA BARK *Shirsh el-Halaweh* The name *Shirsh el-Halaweh*, meaning "the sweet root," refers to their use in the preparation of sweets. When boiled, the root produces a foamy liquid that is the major ingredient in *natef*, a thick, sweet white dip served with Aleppian Semolina Cookies (*see* p. 292).

The active ingredient is a substance called saponin, which is a foaming agent and is still used to make a gentle herbal soap in Europe, used especially for cleaning antique tapestries. Traditionally in the Middle and Near East, the substance was obtained from the roots of certain varieties of the gypsophila plant (a relative of the florist's Baby's Breath, also called Egyptian Soapwort), but due to over-collection of the wild plants, the substance is now mostly obtained from the bark of a South American tree called *Quillaja saponaria* (soapbark tree). The dried bark is known in the Middle East as Panama bark or *bois de Panama*. In Turkey, commercial farming of a plant closely related to the common weed soapwort, *Saponaria arrostii*, yields large amounts of the dried root for Turkish markets. Saponin can be toxic to fish and some animals in high concentrations. Soapwort is on the Poisonous Plants of Mississippi list but the roots are sold in the US as an herbal medicine for ailments such as psoriasis, eczema, boils, acne, and congestion. Recent studies have shown saponin to be toxic to certain cancer cells. The foam is also sometimes used with tahini to make *halaweh* (halva), a common Middle Eastern sweet.

SOUJOK *Soujok* This spiced, dried sausage is said to be of Armenian origin but is consumed extensively in Syria, Lebanon, Jordan, and Egypt. It is made from meat, garlic, and lots of spices. The mixture is stuffed into sausage casings and tied at intervals to form short or long sausages, then dried for 2 or 3 days before being sent to the market. If you can find it, soujok is best consumed fresh, but freezes well, and should be fried directly from the freezer on medium to low heat without the addition of oil.

SOUR CHERRIES *Karaz Washneh* Sour cherries (*Prunus cerasus*) are not commonly cultivated in the world, except for Morello cherries and a variety called *washneh* in Syria. These are grown in Ariha, southwest of Aleppo. The trees bloom in early summer, yielding fruit in June and early July. They are the size of chickpeas with deep red skin, flesh, and juice. They are somewhat bitter and too sour to be consumed raw, but this trait makes them a desirable accompaniment to kebab, especially in the renowned Aleppian dish Meatballs in Sour Cherry Sauce (p. 158). They also make a delicious jam (*see* p. 286) and an excellent liqueur (*see* p. 330).

Fresh ones can be stored in the refrigerator for about 4 days. To be frozen, they must first be pitted; 2 lb/1 kg yields about 28 oz/800 g pitted sour cherries. They are available frozen or dried from Armenian or Middle Eastern stores. Reconstitute the dried ones by soaking them overnight in water.

STRAINED YOGURT *Labneh* This popular dish is yogurt that has been drained of some of its whey, usually by suspending it in a fine mesh strainer or cheesecloth. It is slightly thicker than Greek yogurt and slightly thinner than cream cheese. It is a staple on the Arab mezze table and is often served with Arabic flatbread, scallions, tomatoes, mint leaves or dried mint, and olive oil.

A thicker version of *labneh* is produced by allowing the yogurt to drain for 24 hours or more. It is then formed into balls, sometimes with the addition of herbs like thyme or dried mint, placed in glass jars, and covered with olive oil to preserve. The kind of yogurt used is decisive to the final taste of the *labneh*. Middle Eastern yogurt is slightly sourer than yogurt in the West.

SUMAC *Summaq* With its strong, tangy flavor, sumac is a popular seasoning throughout the Middle East. The Romans used it as a souring agent before the introduction of lemon. It is mixed with dried thyme leaves and sesame seeds to prepare *za'atar*. In Aleppo, it is used in a kibbeh stew (*see* p. 196) and salad (*see* p. 93).

Dried sumac berries are sold whole, or ground with the addition of a little salt. Its color varies from brick red to dark purple, depending on where it is grown. Inferior qualities have more salt in them, so, if possible, taste sumac before buying it. Sumac can be found in most Middle Eastern grocery stores.

TAHINI OR SESAME PASTE *Tahina* This thick, creamy paste is made from ground raw sesame seeds. Tahini has a rich nutty flavor, is high in calories, and comes in varying degrees of beige. *Taratore* is the Arabic name of the sauce prepared by mixing tahini with lemon juice, garlic, water, and salt. The sauce accompanies some fish, rice, and salad dishes, and the famous Egyptian falafel.

Tahini will keep in the pantry until the use-by date, but needs to be stirred vigorously when left for a long time. Storing the container upside down helps. It is indispensable for cooking cold appetizers like Hummus (p. 39), Baba Ghanouj (p. 40), Aleppian Batersh (p. 60), Swiss Chard Stems in Tahini Sauce (p. 106), Chicken in Tahini Sauce (p. 107), and Baked Fish with Tahini Sauce (p. 120). Tahini is available in Middle Eastern stores and most supermarkets.

TAMARIND *Tamer Hindi* The name tamarind is a contraction of the Arabic term *tamer hindi*, meaning Indian date. The name refers to the syrup, paste, and the beverage (*see* p. 333) prepared from the fruit of the tamarind tree. These are long, hard, shiny pods containing a sour pulp and brown seeds. They are a good source of vitamin B and calcium. You can find tamarind in packaged blocks of dark, semi-dried pulp. These are produced in India and have a long shelf life.

THYME MIX *Za'atar* The name *za'atar* refers to both to the herb wild thyme, and a mixture of dried herbs and spices in which wild thyme is the prominent ingredient. The mixture is a staple of many Arab breakfast tables, mixed with olive oil and eaten with bread. *Za'atar* and olive oil is also spread on flatbread dough and baked in the oven to make *man'oushe*, a popular inexpensive breakfast in many parts of the Middle East.

Aleppo, along with Nablus in Palestine, is known for producing the best *za'atar*. The ingredients and quantities vary among vendors, who take great pride in the quality and flavor of their blend. In Aleppo, the main ingredients are typically wild thyme, cumin, anise, fennel, coriander, sesame seeds, and sumac. These are toasted to release their aromas and to dry them out in order to be ground. Some vendors inflate the mix with the less expensive ground chickpeas and citric acid. Others add ground pistachios for extra flavor.

TURMERIC *'Iqdeh Safra* Also called *curcuma*, turmeric is a deep orange-yellow powder, obtained from the dried and ground roots of the plant *Curcuma longo*, which is part of the ginger family and native to India. It is a coloring agent, used as a spice for its mild flavor and as a dye for food and drink. It has a huge array of health benefits and is used as a natural remedy in many countries.

VERJUICE *Hamed al-Husrom (Mayet al-Husrom)* Verjuice is the acidic juice of unripe white grapes. It is softer in flavor and slightly sweeter than lemon juice or vinegar. It has been used since ancient times as a substitute for wine or vinegar in food, though its use has declined due to the availability of flavored vinegars.

The juice is popular in Northern Iran and Azerbaijan, and it is used extensively in Syrian cuisine. There is somewhat of a ritual attached to its production: women gather at the onset of the sour grapes season to chat, drink coffee, and press the sour grapes, bottle the juice, and then distribute it among family members.

Look for the fresh pressed juice, not the verjuice that has been simmered and reduced. A possible substitute is 1 cup/240 ml of water mixed with 3 tablespoons white wine vinegar, 4 teaspoons sugar, and ¼ teaspoon salt. Or replace verjuice with a mixture of lemon juice and water, adding a little sugar.

VERMICELLI *Shi'ariyeh* The word *shi'ariyeh* is a derivative of the Arabic word *sha'ir*, meaning hair. It refers to thin strands of pasta, usually sold in spiral forms, which are broken before cooking, or in short already-broken strands. The pasta is primarily fried until golden and added to raw rice; then both are cooked together. Vermicelli adds a nice nutty taste to plain cooked rice or bulgar (*see* p. 110).

INDEX